50 YEARS
lonely planet
OF TRAVEL

# FINLAND

D1562937



Paula Hotti, John Noble, Barbara Woolsey

# CONTENTS

## Plan Your Trip



## The Guide

Helsinki (p42)

ANASTASIIA AKH/SHUTTERSTOCK ©

Lapland (p187)

LEFT: ROMAN BELIAKOV/SHUTTERSTOCK ©; TOP RIGHT: WASIM KHUZAM/SHUTTERSTOCK ©; BOTTOM LEFT: ANASTASIIA AKH/SHUTTERSTOCK ©

Northern Lights (p232)

## Toolkit



## Storybook

Finnish crowds enjoying live music (p18)

# FINLAND

## THE JOURNEY BEGINS HERE

My first connection to Finland? Wiling out to its hard rock in my teenage angst. Years later, I discovered Finnish metal is deeply culturally significant: it symbolises the 'everyday melancholy of Finnish hearts,'. Finland's postcard-perfect landscapes, thriving forests and translucent waters are certainly not telltale of its devastating, war-torn history. It's made the people *sisu* (an untranslatable word for tough, resilient character) – yet also more warm-hearted, hospitable and fun-loving. Finns joyfully suck every last golden drop out of summer with sports and festivals. Winter is for pub karaoke and getting *pantsdrunk* (tipsy with no trousers on). The beautiful seclusion of Finland's great outdoors, from deserted beaches to trails, is what draws you in, but it will be the locals' spirit that keeps you coming back.

**Barbara Woolsey**

*@xo_babxi*

**My favourite experience** is visiting the Sámi's cultural capital, Inari; meeting northern indigenous peoples and discovering nature through their language and legends, as well as ancient traditions such as reindeer herding.

TOP: HEIKKI WICHMANN/SHUTTERSTOCK ©; BOTTOM: PAULHARDING00/SHUTTERSTOCK ©

## WHO GOES WHERE

Our writers and experts choose the places which, for them, define Finland

RIGHT: YARI2000/SHUTTERSTOCK ©

Kilpisjärvi

I love remote places, so **Kilpisjärvi** is just perfect. The village sits all alone between a lake and a mountain up at Finland's far northwest tip. The day hike across 11km of Arctic wilderness to the triple border of Finland, Norway and Sweden is awe-inspiring with its views of multiple lakes large and small, near and far, shimmering or threatening depending on the colour of the sky.

### John Noble

*@johnnoble11*

*John is a travel writer who has covered more than 20 countries for Lonely Planet. He loves being north of the Arctic Circle.*

RIGHT: ARTBBNV/SHUTTERSTOCK ©

Saimaa Lakeland

The **Saimaa Lakeland** has a beautiful setting: lakes, little coves and rural hotels putting up feasts of local produce. Then there are the small cities, with summer markets and harbours with slow-boat tours. There is another side, too – the endangered Saimaa ringed seals suffering from lessening snowfall in winter and fishing nets in summer, and the outdated mining laws threatening the local environment, both reminders of the fragility of nature.

### Paula Hotti

*@retrotravels*

*Paula is a travel journalist and photographer who lives in Helsinki, and the author of books about Dublin, gin and European coffee-shop culture.*

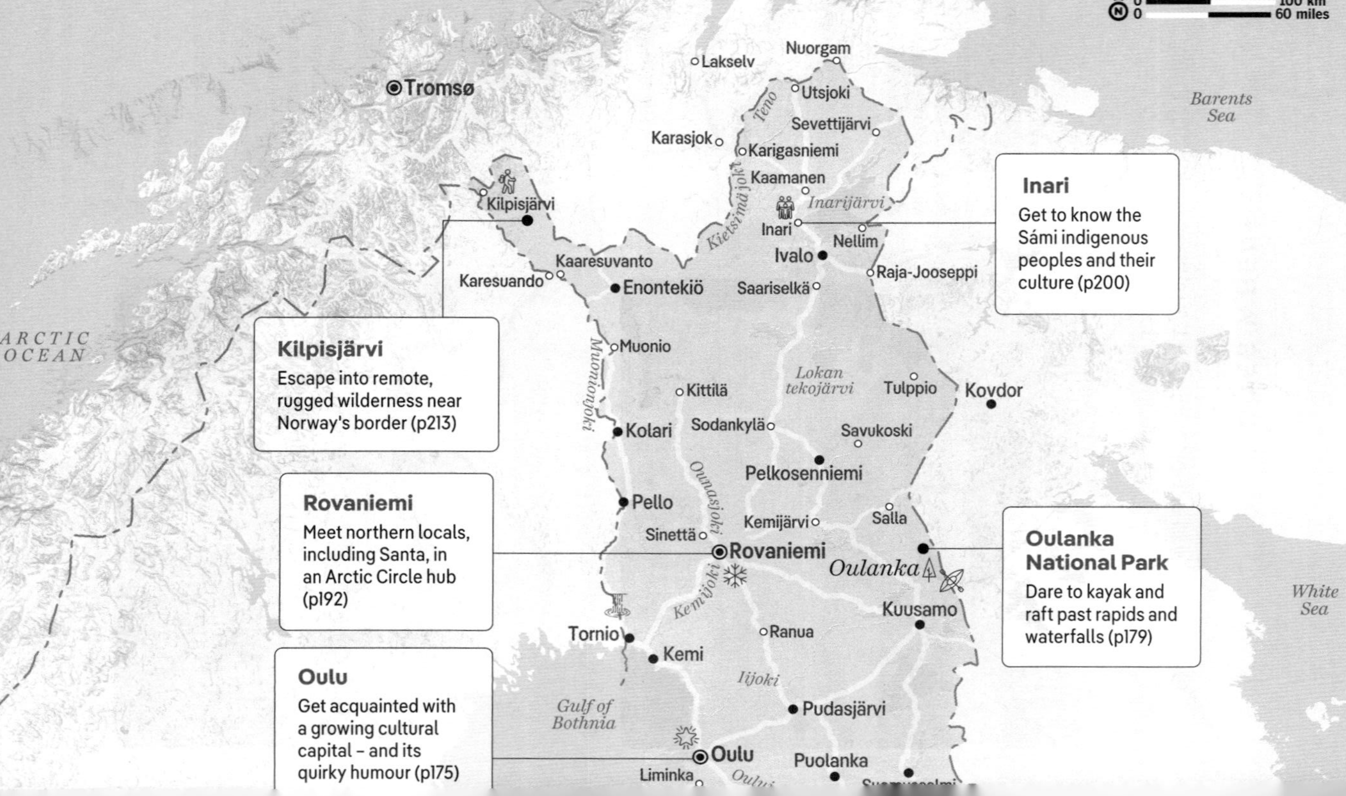
0 100 km
0 60 miles
Barents Sea
White Sea
ARCTIC OCEAN
Tromsø
Lakselv
Nuorgam
Utsjoki
Teno
Sevettijärvi
Karasjok
Karigasniemi
Kaamanen
Inarijärvi
Kietsimäjoki
Inari
Nellim
Ivalo
Raja-Jooseppi
Saariselkä
Kilpisjärvi
Kaaresuvanto
Karesuando
Enontekiö
Muonio
Muonionjoki
Lokan tekojärvi
Kittilä
Tulppio
Kovdor
Kolari
Sodankylä
Savukoski
Pelkosenniemi
Ounasjoki
Pello
Kemijärvi
Salla
Sinettä
Rovaniemi
Oulanka
Kemijoki
Kuusamo
Tornio
Ranua
Kemi
Iijoki
Gulf of Bothnia
Pudasjärvi
Oulu
Puolanka
Liminka
Inari
Get to know the Sámi indigenous peoples and their culture (p200)
Kilpisjärvi
Escape into remote, rugged wilderness near Norway's border (p213)
Rovaniemi
Meet northern locals, including Santa, in an Arctic Circle hub (p192)
Oulanka National Park
Dare to kayak and raft past rapids and waterfalls (p179)
Oulu
Get acquainted with a growing cultural capital – and its quirky humour (p175)

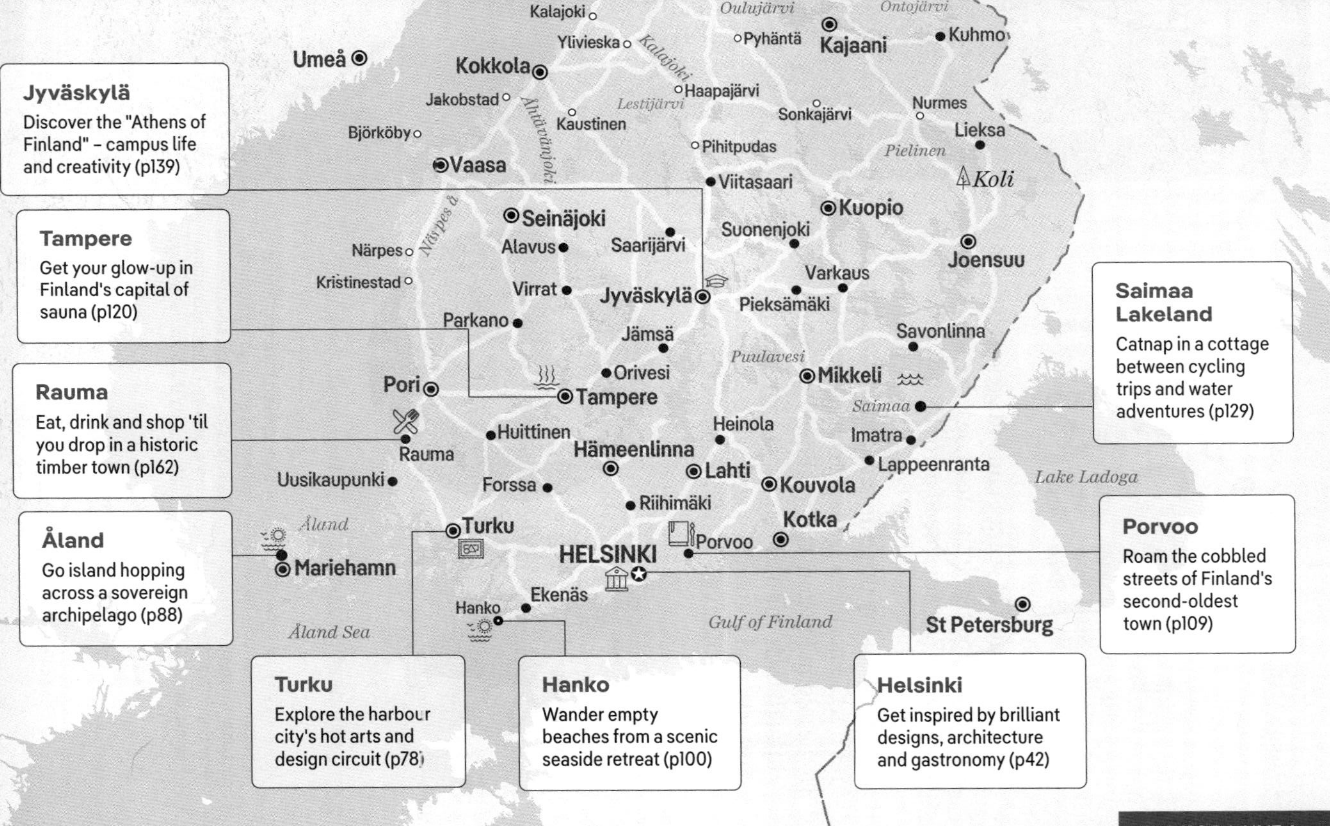
Jyväskylä
Discover the "Athens of Finland" – campus life and creativity (p139)
Tampere
Get your glow-up in Finland's capital of sauna (p120)
Rauma
Eat, drink and shop 'til you drop in a historic timber town (p162)
Åland
Go island hopping across a sovereign archipelago (p88)
Turku
Explore the harbour city's hot arts and design circuit (p78)
Hanko
Wander empty beaches from a scenic seaside retreat (p100)
Helsinki
Get inspired by brilliant designs, architecture and gastronomy (p42)
Porvoo
Roam the cobbled streets of Finland's second-oldest town (p109)
Saimaa Lakeland
Catnap in a cottage between cycling trips and water adventures (p129)
Kalajoki
Oulujärvi
Ontojärvi
Kuhmo
Kajaani
Pyhäntä
Ylivieska
Kalajoki
Umeå
Kokkola
Haapajärvi
Jakobstad
Lestijärvi
Kaustinen
Ähtävänjoki
Sonkajärvi
Nurmes
Björköby
Pihitpudas
Lieksa
Pielinen
Vaasa
Viitasaari
Koli
Kuopio
Seinäjoki
Närpes å
Närpes
Alavus
Saarijärvi
Suonenjoki
Joensuu
Kristinestad
Virrat
Jyväskylä
Varkaus
Pieksämäki
Parkano
Jämsä
Savonlinna
Puulavesi
Pori
Orivesi
Mikkeli
Tampere
Saimaa
Huittinen
Heinola
Imatra
Rauma
Hämeenlinna
Lahti
Lappeenranta
Uusikaupunki
Forssa
Kouvola
Lake Ladoga
Riihimäki
Kotka
Åland
Turku
Porvoo
Mariehamn
HELSINKI
Ekenäs
Hanko
Åland Sea
Gulf of Finland
St Petersburg

# LAND OF THE SÁMI

Over thousands of years, Sámi indigenous peoples have maintained an intimate knowledge of northern landscapes. They are spread across Norway, Sweden, Finland and Russia's Kola Peninsula, with around 4000 (speaking three different Sámi languages) residing in northern Lapland, considered the Sámi Homeland in Finland. Get to know the modern Sámi through their cultural centres in Inari, their crafts and arts, and through experiencing contemporary Sámi lifestyles at their reindeer farms.

### Reindeer herding

Today, a significant percentage of Sámi are involved in reindeer husbandry. Herders keep track of their free-wandering stock with earmarks and GPS collars.

### Homespun treasures

Sámi handicrafts, recognised as indigenous art, range from beautiful Sámi hats to jewellery, silverware and more. Genuine handicrafts around Lapland carry the 'Sámi duodji' logo.

### Traditional clothing

Sámi's beautiful embroidered costumes are now mostly worn on special occasions.

FAR LEFT: EKATERINA POLISCHUK/SHUTTERSTOCK ©; LEFT: O.C RITZ/SHUTTERSTOCK ©; RIGHT: PETER GUDELLA/SHUTTERSTOCK ©

Sajos (p202), Inari

## BEST CULTURAL EXPERIENCES

Discover Sámi culture and history at the state-of-the-art **Siida** ❶ museum featuring exhibition halls and original buildings such as farmhouses and storage huts. (p201)

At the **Sajos** ❷ cultural centre, visit the seat of Sámi Parliament and peruse the excellent Sámi duodji crafts shop. (p202)

Explore Sámi life at **Tuula Airamo's** ❸ lakeside home. Feed reindeer, chat about folklore, and discover traditional handicraft from natural materials. (p207)

Learn about reindeer husbandry from Petri Mattus and his family at their **reindeer farm** ❹. (p207)

Visit Sámi artisan Kikka Laakso at **Kammigalleria** ❺ where she crafts fabulously detailed jewellery from antlers and leather. (p207)

Lapland (p187)

LEFT: YAUHEN_D/SHUTTERSTOCK ©; RIGHT: MARAT LALA/SHUTTERSTOCK ©; FAR RIGHT: R.CLASSEN/SHUTTERSTOCK ©

# CHILLS & THRILLS

The Arctic winter's charm is undeniable. From frost-tipped trees to frozen lakes, Finland's northern wilderness sparkles once the temperatures drop. The best way to thrive in subzero conditions? Bundling up and getting busy outdoors, from snow sports to spotting the aurora borealis (Northern Lights).

### Snowed in

It's possible to spend the night in a room made of ice in one of Lapland's 'snow hotels'. If that's too hardcore, hit their ice bars instead.

### Frosty fun

Lapland is covered in snow for up to eight months a year, making for the ultimate snow-sports destination. From March, hours of daylight increase dramatically.

### BEST ARCTIC WINTER EXPERIENCES

Explore some of the 150km of cross-country ski tracks around **Saariselkä ❶**, or hit the downhill slopes of the Ski Saariselkä resort. (p210)

At **Konttaniemen Porotila ❷** reindeer farm feed reindeer and go on a winter sleigh ride. (p198)

Watch the aurora borealis from a 0°C, glass-igloo room at the **Arctic Snow Hotel ❸**. (p199)

Cheer on reindeer and their skiing 'jockeys' at the '**Royal Reindeer Race**' **❹**. (p207)

Go on a mushing ride with huskies at **Ride North Inari ❺**. (p208)

# SAUNA CULTURE

Nothing is more integral to Finnish culture, psyche and wellbeing than the sauna. From fire-heated chimney saunas in rustic summer cottages, to modern electric saunas in most homes, getting sweaty is an everyday ritual for the body and soul. With more than two million saunas around the country, there's no excuse not to sneak in a session.

## Lakeside saunas

The best saunas are near water for you to jump in. Yes, the about-face from hot to cold is brutal, but that's just how it's done.

## Sacred ritual

For hundreds of years, saunas have been a place in which to meditate, warm up, bathe and even give birth. Respect sauna etiquette (p233) accordingly.

## Bundle blunders

Sauna whisks (twig bunches) are called '*vihta*' in Finland's west and '*vasta*' in the east. Avoid making a cultural faux pas by using the right term.

3

4

1 2 5

## BEST SAUNA EXPERIENCES

**Kotiharjun Sauna** 1 Helsinki's only original traditional public wood-fired sauna, dating back to 1928, is a winner for its traditional atmosphere and optional scrub-down. (p71)

At **Löyly** 2, on Helsinki's Hernesaari waterfront, go straight from an electric or traditional smoke sauna into the sea (or a winter ice hole). (p56)

Oulu's **Kesän Sauna** 3 is a rare unisex bathing stop. Float in a wood-burning sauna sitting off Oulujoki's northern bank. (p176)

Tampere's **Rajaportin sauna** 4 is one of Finland's most famous public saunas, regularly heating up the photogenic Pispala neighbourhood since 1906. (p125)

At Helsinki 'scene spa' **Allas Sea Pool** 5, go for a sauna, splash into Baltic seawater and catch events with DJs and full-moon nude swimming. (p50)

# WILDLIFE WONDERS

Time and again, Finland has been recognised by environmental organisations for its conservation efforts – maintaining wonderful natural areas in which to experience wildlife. Dense forests and extensive coastlines are home to plentiful birdlife and myriad impressive mammals. Keep your eyes peeled for elk, foxes and wild swans, or take a dedicated wildlife tour in the east to spot bears, wolverines or the rare Saimaa ringed seal. Sustainable, ethical experiences keep animals, and their natural habitats, intact.

### Seal spotting

Only about 400-odd endangered ringed seals (p132) remain in Saimaa Lakeland, though populations are rising. May is the most likely time to see them moulting on rocks.

### Finland's favourite

The brown bear (*Ursus arctos*) is Finland's national animal. See the bears in the northeast between mid-April and August (but for a little July gap during mating season).

### Kuhmo creatures

Finland's highest number of bears and wolves roam the vast taiga forests running from Kuhmo across Siberia.

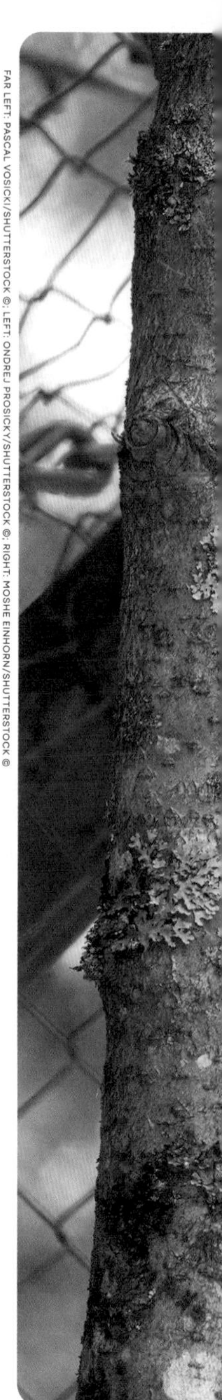

FAR LEFT: PASCAL VOSICKI/SHUTTERSTOCK ©; LEFT: ONDREJ PROSICKY/SHUTTERSTOCK ©; RIGHT: MOSHE EINHORN/SHUTTERSTOCK ©

Owl in Ranua Wildlife Park (p198)

## BEST WILDLIFE-WATCHINGEXPERIENCES

At **Ranua Wildlife Park** ❶ get a chance to see Finnish wildlife, including the brown bear, elk, lynx, wolverine, otter, Arctic fox, owls and eagles. (p198)

In Kuhmo, stay in one of **Bear Centre's** ❷ big viewing cottages in marshland, looking out for bears and wolverines. (p155)

**Lapland Welcome** ❸ is a well-known Rovaniemi-based tour operator with a focus on elk (moose) spotting and wilderness wildlife photography. (p197)

Watch for wild brown bears relaxing by a pond, as well as cheeky fish-eating ospreys, at the comfortable **Karhu-Kuusamo** ❹ hide. (p184)

Gaze at birdlife and wildlife on the vast nature trails of **Kumlinge** ❺ island. Look for cranes, roe deer, foxes and elk. (p98)

LEFT: GRISHA BRUEV/SHUTTERSTOCK ©; RIGHT: ROMAN BABAKIN/SHUTTERSTOCK ©; FAR RIGHT: LIZAVETTA/SHUTTERSTOCK ©

**Helsinki's Design District (p59)**

# INSPIRING DESIGNS

Finnish design is a byword for quality, but it's not just the big-name brands that impress. Helsinki's backstreets are fantastic for getting the creative juices flowing. Numerous ateliers and shops run the gamut from innovative to quirky, what-were-they-thinking and brilliant.

### Design hot spot

The little settlement of Iittala Village, between Tampere and Hämeenlinna, is worth a half-day trip to discover its famous glass factory at the forefront of Finnish design.

### Hit the streets

Helsinki's Design District is a treasure trove of furniture, art, fashion, accessories and homewares. Discover hundreds of shops and galleries mapped on its website (designdistrict.fi).

### BEST CREATIVE EXPERIENCES

Helsinki's **Design Museum** ❶ looks at the roots of Finnish design in the nation's traditions and nature. (p61)

**Korkeavuorenkatu** ❷ road (p56) has antique shops with glassware, watches and more.

**Lokal** ❸ contemporary art gallery-cum-concept store sells wares from local artisans. (p63)

Stock up on sleek Finnish designs at the 'modernist shopping mall' **Lasipalatsi** ❹. (p62)

**Kiasma** ❺ museum exhibits Finnish and international contemporary art. (p50)

# SANTA'S LAPLAND

Situated right by the Arctic Circle, Rovaniemi is the 'official' terrestrial residence of Santa Claus. In the Finnish Lapland's capital, kitschy holiday cheer is an all-year affair with Christmas-themed attractions and accommodation. The centrepiece, of course, is Santa's 'official' village, where thousands of visitors, young and old, get to meet him every year.

### 365 days a year

The sprawling Santa Claus Village encompasses many Christmas-spirit experiences. Snowmobiling and ice sculpting run seasonally, but there's always a little action.

### Meeting Mr Claus

Sitting on Santa's knee is the highlight. Or enjoy a tête-à-tête with Lapland's main man – a worldly, multilingual fellow. It's free, though photos with him aren't.

### Happier times

Rovaniemi was 90% destroyed by the Nazis in WWII. Today's cheesy Christmas cheer and booming tourism must be appreciated against this dark past.

❶❷ ❹❺ ❸

### BEST YEAR-ROUND CHRISTMAS EXPERIENCES

Visit the **Santa Claus Main Post Office** ❶ to send a postcard with Santa's 'official' stamp. Arctic Circle certificates are available around Santa Claus Village. (p197)

Stay in the **Arctic Light Hotel's** ❷ Christmas cabin. All year, it's adorned with a Christmas tree and decorations. (p193)

Enjoy speeding down the 1km summer toboggan track at **Ruka** ❸, or gliding over the fells in the Village2Valley cable car. (p184)

Take a winter sleigh ride with Dasher and Dancer at **Santa Claus Village** ❹ or accompany them on a summer forest walk. (p197)

Learn more about Santa's home in Rovaniemi at Arktikum ❺, a science centre on Lapland nature and local history. (p192)

# ELEGANT BUILDINGS

From great fires to wartime devastation, Finland is no stranger to reconstruction. Its architecture comprises an impressive pastiche of styles and influences across regions, reflecting periods from Swedish and Russian rule to postwar rebirth. Sleek, breathtaking modern architecture has been greatly influenced by Finnish architect Alvar Aalto's philosophy of beauty and functionality. Since the forest is ever-present in Finnish life, cottages and timber homes are designed to blend gloriously into natural landscapes, leaving feelings of awe and ease.

### Going south

Turku, Finland's oldest city, holds the lion's share of historic buildings, and particularly medieval treasures. This is prime territory for exploring the region's past.

### Living artwork

Vanha Rauma is the Nordic region's largest wooden old town. Its 600 houses might be museum-worthy, but it's a lively area, active with residents and visitors alike.

### Legacy of a 'starchitect'

Aalto's democratic view of architecture emphasised it must be attractive yet serve the wellbeing of everyone.

FAR LEFT: IGOR GROCHEV/SHUTTERSTOCK ©; LEFT: FINESTOCK/SHUTTERSTOCK ©; RIGHT: MIKHAIL OLYKAINEN/SHUTTERSTOCK ©

Finlandia Hall (p68)

## BEST ARCHITECTURE-SPOTTING EXPERIENCES

Gape at **Helsinki's diverse architecture** ❶ from downtown art nouveau wonders to the Rock Church and Aalto's magnum opus, Finlandia Hall. (p42)

Stroll **Rovaniemi's riverside**, ❷ taking in 1960s and '70s Aalto masterpieces and admiring an impressive era of rejuvenation after the town was razed in 1944. (p195)

Take in grand villas and **Jugendstil stunners in Hanko**, ❸ a quiet seaside retreat and former spa for Russian nobility. (p105)

Roam around **Vanha Rauma** ❹ and its hundreds of 18th- and 19th-century wooden buildings. Each one has its name above the door. (p163)

Go back to medieval times in **Turku** ❺, exploring the gloriously preserved cathedral and stone castle. (p79)

Savonlinna castle (p130)

# RHYTHMIC PARADISE

From chamber music to head-banging metal, Finland's music scene is among the world's richest. The output of quality Finnish musicians per capita is very high. Summer is a medley of music festivals, while winter is all about live bands in pubs and belting karaoke.

### Summer festivals

In July, Finland's biggest music festivals, such as Savonlinna castle's month-long opera event, Ruisrock (p82) and Pori's music extravaganza (p166), draw famous artists and thousands-strong crowds.

### Symphonic chords

Finland's musical education is among the world's best. Finnish talent is a popular export to top overseas orchestras, and excellent classical-music festivals are held across the country.

### BEST ON-STAGE EXPERIENCES

Legendary Helsinki rock venue **Tavastia** ❶ attracts local acts and bigger international groups. (p61)

Hamina celebrates military music in a fortress during the **Hamina Tattoo.** ❷ (p77)

Sing your favourite tune at a cool **Turku karaoke bar.** ❸ (p83)

Take in Inari's **'Nightless Night'** ❹ indigenous music festival for a full spectrum of Sámi music. (p207)

Find gigs in Jyväskylä, where cosy **live-music pubs** ❺ host folk music and jam sessions. (p141)

FAR RIGHT: MAZUR TRAVEL/SHUTTERSTOCK ©

# COTTAGE IN THE COUNTRY

Tucked away in Finland's forests and shores are half a million *kesämökkejä* (summer cottages), or *mökki* for short. Part holiday house, part sacred place, they are a spiritual home for the Finnish. Lakeland has abundant options, often boasting fishing piers and swimming beaches, but on islands and archipelagos. Scenic retreats are also everywhere.

## Assorted abodes

Pick your pleasure. The simplest rustic cabins have outside loos and water drawn from a well, while the most modern designer bungalows have every creature comfort.

## Paddling adventures

Rental cottages often come with a rowboat that you can use free of charge to investigate the local lake and islands.

## Steamy tradition

There's no better sauna than a *mökki* one: the heat feels much gentler with their wood stoves. Dashing nude into the chilly lake is truly Finnish.

## BEST MÖKKI EXPERIENCES

Stay in a shoreside glass house in Lake Saimaa's **Oravi village ❶**, a launching pad to the Kolovesi and Linnansaari national parks. (p131)

Take a **summer boat cruise ❷** by a sacred Sámi island on the Inarijärvi in northern Lapland. (p203)

Relax in a wilderness hut on Finland's side of the **Three-Country Cairn ❸**, where Finnish, Norwegian and Swedish waters meet. (p214)

Get a taste for Finnish nature staying in a cottage in **Nuuksio National Park ❹**, close enough to Helsinki for an overnight stay. (p52)

Combine seaside cottage stays with island hops and hunting landscapes during Finland's best cycling adventure, Turku's **Archipelago Trail ❺**. (p87)

# REGIONS & CITIES

Find the places that tick all your boxes.

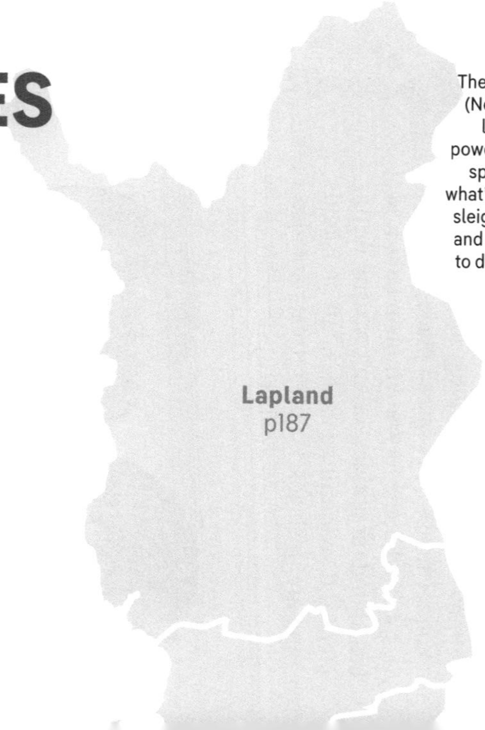

## West Coast & Northern Ostrobothnia

**NATURE'S BOUNTY**

Finland's west coast is a dreamy cache of historic wooden towns, sand-and-stone seaboard, and laidback islands. Northern Ostrobothnia, bordering Russia, offers remote national parks and some of the country's most abundantly beautiful scenery. With tumbling rivers, isolated lakes and dense forests, look no further for energetic, al fresco escapes.

p157

Lapland
p187

## Lapland

**ARCTIC WONDER**

The midnight sun, aurora borealis (Northern Lights) and awesome latitudes combine to cast a powerful spell. The sense of empty space, pure air and big skies is what's memorable here. Spend days sleighing, sledding, snowmobiling and reindeer spotting. Head north to discover the ancestral home of the Sámi people.

p187

## Turku, the South Coast & Åland Archipelago

**MARINE HERITAGE**

Discover Finland's seafaring southern charm and distinctive little port towns strung along the coast and archipelago. Unique historical features include captivating castles, fortresses and sailboats, plus former bruk (ironworks) buildings revamped for modern times. Get in touch with warm-hearted, Swedish-speaking islanders and their unique maritime traditions.

**p73**

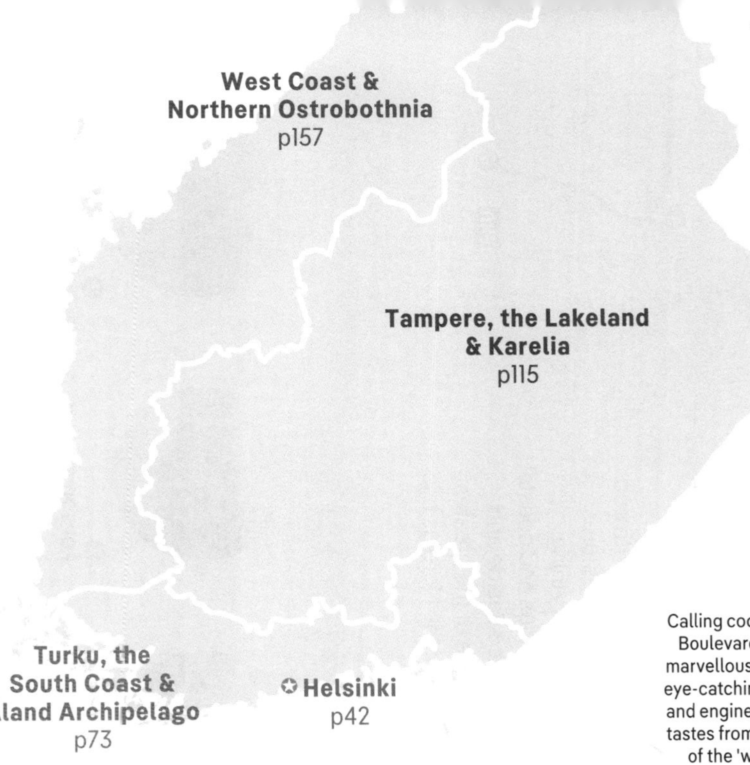

## Tampere, the Lakeland & Karelia

**IDYLLIC OUTDOORS**

Get in touch with nature – both in city centres and delightfully remote forests. With some 180,000 lakes, much of Finland is lakeland, but these parts boast the most glorious aqua. Discover trendy waterside haunts in Tampere and alfresco pursuits, from wildlife spotting to hiking, eastwards to Kuhmo, near the Russian border.

**p115**

## Helsinki

**COASTAL CAPITAL**

Calling cool hunters: Helsinki aims to inspire. Boulevards and backstreets overflow with marvellous architecture, hip gastronomy, and eye-catching design. Delight in impressive art and engineering, nearby lake life and exciting tastes from farm to forest. Here, in the capital of the 'world's happiest country', there's something for everyone.

**p42**

ITINERARIES

# Essential Suomi

**Allow:** 7 days
**Distance:** 957km

This greatest-hits list roves around the country's south and central regions, and features a little taster of everything: typical Finnish cities and coastal living across the seaside and lakes, plus some of the greatest historical sights the Nordics has to offer.

❶

### HELSINKI ⏱ 2 DAYS

Kick things off in **Helsinki** (p42). The capital is an electrifying urban space with world-renowned design and music scenes. Discover a spectacular ensemble of modern and stately architecture, stylish and quirky bars, and lavish spas with Baltic Sea views. Your meals in Helsinki will be memorable – devour the 'new Suomi' epicurean scene in all its farmed and foraged glory. Tampere, Finland

*50-minute drive*

❷

### PORVOO ⏱ ½ DAY

Helsinki and **Porvoo** (p72) are a smart package deal. Finland's second-oldest city is a real charmer in its own right, though, famed for the enchanting wooden buildings stacked around its historic old town. Treat yourself to a fantastic lunch (Porvoo's gastronomy scene is currently the talk of Finland) and a few containers of local homemade sweets for the road.

*3¼-hour drive*

❸

### SAIMAA LAKELAND ⏱ 1½ DAYS

Make your way eastwards to **Saimaa Lakeland** (p129), where the shiny bodies of water come in all cuts and shapes. Lake Saimaa, Finland's largest lake, has a solid pick of cute shorelines and abundant *mökki* (cottages) to call your sanctuary. The region offers epic drives and summer boat trips – a stop in Savonlinna, with its stunning medieval castle, is essential.

*4-hour drive*



FROM LEFT: RITTIS/SHUTTERSTOCK ©, SURATWADEE RATTANAJARUPAK/SHUTTERSTOCK ©, DIMM3D/SHUTTERSTOCK ©

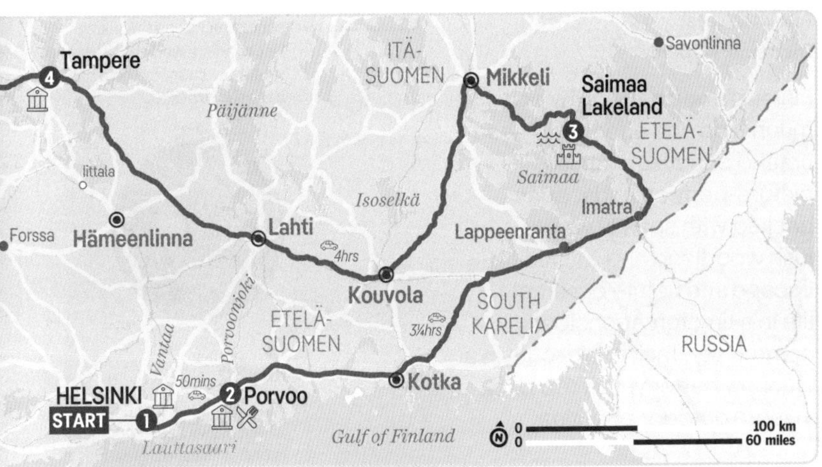

❹
**TAMPERE** 1 DAY

Loop west to **Tampere** (p120), where a groovy model of post-industrial regeneration awaits. A peek into Finland's industrial origins is rounded out by the city's bohemian vibe and stunning lakescapes. Explore former fabric mills and warehouses revamped into gastronomy hot spots, eye-worthy shops and unusual museums. Enjoy a coffee to go on the city-centre banks of the Tammerkoski rapids.

*2-hour drive*

❺
**RAUMA** 1 DAY

**Rauma's** (p162) old-town district, Vanha Rauma, is the largest preserved Nordic wooden town. Your pleasure mission here is simply meandering the quaint streets of this Unesco World Heritage Site, popping into shops, perhaps a cosy cafe, and spying on artisans working in their small studios. Try to visit between Tuesday and Saturday, when everything's open and humming with life.

*1¼-hour drive*

❻
**TURKU** 1 DAY

Cut southwards to **Turku** (p78). Finland's oldest city (and technically its original capital) is an essential Suomi 'hit parade' stop for its grand medieval seats, Swedish origin stories and showy harbour vistas. In this buzzy university city, you'll find plenty of action at live-music pubs, galleries and gratifying riverside restaurants. Not done exploring? Hop a ferry to the Åland Islands from here.

FROM LEFT: PYSTO_PHOTOGRAPHY/SHUTTERSTOCK ©, HARRY HYKKO/SHUTTERSTOCK ©, MARCO TALIANI DE MARCHIO/SHUTTERSTOCK ©

ITINERARIES

# Call of the Wild

**Allow:** 12 days

**Distance:** 1420km

Finland's north is worthy of much time and affection. These upland beauties promise picture-perfect landscapes packed with sparkly waters, lush woodland and wildlife. Escape into nature or sample life in a tiny, forest-enclosed community. Tackle this route in a week, or better yet two to pack in more outdoor activities.

**Koli National Park**

LEFT: MAZUR TRAVEL/SHUTTERSTOCK ©

## 1 KOLI NATIONAL PARK

2 DAYS

**Koli National Park** (p162), Finland's most scenic turf, is a strong starter to getting wild in Suomi. Its 347m-high mountain inspired Finland's artistic National Romantic era. These rich primeval forests are superb for hitting the hiking tracks (90km worth!), observing wildlife or strapping on a pair of snowshoes or skis.

*2-hour drive*

## 2 KUHMO

2 DAYS

Head north to **Kuhmo** (p155), where brown bear–watching is one of Finland's greatest wildlife experiences. Vast taiga forests, running from here across to Siberia, provide more wildlife-watching (wolves, lynx, wild reindeer, for example). Hike, swim and cycle in Karelia's pristine green.

*Detour: Discover Finland's 'capital of the north', **Oulu** (p175).*

*4-hour drive*

## 3 OULANKA NATIONAL PARK

2 DAYS

Cut further north to **Oulanka National Park** (p179), for some serious trekking. The Karhunkierros (Bear's Ring), one of the oldest and best-established trekking routes, offers breathtaking scenery. You can also go canoeing or white-water rafting – and in winter, snowshoeing and cross-country skiing. At night, curl up in a wilderness hut.

*2½-hour drive*



ABOVE: WAYNE MARINOVICH/SHUTTERSTOCK ©

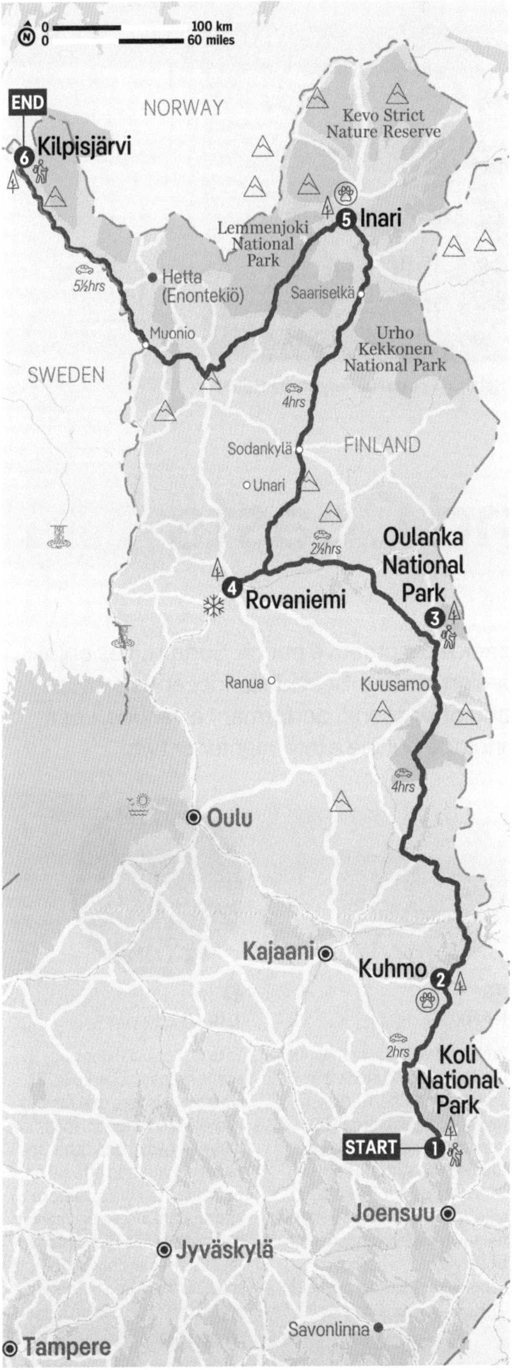

0 100 km
0 60 miles
END
NORWAY
Kevo Strict Nature Reserve
6 Kilpisjärvi
Lemmenjoki National Park
5 Inari
5½hrs
Hetta (Enontekiö)
Saariselkä
Muonio
Urho Kekkonen National Park
SWEDEN
4hrs
Sodankylä
FINLAND
Unari
2½hrs
Oulanka National Park
4 Rovaniemi
3
Ranua
Kuusamo
4hrs
Oulu
Kajaani
Kuhmo 2
2hrs
Koli National Park
START 1
Joensuu
Jyväskylä
Savonlinna
Tampere

❹

## ROVANIEMI ⏱ 2 DAYS

Head to **Rovaniemi** (p192), capital of Lapland, and a great base for outdoor activities. Communicate with Arctic nature and get acquainted with northern climes: visit lakeside reindeer and husky farms, forage berries and mushrooms in the forest, and search for wildlife such as elk. During winter, cross your fingers for the clearest skies possible to witness the shimmering aurora borealis (Northern Lights).

*4-hour drive*

❺

## INARI ⏱ 2 DAYS

**Inari** (p200) is where unforgettable Arctic adventures take place. This tiny village in Lapland is a cultural capital for the Sámi people. Prime yourself for guided nature tours, visits to reindeer farms and a cosy log-cabin stay. Get even more off the beaten track with a foray into the remote wilderness of Lemmenjoki and Urho Kekkonen national parks.

*5½-hour drive*

❻

## KILPISJÄRVI ⏱ 2 DAYS

Head northwest to remote **Kilpisjärvi** (p213); pictured above. Wedged between its namesake lake and the magnificent fells, this is the country's highest village. Take the boat to the remote border point where Finland meets Norway and Sweden in the shadow of fearsome Norwegian mountains, then walk 11km back across electrifyingly beautiful Arctic wilderness.

ABOVE: HENRYBON/SHUTTERSTOCK ©

GRISHA BRUEV/SHUTTERSTOCK ©

Helsinki Central railway station (p53)

ITINERARIES

# Cities and Coasts

**Allow:** 7 days **Distance:** 661km

Finland's urban centres pack a big creative punch. Suomi cities enjoy thriving arts, music and design scenes. Seaside landscapes provide artisans with inspiration and offer scenic performance venues. Let's face it, this itinerary may include pulling a late-nighter or two.

### 1 HELSINKI ⏱ 2 DAYS

In **Helsinki** (p42), you'll get a fix of Finland's distinctive brand of Nordic urban living through bold architecture, fascinating museums and the Design District's studios and boutiques. Get fired up on innovative, indulgent fine dining. Quirky bars, plus the Finnish tendency for warming up after a few drinks, promise good times.

*1¾-hour drive*

### 2 HANKO ⏱ 1 DAY

Small yet vibrant communities like **Hanko** (p72) stock the country's southern areas, revealing a past forged by ironworks and foreign rule. Cherish this seaside escape with a stay in a former tsarist villa, a spa treat and a dose of the town's important wartime history. Catch a harbour sundowner before a pub night.

*2-hour drive*

### 3 TURKU ⏱ 2 DAYS

Take in the social drinking scene in coastal **Turku** (p78), where locals lose that famous reserve after a *tuoppi* (half-litre glass) or two of beer. The city is full of original and offbeat bars boasting live music, karaoke and student life. At the market hall, a centuries-old fish-soup recipe cures any hangover, and will help for taking in Turku's superb arts and design circuit.

*1¼-hour drive*

FROM LEFT: XSEON/SHUTTERSTOCK ©,, TSUGULIEV/SHUTTERSTOCK ©,, MAHMOUD SUHAIL/SHUTTERSTOCK ©

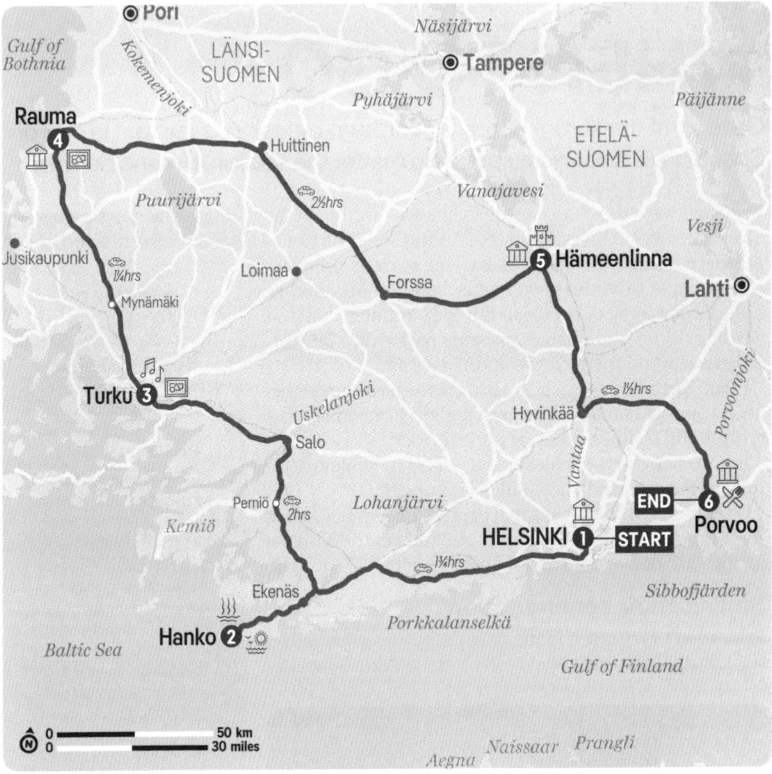

Pori
Gulf of Bothnia
Kokemenjoki
LÄNSI-SUOMEN
Näsijärvi
Tampere
Pyhäjärvi
Päijänne
ETELÄ-SUOMEN
Rauma 4
Huittinen
2½hrs
Puurijärvi
Vanajavesi
Vesji
Uusikaupunki
1¼hrs
Loimaa
Forssa
5 Hämeenlinna
Lahti
Mynämäki
Turku 3
Uskelanjoki
1½hrs
Hyvinkää
Porvoonjoki
Salo
Vantaa
Perniö
2hrs
Lohanjärvi
END 6
Porvoo
Kemiö
HELSINKI 1 START
1¾hrs
Ekenäs
Sibbofjärden
Porkkalanselkä
Hanko 2
Baltic Sea
Gulf of Finland
0 50 km
0 30 miles
Naissaar
Prangli
Aegna

**4**

## RAUMA 1 DAY

**Rauma** (p162), the largest wooden old town in the Nordic countries, deserves its Unesco World Heritage status. Amid the lovely 600 houses are low-key cafes, shops, museums and artisans' workshops. Tune your ear into Rauman giäl, an old sailors' lingo.

***Detour**: Discover trendy **Tampere's** (p120) quirky museums, pubs and cafes.*

*2½-hour drive*

**5**

## HÄMEENLINNA ½ DAY

**Hämeenlinna** (p146), Finland's oldest inland city is a picturesque place to recharge. Don't miss the namesake castle, an ancient Swedish stronghold of historical importance, and a museum or two. Hämeenlinna also makes an excellent pit stop between Helsinki and Tampere.

*Discover Aalto architecture in the 'Athens of Finland', **Jyväskylä** (p139).*

*1½-hour drive*

**6**

## PORVOO ½ DAY

**Porvoo** (p109) is a solid finish to your Finnish itinerary (it's less than 50km from Helsinki's airport). Stroll lovely cobbled lanes and riverside wooden warehouses lining the old town. Grab a fabulous last meal at one of its many up-and-coming gastronomic venues. Don't forget to load up your luggage with chocolate boxes (the local speciality) and other handmade souvenirs.

FROM LEFT: MIKKO LEMOLA/SHUTTERSTOCK ©, JANUS ORLOV/SHUTTERSTOCK , MCAJAN/SHUTTERSTOCK ©

# WHEN TO GO

Gaze up at the aurora borealis (Northern Lights), or camp out in one of Scandinavia's sunniest spots. No matter the season, Finland delivers.

The Sámi have some 200 words for snow – hinting at the diversity of these climes. Inside the Arctic Circle, the Sámi's northern ancestral home sees extreme seasons, from 24-hour daylight to winter polar nights. Southern regions like Åland enjoy some of northern Europe's sunniest, mildest weather. Cities and villages, pristine parks and the lakes in between find their groove at different times of year.

Head north from March to April for the best shot at seeing the aurora borealis (Northern Lights). From April, boat cruises and southern coastal festivals kick off.

In October, ports get sleepy but this is a fabulous time to have beaches and viewpoints to yourself.

Winters are prone to seasonal depression – in December, the Arctic sun never rises. Southern and central Finland are privy to downpours and six-hour windows of sunlight.

## Saving on Accommodation

Prices don't vary much in the year. Campsites offer budget stays, including caravans and cabins in the warmer months.

I LIVE HERE

### SUMMER SOLSTICE

**Helsinki-born artist Isabella Chydenius spent her childhood summers in Hanko @isabellachydenius**

"Summer mornings start by deciding which beach to cycle to. Bellevue beach has shallow waters, with dunes for lounging by the warm sea and reading between ice-cream breaks. Although Hanko (Hango) is famous for its beaches and villas, what's special to me are its large, round rocks and cliffs. They're warm to sit on in summer, telling stories of another time."

Reindeer in Lapland (p187)

### BRIGHT DEAD OF NIGHT

The midnight sun – when the sun remains visible at midnight inside the Arctic Circle – goes from about mid-May to late July, bringing darkness down to five hours per night. In the far north, the sun doesn't set at all.

RIGHT: ANTEROVIUM; FAR RIGHT: FUJILOVERS/SHUTTERSTOCK ©

## Weather through the year (Helsinki)

| JANUARY | FEBRUARY | MARCH | APRIL | MAY | JUNE |
|---|---|---|---|---|---|
| Ave. daytime max: **-2°C** | Ave. daytime max: **-2°C** | Ave. daytime max: **2°C** | Ave. daytime max: **8°C** | Ave. daytime max: **14°C** | Ave. daytime max: **18°C** |
| Days of rainfall: 12 | Days of rainfall: 9 | Days of rainfall: 8 | Days of rainfall: 7 | Days of rainfall: 7 | Days of rainfall: 9 |

### AURORA BOREALIS QUESTS

In Lapland, October, November and March, between the hours of 9pm and 2am, are the best times to watch the lights of the aurora borealis dance (p232). The region's ancient inhabitants believed the streaky skies were caused by a giant fox swishing its tail above the Arctic tundra.

## Biggest Celebrations

**Juhannus** (Midsummer) is the most important annual celebration for Finns. The country shuts down as people head to cottages to celebrate the longest day of the year with bonfires and dancing. On the Åland islands, see villagers adorn maypoles in flowers. **July**

The **Savonlinna Opera Festival** (p130) is Finland's most famous festival. Month-long performances take place in the romantic covered courtyard of Olavinlinna Castle. **July**

Join thousands of spectators at the **Ruisrock** (p82) rock festival on an island outside Turku. Line-ups are stacked with big acts. **July**

In the weeks leading up to the Yuletide holidays, cobblestone town squares host traditional **Christmas markets** with wooden stands selling treats and decorations. Drink a *glögi* (hot punch) in Porvoo's Old Town. **December**

### I LIVE HERE

### WINTER PASTIME

**Irene Kangasniemi designs jewellery and home decor from natural forest materials. She lives near Rovaniemi @kangasniemihornwork**

"Winters are best when we have a lot of snow. The more snow, the better the berries are next summer. This time of year, I cook with my wood oven. Moose meat with *rieska* bread is my favourite winter dish. Moose eat forest plants such as berries...they are thankful for winter, too."

***Rieska* bread**

## Local Festivals & Celebrations

Head to Inari for the '**Royal Reindeer Race**' (p207), the grand finale of Finnish Lapland's reindeer-racing season over the frozen Inarijärvi. **March or April**

Traditionally a festival of students and workers, **Vappuaatto** (May Day Eve) followed by **Vappu** (May Day) mark the beginning of summer with plenty of sparkling wine and merrymaking by lakes and in parks. **April to May**

In the southern port town of Naantali, **National Sleepyhead Day** is marked by villagers dousing each other with water and getting tossed out to sea. A lively carnival atmosphere includes dancing, live music, a bake-off and more. **July**

The three-day **Skábmagovat** indigenous peoples' film festival holds screenings at an open-air snow theatre. It takes place in Lapland, in the Sámi capital of Inari. **January**

### LUSH LAKE LIFE

The average Finn spends less than two days in a hotel each year, but several weeks in cottages. July is the busiest month on the coast and around lakes, as this is when Finns tend to enjoy their summer holidays.

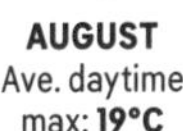

| JULY | AUGUST | SEPTEMBER | OCTOBER | NOVEMBER | DECEMBER |
|---|---|---|---|---|---|
| Ave. daytime max: **21°C** | Ave. daytime max: **19°C** | Ave. daytime max: **14°C** | Ave. daytime max: **9°C** | Ave. daytime max: **4°C** | Ave. daytime max: **0°C** |
| Days of rainfall: 7 | Days of rainfall: 10 | Days of rainfall: 9 | Days of rainfall: 10 | Days of rainfall: 12 | Days of rainfall: 12 |

LEFT: TSUGULIEV/SHUTTERSTOCK ©; RIGHT: ANDREAS RENTZ/GETTY IMAGES ©

Oulanka National Park (p179)

# GET PREPARED FOR FINLAND

Useful things to load in your bag, your ears and your brain

## Clothes

**Casual attire:** Finns are masters of practicality. In the heart of Helsinki, fashion is sleek yet functional and minimalistic, with a penchant for textiles that are sustainable and long lasting. There's no need to pack lots of fancy clothes, especially when planning to spend time alfresco.

**Comfy clothes:** Blend right in during warmer months with outfits that translate well from urban patios to *mökki* (summer cottage) such as comfy sandals and a light jacket. Sturdy walking shoes are a must.

**Layers:** Pack for seasonal extremes. For northern climes, make sure you have items in which to bundle up, such as thermals, wool socks and other knitwear, windproof items and a parka.

**Swimwear:** Don't forget your trunks and goggles. In saunas, swimwear is optional – bring flip-flops for showering.

### Manners

**Finnish culture is rather polite and reserved.** Finns believe in comfortable silences. There's no need for small talk.

**Finns love to have fun.** It's not that Finns don't talk. Once they get a couple of pints in, that reserve tends to go out the window.

**And they're known for quirky and dark humour.** Self-deprecating jokes and well-timed jibes will be deeply appreciated.

## READ

**Sisu: The Finnish Art of Courage** (Joanna Nylund; 2018) All you need to know about the nation's defining trait and resilience.

**Tales from Moominvalley** (Tove Jansson; 1962) This is one of the most beloved Moomin books in Finland and beyond.

**Frozen Hell: The Russo-Finnish Winter War of 1939–1940** (William R Trotter; 2013) Finland's fight to keep its independence.

**Kalevala** (Elias Lönnrot; 1835) Finland's national epic, compiled from bard songs, telling all from the world's origins to how to home brew.

## Words

**'hei'** (hay) is how you say 'hello' in Finnish.
**'näkemiin'** (na·ke·meen) means 'goodbye'.
**'hyvää päivää'** (hy·vah pai·vah) means 'good day'.
**'hauska tavata'** (hau·ska ta·va·ta) means 'nice to meet you'.
**'kiitos (paljon)'** (kee·tos (puhl·yon)) is 'thank you (very much)'.
Order in a restaurant by saying **'saisinko...'** (sai·sin·ko) or 'I would like...'.
**'pullon (olutta)'** (pul·lon (o·lut·tuh)) is a bottle (of beer).
**'(kupin) kahvia'** (ku·pin) kuh·vi·uh) is a (cup of) coffee.
**'(kupin) teetä'** (ku·pin) tay·ta) is a (cup of) tea.
**'kippis!'** (kip·pis) means 'cheers!'
In saunas, **'kauha'** (kau·ha) is the ladle, and the steam is called **'löyly'** (löy·ly). The bunch of twigs for hitting oneself is a **'vasta'** (vas·ta) in eastern Finland, and **'vihta'** (vih·ta) elsewhere.
**'kalsarikännit'** (kal·saree·kahn·it) is drinking at home with no pants or getting 'pantsdrunk'.
**'sisu'** (si·su) is a Finnish trait often translated as 'guts', or the resilience to survive prolonged hardship.
**'kaamos'** (kaa·mos) is a 'polar night'.
**'kuksa'** (kuk·sa) is a traditional, hand-carved wooden cup for drinking outdoors.

## WATCH

**The Unknown Soldier** (Aku Louhimies; 2017) Third adaptation of Finland's most revered fictional novel about the Winter War.

**Hanna** (Joe Wright; 2011) A psychological thriller about a young girl raised by her father as an assassin in northern Finland.

**The Man Without a Past** (Aki Kaurismäki, pictured; 2002) Comedic drama about a man who finds himself, post-coma, in Helsinki.

**Bordertown** (Miikko Oikkonen; 2016) 'Nordic noir' crime-drama set in a town by the Russian border.

**Road North** (Mika Kaurismäki; 2012) Estranged father-and-son's road trip across northern Finland.

## LISTEN

**Mastering Finland** (2019) For expats in Finland by expats in Finland – a podcast exploring what it's like to live and work here.

**Very Finnish Problems** (Joel Willans; 2017) Podcast (plus book and popular Instagram account of the same name) delving into Finland's cultural quirks.

**Mún** (Wimmi; 2009) Kelottijärvi-born artist Wimme Saari explores the Sámi *'joik'* vocal tradition with hypnotic ambient beats.

**Sibelius: Finlandia** (Thomas Søndergard; 2018) Modern orchestra performance of the Jean Sibelius tone poem that has shaped national identity.

FANFO/SHUTTERSTOCK ©

Traditional Finnish fare

# THE FOOD SCENE

**Finland's landscape is dominated by lakes and forests, which also influences the country's cuisine; prepare your palate for earthy flavours.**

In recent years, Finnish chefs have turned to respecting and reinventing Finland's traditional gastronomy. And not just the Michelin-starred Helsinki establishments: you will find country house manors, restaurants and hotels all over the country offering the best of local produce – often in a picture-perfect setting, too.

Whether you are ordering seafood, meat or vegetarian dishes, it's all about simplicity and seasons here.

Think locally fished cod, summery strawberries and autumnal mushrooms from the nearby forests, rich meats of moose or reindeer, with a hint of spruce tree and smoke lingering in the background, and you'll get the gist of Finnish cuisine.

Market halls in cities such as Helsinki, Tampere, Turku and Kuopio still offer a glimpse of the traditional Finnish dishes, from vendace (freshwater fish) to cinnamon buns or Karelian pies served with simple filter coffee, but nowadays there are also stalls serving gourmet versions of the old Finnish classics, as well as other ethnic flavours from around the globe.

## Finnish food traditions

Finnish home cooking has traditionally been a simple affair, varying from hearty meat stews and hefty casseroles in the winter to lightly fried pikeperch and delicate new potatoes in the summer.

Many homeowners also grow berries and apples, and dedicate time in the autumn to make jams and juices for the winter

**Best Finnish dishes**

**KARJALANPAISTI**
Meat cubes stewed overnight with vegetables. Served with potatoes.

**LOHIKEITTO**
Salmon soup with a clear/creamy broth, served with dill.

**KESÄKEITTO**
Summer soup with season's vegetables, such as peas and cauliflower.

months. Some go hunting, with restricted licences for hunting moose and bear yearly, and the fines for poaching are hefty. People actively forage too, and fill their freezers with frozen vitamin bombs, such as bilberries and sea buckthorn berries.

In fact, foraging isn't just a trend in Finland, but a skill often passed from one generation to the other. Visitors can also easily participate in this activity, as foraging courses are organised all over Finland.

Another skill typically passed from one generation to the next is bread making, with some families holding dear a heritage starter dough to make rye or white bread.

## Ethical eating

Helsinki is a haven for responsible eating, as the city offers plenty of choices for vegetarians and vegans – other bigger cities, such as Turku and Tampere, follow close behind. In more remote towns forward-thinking vegetarian and vegan establishments are popping up, but tasty veggie dishes might still turn out to be a rarity.

In rural areas, such as Saimaa Lakeland, Lapland, Karelia and the Åland Islands, instead of vegan joints, you are likely to find restaurants taking pride in offering locally sourced organic food, varying from fish and meat to vegetables and berries, served in quaint settings.

Another way of tackling environmental issues in Finland is concentrating on food waste. Restaurants such as Nolla (meaning zero), with its zero-waste ethos, lead the way in Helsinki. You can also download the ResQ app and pick up a leftover restaurant meal at a reduced price. The app covers all of Finland, from Helsinki to Lapland's Ivalo.

**Foraging in Finland**

RIGHT: MAJNA/SHUTTERSTOCK ©, BOTTOM LEFT: TANHU/SHUTTERSTOCK ©

### FOOD & WINE FESTIVALS

**Helsinki Herring Market** (*silakkamarkkinat.fi; early October*) Helsinki city-centre market combines traditional atmosphere with modern foodie finds into a joyful ode to one small fish, the herring.

**Kuopio Wine Festival** (*kuopiowinefestival.fi; late June–early October*) Finland's biggest wine and food festival is set in Kuopio Harbour.

**Ahvenanmaan sadonkorjuujuhlat** (*skordefest.ax; September*) A harvest festival in the Åland Islands celebrates this foodie island's local produce. Restaurants, breweries, farmhouses and pop-ups participate.

**Hillamarkkinat** (*hillamarkkinat.fi; August*) Ranua is Lapland's unofficial cloudberry capital and holds a festival for this 'gold of Lapland' on the first weekend in August.

**Smaku** (*smakufestivals.com; various*) Set in quaint Porvoo, Loviisa (Lovisa) and Naantali, all famed for their wooden-house architecture; local restaurants serve dishes priced from €5 to €7.

**PORONKÄRISTYS** Sautéed reindeer from the Sámi area. Served with lingonberries/pickled cucumber.

**PAISTETUT MUIKUT** Small fish rolled in rye flour and fried in butter.

**GRAAVILOHI** Thinly sliced cured salmon; can be served with rye bread.

**LIHAPULLAT** Finnish meatballs served with mashed potatoes, brown sauce and lingonberries.

**PANNUKAKKU** Thick pancake baked in the oven, served with jam and cream.

## Specialities

Sweet or savoury, Finnish food delivers.

### Snacks

**Lihapiirakka, lörtsy:** (deep-fried doughnut-like pie filled with minced meat and rice)
**Omenalörtsy:** (same as above but with sweet apple jam filling)
**Ruisleipä:** (rye bread)
**Ahvenanmaan mustaleipä:** (sweetened and malty black bread from the Åland Islands)
**Ohrapuuro:** (pearl barley porridge stewed overnight)
**Kalakukko:** (traditionally vendace or European char and pork baked in a rye crust)
**Karelian pie:** (thin rye crust filled with rice porridge)
**Munavoi:** (boiled eggs with butter, served with Karelian pies)
**Rönttönen:** (Karelian pie made with rye or barley flour and filled with sweetened potato and berries)
**Kaalikääryle:** (cooked cabbage leaves filled with minced meat and rice)
**Viili:** (fermented milk, similar to yoghurt but sour; can be served with jam or sugar and cinnamon)

### Favourite sweet treats

**Leipäjuusto:** (squeaky baked cheese served hot/cold with cloudberry jam)

Korvapuusti

**Mustikkakukko:** (blueberry pie baked in rye crust)
**Korvapuusti:** (cinnamon bun)
**Munkki:** (doughnuts with a jam filling)
**Lakkakakku:** (sponge cake with cloudberries and cream, sometimes with a caramel topping)

### Dare to try

**Mustamakkara:** (blood sausage served with lingonberry jam)
**Salmiakki:** (salty and strong-flavoured liquorice candy)
**Salmiakkisnapsi:** (a vodka schnapps made of liquorice)
**Mämmi:** (Easter-time dessert made of rye flour and powdered malted rye, served with sugar and cream)

### MEALS OF A LIFETIME

**Laanilan Kievari (p208)** Imaginative preparations of Lapland reindeer, elk and lake fish, plus veggie options, in a wooden cottage near Saariselkä.

**Finnjävel (p71)** Michelin-starred restaurant in Helsinki; Finnish traditional cuisine with a modern take.

**Kalaliike S Wallin (p81)** Sit on a bar stool in Turku Market Hall and order from Finland's second-oldest fish shop (1896).

**Tertti Manor (p130)** The best of Finnish manor house hospitality in a rustic setting.

**Kolin Ryynänen (p153)** Experience a warm-hearted Karelian ambience and *mustikkakukko* dessert in the gastro-pub near Koli National Park.

**Sydvest (p160)** Local and global ingredients combine in this tasteful, bistro-style restaurant in old Rauma.

LEFT: KATTY S/SHUTTERSTOCK ©; RIGHT: ALEXANDERPHOTO7/SHUTTERSTOCK ©

### THE YEAR IN FOOD

**SPRING**

Spring kicks off in Finland with a 1st of May (or Vappu) party, when you will see people picnicking and sipping on *sima*, a fermented lemony soda, and feasting on freshly baked doughnuts.

**SUMMER**

Finnish summer truly kicks in when strawberries appear in the markets in June. Also try freshly caught pikeperch with the summer season's delicately sweet new potatoes.

**AUTUMN**

Autumn marks the end of the foraging season, with people heading to forests to pick up the last of the chanterelles and berries, such as sea buckthorn, lingonberry and juniper berry.

**WINTER**

In December, visit Finnish Christmas markets and sample the season's delicacies, such as *glögi*, the Finnish version of mulled wine, served with raisins and almonds and, if you like, a dash of vodka.

FROM LEFT: THE ART OF PICS, JOPPO, PAULA SAVELIUS, LENISECALLEJA.PHOTOGRAPHY/SHUTTERSTOCK ©



**Right: Cafe Regatta, Helsinki (p67)**

REGATTA
OPEN
CAFE
Have a Happy day

TSUGULIEV/SHUTTERSTOCK ©

Repovesi National Park (p137)

# THE OUTDOORS

Stretching for 1157km from south to north, Finland's landscape varies from the relatively flat lakesides of the south to the fells and waterfalls of the north.

With three-quarters of Finland covered with forests, and the rest of the land holding some 188,000 lakes, almost the whole country is an outdoorsy backyard awaiting exploration, whether that be by foot, skis, bike or paddle. It can be as simple as popping to Nuuksio National Park from Helsinki for a day hike, or packing a tent for a multiday hike, with everyman's rights giving you the freedom to roam, forage and enjoy the land for free.

## Hiking

Finland's old-growth, coniferous forests, clean air and network of lakes and rivers make a beautiful setting for hikes. Walking in nature is part of the Finnish identity, and may even contribute to the people's happiness levels, with Finland consistently ranking among the happiest nations on earth.

The best time for hiking is from May to October, although during summer months, mosquito repellent is a must. The spectacular show of autumn foliage begins in Lapland in early September and reaches southern Finland by the beginning of October.

Finland's 41 national parks cover over a million hectares of land, and there is a national park or two near all major cities.

Arctic wilderness with vast boglands and bare fells can be experienced in any part of Lapland, whereas further south you will

## Wildlife watching

**BEAR-WATCHING**
Stay overnight in one of the huts or cottages in the wilderness surrounding **Kuhmo** (p155) in eastern Finland.

**BIRDWATCHING**
**Kylmäpihlaja island** (p166) in Rauma's archipelago is home to 28 nesting bird species.

**SEAL SPOTTING**
Look for endangered Saimaa ringed seals on an eco-boat trip around the **Saimaa archipelago** (p129).

## FAMILY ADVENTURES

**Hire a kayak or SUP** from **Cafe Regatta** (p67) and explore Helsinki's seaside – in winter, take a hike on the ice and then enjoy hot chocolates and cinnamon buns after.
**Head to a lighthouse** on Oulu's popular summer spot, **Hailuoto island** (p178).

**Stroll around Moomin central** at **Muumimaailma** (p85). Moomins sleep in the wintertime, but the area is still accessible.
**Say hello to Santa** and then ride a reindeer sled at the **Santa Claus Village** (p197).

**Ranua Wildlife Park** (p198) homes arctic animals varying from brown bears and lynxes to Arctic foxes.
**Chill out** on 6km-long **Yyteri beach** (p168), with a host of activities for children, from horse riding to a water trampoline and climbing park.

find serene lakes lined with enchanting pine, spruce and birch forests.

An extensive network of wilderness huts (p210) makes multiday hikes easier.

In summer, you can enjoy a forest setting by spending a night in a wilderness hut. It's the perfect chance to discover Finland and is also one of the best places in Europe for bear-watching.

## Snow Activities

There's something mesmerising about a white, snow-covered landscape, which lasts approximately from late November to April in southern parts of Finland and October to May in Lapland. For adventurous skiers, Lapland's slopes, such as Ounasvaara near Rovaniemi, offer the rush of adrenalin, while cross-country tracks wind around rural and urban landscapes all over Finland.

Many hotels and rental spots provide snowshoes to tackle the terrain at a slower pace. Or you could have a once-in-a-lifetime experience, hopping on to a sled pulled by reindeer or huskies and racing through Lapland's Christmas-card scenery. Further south, Koli National Park's peaks offer Lapland-like winter activities as well as scenery with its snow-laden tree branches.

**BEST SPOTS**
For the best outdoor activities and routes, see page 38.

Snowshoeing in Lapland (p187)

NBLX/SHUTTERSTOCK ©

## Water Sports

Finland's lakes, rivers and rapids offer multiple ways to explore the country from water level, whether you're a beginner or a heavyweight paddler. Kayak, canoe and SUP rentals are easy to find across the country, from Helsinki's city centre to Lapland's wilderness. Or, if you want to take it easy, hop aboard a slow boat in Savonlinna to navigate the lakes and canals of the Finnish Lakeland.

The lakes freeze over in winter (about December to April) and offer other activities: ice-hole fishing and, for the more daring, ice-hole swimming, which can be experienced in all major cities plus some hotels and cottage rentals across the country.

**MOOSE SPOTTING**
In **Rovaniemi** (p197), Lapland Welcome provides nature trips, including one focused on moose spotting and wildlife photography.

**REINDEER FARMS**
Visit a Sámi reindeer farm in **Inari** (p207), close to the northern tip of Lapland.

**MORE BEAR-WATCHING**
Finland's most popular ski resort, **Ruka** (p183), also offers bear-spotting trips.

**LOON BIRDWATCHING**
Birdwatchers head to **Olhavanvuori in Repovesi National Park** (p137), where flocks of red-throated loons live by an imposing cliff.

# ACTION AREAS

Where to find Finland's best outdoor activities.

### Snow Activities

1. Ruka skiing (p183)
2. Rovaniemi sleigh rides (p192)
3. Kiilopää cross-country skiing (p211)
4. Snowshoe safaris in Kuhmo (p155)
5. Ice-hole swimming in Helsinki (p56)

### Northern Lights Hunting

1. Saariselkä (p210)
2. Rovaniemi (p192)
3. Inari (p200)
4. Ruka (p183)

### National Parks

1. Urho Kekkonen National Park (p211)
2. Oulanka National Park (p179)
3. Hossa National Park (p185)
4. Ekenäs Archipelago National Park (p107)
5. Nuuksio National Park (p52)

Water Activities
1 Canoeing in Saariselkä (p211)
2 Saimaa Canoeing (p131)
3 Boating through Lemmenjoki National Park (p208)
4 Kayaking in Rauma archipelago (p166)
5 Savonlinna slow boats (p130)
Hiking
1 Kilpisjärvi (p213)
2 Pieni Karhunkierros (p180)
3 Mäkrän kierros (p153)
4 Korpinkierros (p114)
5 Njurgulahti to Ravadasköngäs (p209)
Umeå
Kokkola
Kalajoki
Ylivieska
Kalajoki
Oulujärvi
Pyhäntä
Kajaani
Ontojärvi
Kuhmo
Jakobstad
Haapajärvi
Lestijärvi
Sonkajärvi
Nurmes
Björköby
Ähtävänjoki
Kaustinen
Lieksa
Pihitpudas
Pielinen
Vaasa
Viitasaari
Kuopio
Seinäjoki
Suonenjoki
Närpes
Närpes å
Alavus
Saarijärvi
Joensuu
Kristinestad
Virrat
Jyväskylä
Varkaus
Pieksämäki
RUSSIA
Parkano
Jämsä
Savonlinna
Puulavesi
Mikkeli
Saimaa
Orivesi
Pori
Tampere
Heinola
Imatra
Huittinen
Rauma
Hämeenlinna
Lahti
Kouvola
Lappeenranta
Lake Ladoga
Uusikaupunki
Forssa
Riihimäki
Åland
Kotka
Turku
SWEDEN
Porvoo
Mariehamn
Ekenäs
HELSINKI
St Petersburg
Hanko
Åland Sea
Gulf of Finland
ESTONIA

NBLX/SHUTTERSTOCK ©

FINLAND

# THE GUIDE

Chapters in this section are organised by hubs and their surrounding areas. We see the hub as your base in the destination, where you'll find unique experiences, local insights, insider tips and expert recommendations. It's also your gateway to the surrounding area, where you'll see what and how much you can do from there.

# HELSINKI

## NORTHERN COOLNESS WITH A NEIGHBOURLY TWIST

**The seaside capital is coolly becoming a northern hot spot for food and design, while also attracting visitors with its nature-driven lifestyle.**

When the Prussian architect Carl Ludwig Engel set foot in Helsinki in 1816, the city held a mere 4000 inhabitants. Seven years earlier, Finland had been annexed to Russia, after more than 600 years of Swedish rule, and Alexander I of Russia was keen to transfer Finland's capital from Turku to a place closer to home. He chose Helsinki, appointing Engel to upgrade its buildings. When the architect arrived, he didn't like what he saw, but he was on a mission: to create a worthy capital for the new Grand Duchy of Finland.

In the end, Engel reluctantly stayed in Helsinki for the rest of his life and completed about 30 buildings in the city. Some 50 years later, Helsinki's population had grown to 70,000 inhabitants, and the city began to fill with other types of buildings, such as the Helsinki Central railway station, designed by Eliel Saarinen, and the Stockmann department store, the largest such store in the Nordic countries, designed by Sigurd Frosterus. The city also saw the emergence of the Jugendstil or art nouveau style between Engel's neoclassical architecture and these early-20th-century creations.

All this grand architecture is just a backdrop to everyday life in the seaside city bordered by more than 130km of coastline. With waterfront promenades, cycle lanes, cafes and beaches, the coast is very much a part of Helsinki's lifestyle, as well as the 300 islands scattered nearby, providing natural escapes from the city. Helsinki's many parks, from the posh Esplanadi to small patches of greenery in every neighbourhood, provide calm respite.

During the last few decades, Helsinki's city scene has also changed drastically, and not just because of all the new architecture, from the award-winning Oodi library to the subterranean eye-catcher Amos Rex, but also in the city's atmosphere. There is now more diversity, bursts of joyous festivals, fine-dining restaurants respecting Finnish roots, and bustling cafes. Maybe, if Engel could set foot in Helsinki today, he too would be happy here.

LEFT: MIKHAIL VARENTSOV/SHUTTERSTOCK ©; RIGHT: CANADASTOCK/SHUTTERSTOCK ©

### THE MAIN AREAS

Helsinki city centre

# Find Your Way

Helsinki has only about 500,000 residents, but geographically the city is quite vast to tackle on foot. Luckily, the public transport network is extensive and prompt. To help your exploration, we've highlighted the main areas and landmarks in this seaside city of parks and wide boulevards.

**FROM THE AIRPORT**

From the underground station at the airport, it's a half-hour ride to the city centre. It takes about the same time by car. Allow a little more than 40 minutes for shuttle bus 600 to reach the city.

**WALK**

The best way to explore is on foot, as the city is almost completely flat. If you are up for urban hikes, tackle your city-centre sightseeing on foot – there is plenty to see along the way.

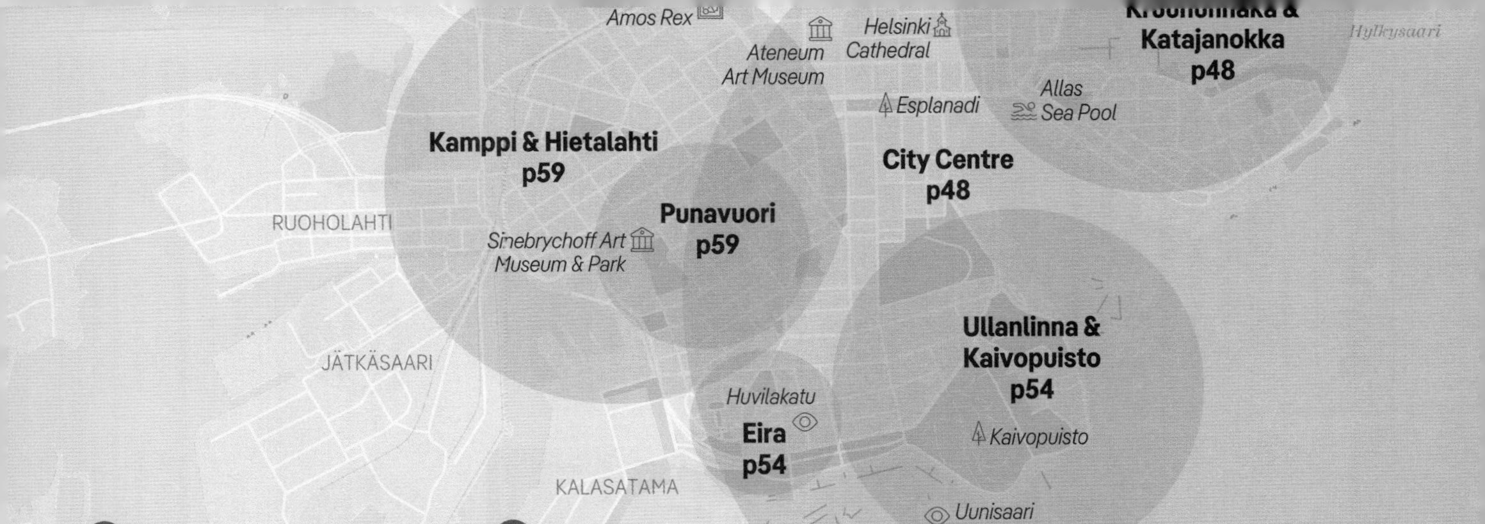

### METRO

Helsinki's retro-style orange metros take passengers from one side of the city to the other in a matter of minutes. If you wish to explore areas outside the city centre, local trains leave from Helsinki Central station.

### TRAM

Trams are a good option to ease the strain on your feet. Line numbers 2, 3, 6 and 7 whisk by many main sights – line 2 is particularly useful, passing the Old Market Hall and Market Square, Senate Square, Amos Rex art museum and Kamppi.

# Plan Your Days

Kick off the days with coffee before venturing out to explore Helsinki's sights, which range from flashy art museums to cosy cafes and seaside saunas.

NOWACZYK/SHUTTERSTOCK ©

Helsinki Cathedral (p48)

## DAY 1

### Morning

- Start in Old Market Hall's **Story** (p51) restaurant before taking in Senate Square, anchored by **Helsinki Cathedral** (p48). Work up an appetite with a spree of shopping in **Torikortteli's boutiques** (p48) and stroll through **Esplanadi park** (p49), where **Kappeli** (p49) is a flashy spot for lunch.

### Afternoon

- Jump on a ferry to **Suomenlinna sea fortress** (p51) and explore the island's museums and fortifications. Have a cinnamon bun in **Cafe Silo** (p51) before heading back to the city.

### Evening

- Round out the day in Punavuori's **Nolla** (p64), a zero-waste restaurant, followed by cocktails in **Bar Mate** (p65).

### YOU'LL ALSO WANT TO...

Embrace small neighbourhood finds, watch the Finns going crazy at a hockey game, and enjoy a cinematic experience.

### WATCH THE ICE HOCKEY

Starting in September and ending in March, the SM league (Finnish Elite League) provides thrills in Helsingin Jäähalli.

### LEARN SOMETHING NEW

In Helsinki's neighbouring city, Vantaa, Heureka science centre's take on science is fun for all ages.

### GO TO A CINEMA

Helsinki's most hedonistic cinema, Riviera, in Kallio and Punavuori, comes with a bar, restaurant and velvet seats.

FROM LEFT: AIJA LEHTONEN/SHUTTERSTOCK ©, ELINA/SHUTTERSTOCK ©, RIVIERA/MIKKO RASKINEN ©

## DAY 2

### Morning

- Head to Kallio to find the popular breakfast spot, **Way Bakery** (p71). Take a ride on the wooden roller-coaster at **Linnanmäki amusement park** (p70) before catching tram 3 or 9 to the **Ateneum Art Museum** (p50) and **Museum of Contemporary Art Kiasma** (p50) in the city centre. Have a late lunch at **Finnjävel Sali** (p71).

### Afternoon

- Continue indulging in art by visiting **Taidehalli** (p69), which focuses on contemporary Finnish art, design and architecture. Then, quieten down in **Temppeliaukion church** (p69).

### Evening

- Head back to Kallio to take the heat in **Kotiharjun sauna** (p71). Stop for dinner at nearby **Konepaja** (p70), with restaurants, a hotel and the rooftop bar **Loi Loi** (p70).

## DAY 3

### Morning

- Kick off the day with coffee and a croissant in Helsinki's oldest cafe, **Ekberg** (p64), before descending to the **Amos Rex** (p59) museum. Continue to **Oodi library** (p53) then head to lunch in **Hietalahti market hall** (p62).

### Afternoon

- Stroll around **Punavuori** (p59), popping into its design boutiques and art galleries, and the vintage shops in **Iso Roobertinkatu** (p60). In the neighbouring Ullanlinna district, climb to **Tähtitorninvuori** (p55) to take in the views towards Market Square and Helsinki Cathedral's turquoise dome.

### Evening

- Join the locals for dinner in **Spis** (p52) and sneak in for speakeasy-style cocktails at **Trillby & Chadwick** (p48).

### COUNT SHEEP

Visit Lammassaari 'sheep island' nature reserve. The duckboards make it accessible to wheelchairs. How many sheep are here? None.

### SEE STREET ART

The best street art is along Baana pedestrian and bicycle path running from the Museum of Contemporary Art Kiasma to Ruoholahti.

### BE A FOODIE

Around the city's old slaughterhouse, Teurastamo in Kalasatama has eateries including smokeries, bakeries and a distillery.

### SAIL TO ZOO ISLE

Korkeasaaren eläintarha (Korkeasaari Zoo) is on an island, reached by a ferry from June to August; or else metro (1, 2) or bus (16) go close by.

FROM LEFT: VERNAIO/SHUTTERSTOCK ©, ESTAM/SHUTTERSTOCK ©, EMMA LIPASTI/SHUTTERSTOCK ©, KEKYALYAYNEN/SHUTTERSTOCK ©

# CITY CENTRE, KRUUNUNHAKA & KATAJANOKKA

## ART AND ART NOUVEAU

Looking at the magnificent buildings of Kruununhaka, it's hard to believe the area was no more than a modest harbour and pastureland for the Crown's horses when the Swedish count Per Brahe the Younger decided to transfer Helsinki here from its original spot some 6km away in 1640. Now, Kruununhaka and its neighbours, the city centre (consisting of Kluuvi and Kaartinkaupunki) and Katajanokka, contain many of Helsinki's main sights, and are easily explored on foot, with many cafes and restaurants along the way. Most of the tourist activities here focus on Senate Square and its centrepiece, Helsinki Cathedral. Another hub is nearby Esplanadi park, lined with stylish cafes and restaurants. The park leads towards Katajanokka, with its residential buildings representing some world-class examples of art nouveau architecture.

### TOP TIP

Katajanokka is an island connected to the mainland by bridges, and includes some of Helsinki's major sights. But venture beyond, and you will find art nouveau quarters dotted with eye-catching details. Finish your walk on the island's northern harbour, with restaurants, cafes and a quay for icebreakers.

TOP LEFT: MAY_LANA/SHUTTERSTOCK ©
BOTTOM RIGHT: VERMETTE108/SHUTTERSTOCK ©

Helsinki Cathedral

## Helsinki Cathedral

GRAND CITY-CENTRE ARCHITECTURE

Helsinki Cathedral, or Tuomiokirkko, dominates the city's skyline. The cathedral was built from 1830 to 1852 in honour of Tsar Nicholas I of Russia, the Grand Duke of Finland. On the cathedral's roof, 12 statues of the Apostles keep an eye on people photographing the building. The cathedral was designed by CL Engel, but the statues were a later addition – after Engel's death, it was noticed the church's proportions were not in perfect symmetry.

## Trillby & Chadwick

HISTORIC SETTING

Down the cobblestoned Katariinankatu from Helsinki Cathedral is Trillby & Chadwick, a speakeasy with a 19th-century detective-fiction theme. The dimly lit interior features comfy sofas and armchairs, and super-retro phones. The menu offers an intriguing backstory for each cocktail.

Katariinankatu

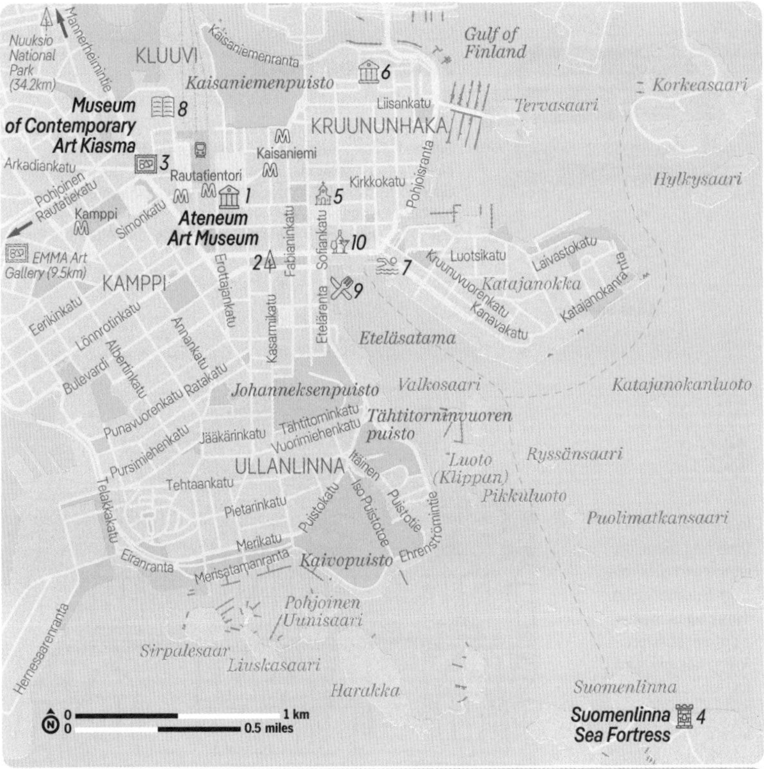

**HIGHLIGHTS**
**1** Ateneum Art Museum
**2** Esplanadi
**3** Museum of Contemporary Art Kiasma
**4** Suomenlinna Sea Fortress

**SIGHTS**
**5** Helsinki Cathedral
**6** Ruiskumestarin taloe

**ACTIVITIES, COURSES & TOURS**
**7** Allas Sea Pool
**8** Oodi Library

**EATING**
**9** Old Market Hall

**DRINKING & NIGHTLIFE**
**10** Trillby & Chadwick

## Esplanadi

HELSINKI'S POSH PARK

Esplanadi

The leafy Esplanadi park, lined with cafes and shops, is a breath of Central European sophistication in the middle of Helsinki. This is where Finland's cultural elite has gathered since the time when the Finnish language and cultural identity – in opposition to Swedish and Russian ones – were being promoted in the late 19th and early 20th centuries. These figures, from composer Jean Sibelius to painter Akseli Gallen-Kallela, met in Esplanadi's fabulous Kappeli glass building, adorned with glittering chandeliers, eating and drinking till the small hours of the morning. Kappeli means 'chapel' in Finnish, and the restaurant here is truly a holy institution, beloved by locals and visitors.

RIGHT: MIKKO RYYNANEN / SHUTTERSTOCK ©

Allas Sea Pool

## Allas Sea Pool

OUTDOOR SWIMMING IN AN URBAN SETTING

Open year-round, Allas Sea Pool is an urban sauna and spa oasis beside Market Square. The spa features fresh and saltwater pools, as well as sauna and wellness facilities. The pools are open till 9pm, which, especially in autumn and winter, offers memorable possibilities for moonlight swims. For less wellness and more wow, take in Helsinki's city lights from Allas Sea Pool's upper-floor bar.

### LONNA

In summer, make time for Lonna, an island just offshore from Suomenlinna. Tiny Lonna makes a cute excursion from Helsinki, and its public loft saunas have calming sea views. The sauna, which can be combined with dips in the sea, is open from Tuesday to Saturday and pre-booking is advised – note that on Tuesday and Friday it's a mixed sauna for all genders. Bring your own swimsuit, if you wish. The ferry (10 minutes) leaves from Kauppatori (Market Square) and is operated by Suomen saaristokuljetus.

Ateneum Art Museum

TOP LEFT: STUDIO MDF/SHUTTERSTOCK ©, LEFT: KIEVVICTOR/SHUTTERSTOCK ©

## Ateneum Art Museum & Kiasma

FINNISH CLASSICS NEAR CENTRAL STATION

Opposite Helsinki Central railway station, Ateneum Art Museum forms a part of the Finnish National Gallery. The museum's art collection spans from 18th-century rococo to 20th-century art movements, and provides a crash course on Finnish art. Notable Finnish works include Eero Järnefelt's scenes from Koli National Park, Akseli Gallen-Kallela's paintings of Finland's national epic *Kalevala*, and Helene Schjerfbeck's striking portraits as well as masterpieces from the likes of Paul Cézanne to Edvard Munch. Right nearby, the Museum of Contemporary Art Kiasma has a mix of foreign and Finnish exhibitions and runs tours in English every other Friday.

RIGHT: MAISICON/SHUTTERSTOCK ©

Suomenlinna Sea Fortress

## Old Market Hall

FINE FINNISH FOODS

Next to the bustling Kauppatori (Market Square), Vanha Kauppahalli (Old Market Hall) features stall after stall selling traditional Finnish foods and international flavours. Built in 1889, the market hall retains its revered knowledge of modern food trends – it has featured in listings of the world's best food spots.

Try the traditional creamy salmon soup at Story restaurant, or sit at Erikssonin osteribaari for oysters hailed as the best in Helsinki. There is a selection of Finnish meats such as moose, bear and reindeer on offer, as well as local delicacies like Karelian pies and fried vendace.

## Suomenlinna Sea Fortress

EXPLORE HELSINKI'S ARCHIPELAGO

Helsinki has more than 300 islands, and the main sight among them is Suomenlinna sea fortress, dating from the 1740s and Helsinki's only Unesco World Heritage Site.

On the island, be prepared to walk as Suomenlinna's fortifications and barracks host multiple little museums, from toy and military collections to Suomenlinna Museum, which showcases the fortress' history. Peek inside the WWII Vesikko submarine, and wander around the old walls and cannons. Luckily, there's also a dozen different cafes and restaurants at which to rest your feet. If you fancy a tasty cinnamon bun, try Cafe Silo, located near the main entrance.

Suomenlinna is accessible throughout the year. Spring and summer draw in crowds with picnic baskets. Autumn foliage transforms the island into a romantic getaway. Suomenlinna is at its most magical in winter, with the pink barracks covered with snow and the island surrounded by a frozen sea.

HSL (Helsinki Regional Transport Authority) ferries leave from Kauppatori (Market Square), where tickets can also be bought.

### NAKED OR NOT?

Finns often sauna in mixed groups, and nudity in this environment is not sexualised. It's also acceptable to arrive in your swimsuit, or wrapped in a towel – you might attract some harmless chuckles, but Finns do know that naked saunas are not for all nationalities. See more about sauna etiquette on p233.

**BEST RESTAURANTS IN THE CITY CENTRE, KRUUNUNHAKA & KATAJANOKKA**

**Magu**
Vegan fine dining with set menus that won't blow your budget, especially the lunch (Wednesday to Saturday). €€

**Ravintola Kolme Kruunua**
Beloved neighbourhood gem serving homey Finnish dishes from meatballs to fried vendace. €€

**Spis**
Unfussy fine dining with a set menu full of local flavours. €€€

**Palace**
Finland's only two-Michelin-starred restaurant serves seasonal Nordic cuisine and has stellar balcony views. €€€

**The Cock**
Unfussy fine dining with a set menu full of local flavours. €€€

**Social Burger Joint**
Award-winning burgers, including vegan ones, from Finland's MasterChef winner. €

MORE IN CITY CENTRE, KRUUNUNHAKA & KATAJANOKKA

## Train to EMMA

GRAND ART INSIDE GRAND ARCHITECTURE

To visit Finland's biggest art museum, jump onto metro M1 or M2 at Helsinki Central station and head towards Espoo, Helsinki's neighbour city and part of Greater Helsinki. From the station at Tapiola – Espoo's urban centre, built in the 1950s and '60s – it's a 15-minute walk to EMMA, the Espoo Museum of Modern Art. EMMA's contemporary art and design works are exhibited in a former printing house, a 1960s architectural masterpiece in concrete. Admission is pricey (€20 for adults aged over 29) but the exhibits are worth every cent – check out EMMA's website (emmamuseum.fi) for evenings when entry is free. The museum is closed on Mondays.

## Nuuksio National Park

NATURE ON THE URBAN DOORSTEP

Nuuksio National Park makes a peaceful day's outing from Helsinki, with landscapes varying from ponds and lakes with clear waters to age-old forests, cliffs and gorges. To get here, take bus 245 from Espoo to Suomen luontokeskus Haltia (Finnish Nature Centre Haltia), where you can get park maps. The bus ride takes about 20 minutes. Around Haltia, there are several loop trails with viewpoints and campfire spots, as well as a centre for downhill mountain biking. You can also get off the bus in Kattila and walk along trails to the nature centre. There are a few accommodation providers in the park should you wish to relax in nature overnight.

## Helsinki City Museum & Children's Town

HISTORY THROUGH PLAY

Free of charge and open daily, Helsinki City Museum's exhibits, such as the immersive experience of the work of Finland's first female photographer Signe Brander, bring the city's history to life. Part of the museum, Children's Town tells the city's history through play – let your kids enjoy, and you can relax for an hour or two.

**WHERE TO STAY IN THE CITY CENTRE, KRUUNUNHAKA & KATAJANOKKA**

**Hostel Suomenlinna**
Mixed and female dorms, plus double and family rooms, on the World Heritage fortress island of Suomenlinna. €

**Hotel Haven**
Five-star hotel with one of the city's best breakfast views over Old Market Hall and Market Square. €€€

**Hotel Fabian**
A fabulous part of the Helsinki-based Kämp collection hotels, with a great lobby bar. €€

## LIBRARIES OLD & NEW WALKING TOUR

Helsinki's central libraries epitomise the country's long dedication to learning. Start from the modern, award-winning **1 Oodi library**, which hides an airy space for books and games behind its curvy contours. There is a cafe and a terrace upstairs, with views towards the imposing Parliament House, which was built in the 1920s, as well as the glassy concert hall Musiikkitalo, where you can also find the shop Fuga Musiikki, specialising in classical music.

After Oodi, walk past the adjoining **2 Helsinki Central railway station**, dating from 1919. The station, with grand granite statues guarding its entrance, is often named on lists of the world's most beautiful railway stations. The station is by a square, where in winter you can test your skating skills on an ice rink. You will see a statue of the author Aleksis Kivi, in front of the Finnish National Theatre.

Continue uphill on Kaivokatu street, which is lined with restaurants and cinemas. At the top of the street, check out the modern **3 University Library Kaisa** with its striking staircases and windows, and then continue to the **4 National Library of Finland**, by Senate Square. The library's sturdy wooden doors lead into a book shrine with vaulted, decorative ceilings, wooden banisters and Corinthian columns.

The oldest part of the building was designed by CL Engel in the 1840s. By Finnish law, the library also functions as a depository for all Finnish printed and audiovisual material, apart from films.

Because the collection began before Finland gained its independence from Russia in 1917, the library holds the world's largest collection chronicling the Russian Empire, a popular research topic among Finnish scholars and writers.

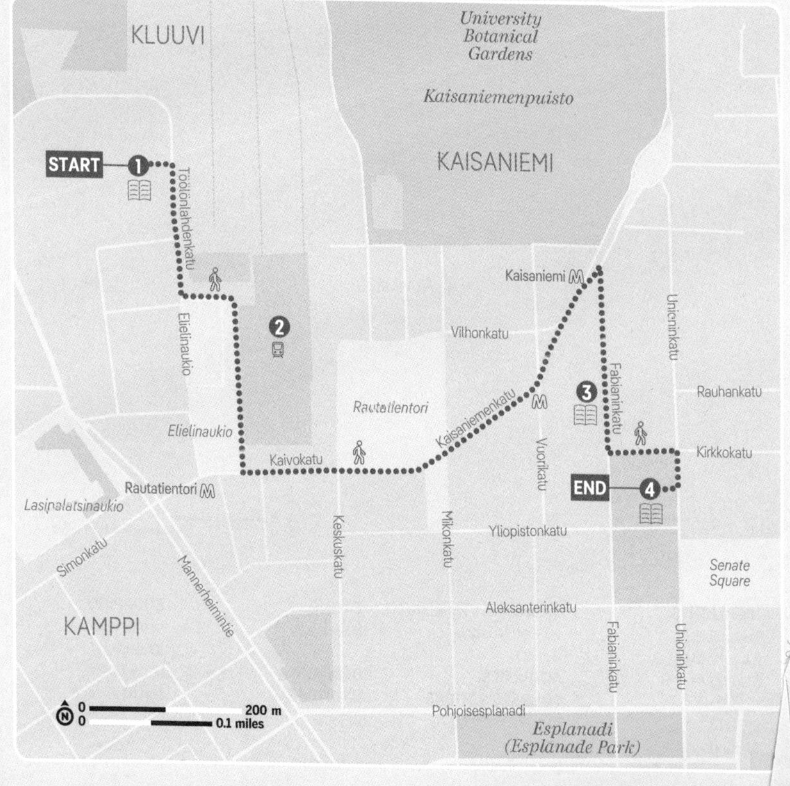

# EIRA, ULLANLINNA & KAIVOPUISTO

## PRESTIGIOUS SEASIDE SETTING

These neighbourhoods form part of Helsinki's most prestigious areas, with plenty of architectural treasures to discover. And yet the seaside is their greatest lure. The shoreline here stretches from Kaivopuisto past Ullanlinna all the way to Eira and beyond.

Walking and cycling tracks line the shore along this southern part of Helsinki's city centre. In warmer months, people exercise or buy snacks and ice creams from the handful of seaside cafes and kiosks. Or you can pack a swimsuit and join others for a sunbathe and a quick dip in the sea – an activity you can also try in the winter months when the seaside transforms into winter magic with snow covering the shores and the water freezing over.

Leaving the coast, you will find a bunch of little shops, restaurants and cafes varying from upscale bakeries to kiosks.

### TOP TIP

One of the best ways to feel the sea breeze on your skin is to rent a city bike. The yellow bikes are dotted around the city and work with the HSL app (hsl.fi). Start from the Old Market Hall, and within 3km you'll have passed cafes, parks and beaches. The best bit? At the end you can have a sauna at Löyly (p56).

**HIGHLIGHTS**
**1** Huvilakatu
**2** Kaivopuisto
**3** Uunisaari

**SIGHTS**
**4** Eiranpuisto
**5** Mannerheim Museum
**6** Tähtitorninmäki

**ACTIVITIES, COURSES & TOURS**
**7** Löyly

**EATING**
**8** Seahorse

**DRINKING & NIGHTLIFE**
**9** Mattolaituri

**SHOPPING**
**see 10** Fasaani
**10** Helsinki Secondhand
**see 10** Vintage Kelloliike Longitudi

## Kaivopuisto

BELOVED PARK BY THE SEA

Kaivopuisto is one of Helsinki's best-loved parks, lined by the Baltic Sea and some of the city's most grandiose buildings.

The park became a bourgeois destination for leisurely strolls and spa treatments in the 19th century. Now Helsinki's inhabitants from every walk of life visit the park with their dogs, friends and picnic baskets, especially during Labour Day celebrations from 30 April to 1 May, when tens of thousands of people gather here.

TOP RIGHT: ROBERTO LO SAVIO/SHUTTERSTOCK © BOTTOM LEFT: THE ART OF PICS/SHUTTERSTOCK ©

**View from Kaivopuisto park**

## Mannerheim Museum

PRESIDENTIAL VILLA

Finland's revered president and war hero, CGE Mannerheim, who steered the nation out of WWII, lived in this Kaivopuisto villa from 1924 to his death in 1951.

Most of the villa remains as it was when Mannerheim lived here. Anyone with a sweet tooth will also appreciate the fact that the villa is owned by the Finnish chocolate manufacturer Fazer – before Mannerheim, Fazer's workers used to live here.

Mannerheim Museum is open on Friday, Saturday and Sunday, and admission is only by guided tour.

**Kaivopuisto park**

## Tähtitorninvuori

SUBLIME SUNSET VIEWS

Rising next to the terminal for ferries to Stockholm, Tähtitorninvuori is one of Helsinki's best-kept secrets for views.

Climb the 30m hill with your loved one, or a camera, to find fabulous views towards the turquoise-domed Helsinki Cathedral. Pathways crisscross the hilltop park, and it's hard to imagine that the parking hall carved into the rock beneath also functions as an air-raid shelter.

The most dominant building on the hill is the observatory, dating from 1834.

When it was built, the observatory was ahead of its time. Now, as Helsinki's light pollution obliterates the prospects of spotting stars, the tower functions as an astronomy visitor centre, open from Thursdays to Saturdays.

Löyly

## Löyly

MODERN SAUNA BY THE SEA

Löyly (meaning 'the steam' or 'the heat of sauna') is an urban sauna and restaurant complex located by the Baltic Sea in the developing harbour area next to Eira. Dipping into the ocean during your sauna session is made easy here: book a sauna, take in some heat, plunge into the water from Löyly's platform, and make a dash back to the sauna. Afterwards, enjoy some food and drinks in Löyly's restaurant. Sauna, swimming and food are available year-round – meaning smart possibilities for ice-hole swimming in the winter.

## Eiranpuisto

HIDDEN PARK AND A CULINARY KIOSK

Eira boasts some of Helsinki's most magnificent homes, as well as a bunch of diplomatic buildings.

To rest your eyes from all the grandeur, sit for a moment in Eiranpuisto, a park that feels somewhat hidden and forgotten. The park is very small and offers tranquil moments on benches under the shadowy trees.

If you feel peckish, one of Helsinki's iconic canopy kiosks (*'lippakioski'*) is located beside the park. The functionalist-style kiosks were designed and built in the early decades of the 20th century, and have, such as here, often been used in recent years as summertime foodie hubs.

Grand Helsinki architecture

TOP LEFT: ELENA LYSENKOVA/SHUTTERSTOCK © LEFT: GRISHA BRUEV/SHUTTERSTOCK ©

## Antique Shops

VAUNTED VINTAGE SOUVENIRS

As these districts are some of Helsinki's most fashionable quarters, you can make astounding antique finds. Head to **Korkeavuorenkatu**, said to be the most Parisian street in Helsinki, and you'll find the colourful buildings – mostly in art nouveau and functionalist style – have dozens of cafes, restaurants and small boutiques and antique stores on their ground floors.

In **Helsinki Secondhand** and **Fasaani**, you can buy vintage Finnish glassware or, if your budget – and luggage restrictions – allow, there's a range of exceptional furniture, too. Next door, in **Vintage Kelloliike Longitudi**, you'll find easy-to-carry vintage watches. When you're done browsing here, stroll around and make your own finds!

SEA HORSE OY ©

Seahorse

**BEST BARS IN ULLANLINNA**

**Badger & Co**
Brooklyn-inspired intimate space with a good selection of beers and cocktails, as well as a hot dog menu with a veggie option included. Dogs are welcome. €

**Goldfish**
Old-fashioned library aesthetic meets modern bar, with splashes of velvet and a cocktail list hailing classics and seasonal ingredients. Small snacks available. €€

**La Bottega 13**
Cosy Italian corner with excellent wines, aperitifs and high-quality delicacies, from truffles to meats, from the deli counter. Warm dishes also available. €€

## MORE IN EIRA, ULLANLINNA & KAIVOPUISTO

### Seahorse

TRADITIONAL FINNISH FARE

Located by the small park of Vuorimiehenpuistikko, Seahorse has fed the hungry and the hungry famous – from Finnish artists to writer Jean-Paul Sartre and poet Pablo Neruda – since 1934.

The restaurant has made very few concessions to ever-changing food trends, apart from adding a couple of vegetarian options to the menu.

Some dishes have delighted Seahorse's clientele for decades, including the fried Baltic herrings and pepper steak.

The atmosphere is warm and the food is tasty, but the prices can feel a bit salty.

**WHERE TO FIND CAFES IN EIRA, ULLANLINNA & KAIVOPUISTO**

**RAMS Roasters**
Third-wave coffees with cinnamon buns and savoury pies on the side. €

**Sokerileipuri Alenius**
Traditional cakes, such as the old-time Finnish favourite banana chocolate cake, and pastries with the skills of a true baker. €

**Cafe Ursula**
Seaside Ursula is open throughout the year and serves all-day breakfast and lunch – both with a view. €

**BEST RESTAURANTS IN EIRA & ULLANLINNA**

**Jura**
Intimate restaurant that elevates vegetables to a new level, and does excellent wine pairings and set menus. €€€

**Boneless**
A rare budget find in these neighbourhoods, Boneless serves juicy chicken wings and various types of hamburgers, including vegetarian, in the heart of Ullanlinna. €

**BasBas**
Stylish bistro serving natural wines, with a sibling establishment, BasBas Kulma ('Corner'), next door, using a charcoal grill to up the food game. €€

**Lilla Fabrik**
A restaurant cafe with salad and burger lunch options for vegans through to meat eaters, next to BasBas. €

## Uunisaari

CALM ISLAND ESCAPE

The little island of Uunisaari, just offshore from Kaivopuisto, is a popular spot throughout the year.

In summer, be your own captain and hop aboard a zero-emission, electric Callboat at Kaivopuisto's Merisatama. The boats run automatically, so no sailing experience is needed.

In winter, the way to Uunisaari is no less memorable with a pedestrian bridge stretching across the frozen sea from mid-November to mid-April.

The island has a beach and a restaurant with two saunas; opening times vary according to season.

## Mattolaituri

QUIRKY SUMMER CAFE

Mattolaituri is a seafront restaurant that takes its name from a nearby floating dock where people can wash their carpets.

The restaurant cafe is open in summer months, featuring DJs on weekends, and is a popular spot for drinks, snacks and people-watching.

The concrete building looks like it's been there for decades, but in fact it was only built in 2011.

## Huvilakatu

PHOTOGENIC STREET

Huvilakatu, with its colourful art nouveau buildings, must be one of the most photographed, if not *the* most photographed, streets in Helsinki.

Even if you are not travelling with a camera, it's worth taking a look. The street and its buildings were constructed between 1906 and 1910 and, apart from one change, they have kept their original looks.

**Colourful Helsinki buildings**

Huvilakatu runs for 320m, ending in a green park lining the Baltic Sea.

**BEST CAFES IN EIRA, ULLANLINNA & KAIVOPUISTO**

**Gateau Ullanlinna**
Originating from Sweden, Gateau now has 14 artisanal bakery-cafes in and around Helsinki; card payment only. €

**Café Succès**
This Finnish-style cafe comes with a lovely summer terrace and has served up coffee and cinnamon rolls since 1957. €

**Café Compass**
A family-owned summer kiosk by the shore – the baking takes place underground! €

# PUNAVUORI, KAMPPI & HIETALAHTI

## BOHEMIAN VIBES AND BOUTIQUE FINDS

Shops from high-street brands to design and vintage finds, with art galleries, cafes and restaurants in between: this is Kamppi and Punavuori in a nutshell. But there is more to these two districts than glitzy shop fronts. Punavuori is Helsinki's old bohemian district, once housing the city's workers and threadbare students. This is where secret bars were tucked away in Finland's Prohibition era from 1919 to 1932. Modern Punavuori has been somewhat hipsterfied, and is also the epicentre for Helsinki's Design District, though it's held on to its friendly neighbourhood vibes.

Kamppi has gone through a similar modernisation in recent decades, with world-class museums and a swanky shopping centre, but wander to the side streets and you'll discover edgy cafes, restaurants and galleries. Hietalahti is a bit of a side note to its bustling neighbours but its market square with regular flea markets draws in bargain hunters.

### TOP TIP

To step out of the city centre and check out Helsinki's modern side, head to the neighbouring Jätkäsaari ('bloke island') district, known for its swiftly rising new apartment blocks. Here, you'll find new hotels and restaurants, as well as a terminal for ferries to Tallinn. Kamppi is a few minutes away by tram.

LEFT: FINN STOCK/SHUTTERSTOCK ©, RIGHT: YINGNA CAI/SHUTTERSTOCK ©

**Amos Rex**

## Amos Rex

UNDERGROUND ART, LITERALLY

Built beneath an old bus station, the Amos Rex museum witnessed queues when it first opened in 2018, and those queues persist on busier days (not on Tuesdays, when the museum is closed). And no wonder – the contemporary art exhibitions here are from the top names of the art world, with works that are a perfect match for the somewhat eerie underground museum space.

Above ground, it's all fun and games, with the museum's skylights, bulging from the ground, forming a utopian sight that adults and kids cannot stop exploring.

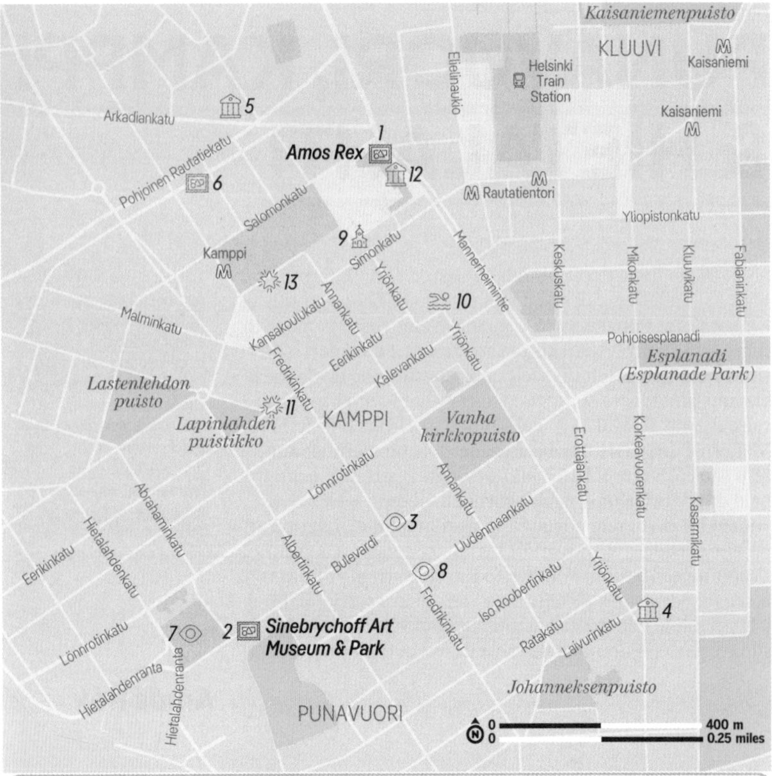

**HIGHLIGHTS**
**1** Amos Rex
**2** Sinebrychoff Art Museum & Park

**SIGHTS**
**3** Bulevardi
**4** Designmuseo
**5** Finnish Museum of Natural History
**6** Helsinki Art Museum (HAM)
**7** Hietalahdentori
**8** Iso Roobertingkatu
**9** Kamppi Chapel

**ACTIVITIES, COURSES & TOURS**
**10** Yrjönkadun Uimahalli

**ENTERTAINMENT**
**11** Cinema Orion
**12** Lasipalatsi
**13** Tavastia

## Iso Roobertinkatu

PUNAVUORI'S ARTERY

**Iso Roobertinkatu**

Iso Roobertinkatu runs through the heart of Punavuori from the leafy Sinebrychoff park to the tiny Kolmikulma park. 'Iso Roba' ('The Big Roba') is mainly a pedestrian street, lined with shops, bars and restaurants. Some of Helsinki's most fabulous vintage shops are here, with flea markets and high-fashion finds guaranteed. Pop into Fida for bargains, Relove for high-street brands and a cup of coffee, and Flea for design and luxury names. Iso Roba has plenty of bars and restaurants, with options varying from Natura's sustainably sourced ingredients to vegetarian dishes in Yes, Yes, Yes! Or sip and soak in the atmosphere in Bar llamas.

## Tavastia

LEGENDARY MUSIC VENUE

The relatively small Tavastia is one of the most coveted music venues in Finland.

Opened in 1970, it is one of Europe's oldest rock clubs, and during its rowdy history, some of music's most influential names have performed here, from the Finnish HIM, Children of Bodom and Nightwish, to the Foo Fighters and Siouxsie and the Banshees. But it's not all megastars, with Tavastia occasionally giving the floor to upcoming bands, too.

Whether the gig is big or small, the atmosphere is always magnificent. On Saturdays at 11.30pm, the disco tunes kick in.

RIGHT: NYC RUSS BOTTOM RIGHT: GRISHA BRUEV, BOTTOM LEFT: ANASTASIA VEREFTENKO/SHUTTERSTOCK©

Horse-drawn carriage in Helsinki

## Designmuseo

FINNISH DESIGN

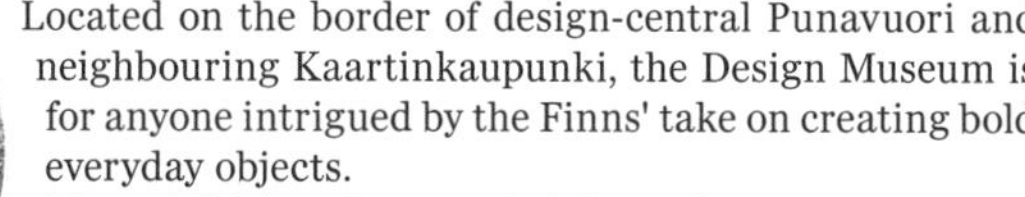

Located on the border of design-central Punavuori and neighbouring Kaartinkaupunki, the Design Museum is for anyone intrigued by the Finns' take on creating bold everyday objects.

The exhibitions have varied from Ilmari Tapiovaara's woodwork and Eero Aarnio's chairs and lamps, to Lotta Nieminen's modern take on design. The museum is closed on Mondays.

For glasswork aficionados, a trip to the Design Museum's satellite space in Arabianranta's Iittala and Arabia Design Centre is a must. Take tram 6 from Central railway station to reach Arabia Design Centre.

Designmuseo

## Sinebrychoff Art Museum & Park

OLD MASTERS AND GENTEEL LIVING

For anyone into old European masters and grand home inspections, a visit to the Sinebrychoff Art Museum is a must. Apart from being an art museum, Sinebrychoff is also the oldest brewery in the Nordic countries.

Around the turn of the 20th century, the brewery was run by Paul Sinebrychoff, and the museum was founded on the art collection of Sinebrychoff and his wife. Walk down the Bulevardi and step inside the refined city manor, which is where Paul and Fanny lived. The museum is part of the Finnish National Gallery and is closed on Mondays.

Be sure to take a stroll around the park behind the museum. In summer, this is a popular gathering place for the city's young and young at heart.

## Lasipalatsi

SHOPPING IN A GLASS PALACE

Lasipalatsi's ('Glass Palace') name might bring to mind grandiose architecture, but this is actually a sober, 1930s functionalist-style building with a glitzy twist.

Lasipalatsi's biggest draw is the Amos Rex museum, but don't ignore the building's little shops – you might leave with a bag full of Finnish fashion, from Karhu sneakers and Makia hoodies to all things Moomin.

There are also cafes and restaurants. At night you can admire Lasipalatsi's retro neon signs.

Finnish Museum of Natural History

TOP LEFT: SARIME, BOTTOM: DREAMERACHIEVERNORATARVUS/SHUTTERSTOCK ©

## Finnish Museum of Natural History

ANIMALS OF ALL SIZES

With an African elephant greeting you in the lobby, families with kids will particularly enjoy visiting the Finnish Museum of Natural History, or Luonnontieteellinen museo. The collection of some 13 million specimens varies from Africa's biggest animals to rocks and fungi.

There are exhibits showcasing Finnish nature, as well as rooms dedicated to nature's diversity around the world. The baroque-revival building was originally a Russian-speaking cadet school until the University of Helsinki established its Natural History Museum here in 1923.

## Hietalahdentori

MARKET SQUARE BY A HARBOUR

At the end of leafy Bulevardi, Hietalahti's seaside vista opens up. The area has a mixed history, with the sea and harbour bringing in fishermen and large industries needing water, such as the Sinebrychoff brewery turned art museum. Today, the harbour hosts an assortment of pleasure boats, varying from little sailboats to boats with saunas and Jacuzzis for private hire. Behind the small harbour lined by walking and cycling lanes looms an industrial harbour where luxury yachts and sturdy icebreakers are built. Still, the heart of Hietalahti is solidly ashore. The Hietalahdentori (market square) buzzes during the summer months but remains open all year. Hietalahden kirpputori (flea market) is especially popular on summer weekends, when you can make fabulous fashion finds as well as stock up with retro knick-knacks and Finnish glassware. Hietalahti market hall is a budget-friendly (by Helsinki's standards) spot for lunch. Döner Harju is popular for kebab, while Petiscaria offers Portuguese feasts and Super Bowl whips up healthy dishes in bowls.

Hietalahti market hall

## Yrjönkadun Uimahalli

ART DECO SWIMMING POOL

It's rare to find a public pool set within 1920s art deco walls and arches, but such is the case in Finland's first natatorium at Yrjönkatu. The building's original features prevail, giving your swim a luxurious feel.

Only one notable change has taken place in the history of Yrjönkadun uimahalli: in 2001 customers were allowed to start using swimsuits, though nude swimming is still possible as there are separate opening hours for men and women. There are saunas, a steam room and private lodges in which to relax and enjoy snacks upstairs.

### I LIVE HERE

**Nina Jatuli**, owner and designer of Design District-based shop Jatuli, shares her tips on the area's best boutique finds.

**Terhi Pölkki**
Gorgeous shop filled with Terhi's namesake shoes; ethical Nordic design with the right kind of edge.

**Lokal**
Gallery meets boutique, changing exhibitions and designer pieces by local artisans.

**Papershop**
Lovely boutique focusing on all things made of paper. A fabulous array of printed items for all paper lovers.

Yrjönkadun Uimahalli

RIGHT: DPA PICTURE ALLIANCE/ALAMY STOCK PHOTO/ALAMY ©

### WHERE TO STAY IN PUNAVUORI & KAMPPI

**Yard Hostel**
With dormitories and private rooms of different sizes, and a central location in Kamppi, this is a good base for exploration. **€**

**Hotelli Mestari**
Excellent-value hotel located close to Kamppi shopping centre, but feeling calm with dim lighting and dark-panelled rooms. **€€€**

**GLO Hotel Art**
Located in a castle-like 1908 stone building, with modern and stylish rooms and beautiful original features elsewhere. **€€**

**BEST FOOD & DRINK IN EERIKINKATU**

**Eerikin Pippuri**
After catching a film in the Orion, pop over for a snack at this popular kebab and falafel spot feeding the city since the 1990s. €

**Viinibaari Apotek**
One of Helsinki's best wine bars is in a pharmacy dating from 1918. In summer, the corner-shop-bar's terrace is especially lively. €

**Goose Pastabar**
The handmade pasta is delicious, but it's more about the friendly buzz in this dimly lit restaurant, which extends out on to the street in warm weather. €

## Bulevardi

FOR FLANEURS AND FLANEUSES

With its Central European atmosphere, Bulevardi is lined with cafes, restaurants, art galleries, hotels and boutiques. Running from Esplanadi park slightly downhill to Hietalahti, the street draws a line between Kamppi and Punavuori districts.

The best way to take in Bulevardi's atmosphere is to stroll without hurry, stopping in **Cafe Ekberg**. This historic cafe dates from 1852, and is a place to see and be seen.

Just before the cafe, there's a charming little park, **Vanha kirkkopuisto** (Old Church Park), also known as Ruttopuisto (Plague Park) as during the plague in 1710, victims were buried nearby. The park itself used to be a cemetery till the early 19th century, but nothing remains of this history: now the park is a calm oasis beside Bulevardi's flutter.

Sinebrychoff Art Museum is located towards the other end of Bulevardi, just before Hietalahti and its market square.

## Kamppi Chapel

SERENE SILENCE IN THE CITY

Beside the busy Kamppi shopping centre, the conical wooden structure that is Kampin Kappeli, or the Kamppi Chapel, is an ecumenical place to promote a very Finnish virtue: silence.

Everyone is welcome to enter and sit in silence, surrounded by some of the busiest parts of the city. Although eye-catching from the outside, the chapel is particularly beautiful inside with its curving wooden walls.

## Helsinki Art Museum (HAM)

ART AND MOVIES

While in Kamppi, you will notice a white hall-like structure with an arched roof. This is Tennispalatsi (Tennis Palace), originally meant as a car maintenance hall for the 1940 Olympic Games (which were subsequently postponed until 1952 because of WWII), but which also included four tennis courts.

The building by Helge Lundström took a long time to gain merit in people's minds, and had been left to deteriorate since the 1960s.

Finally, in the 1990s, the City of Helsinki started to investigate the possibility of transforming the space into a cultural centre, and it now hosts HAM, an art gallery with changing exhibitions and

**OLYMPIAN ARCHITECTURE**

HAM was one of the projects Helsinki undertook to upgrade its infrastructure for the 1952 Olympic Games. For the significance of the Games to Helsinki's development, see p241.

**WHERE TO EAT IN PUNAVUORI**

**Nolla**
Zero-waste fine dining with a microbrewery and inventive use of ingredients (think malt bread ice cream with candied celeriac and smoked caramel). **€€**

**Levain**
Beloved bakery, cafe and restaurant with airy space close to Eira and the seaside – the *pastéis de nata* (custard tarts) are a hit. **€**

**Georgian Kitchen**
A warm-hearted feeling and Georgian flavours are guaranteed, sealed with Georgian tea and Turkish-style, Georgian coffee. **€€**

CHRISTINA VARTANOVA/SHUTTERSTOCK ©

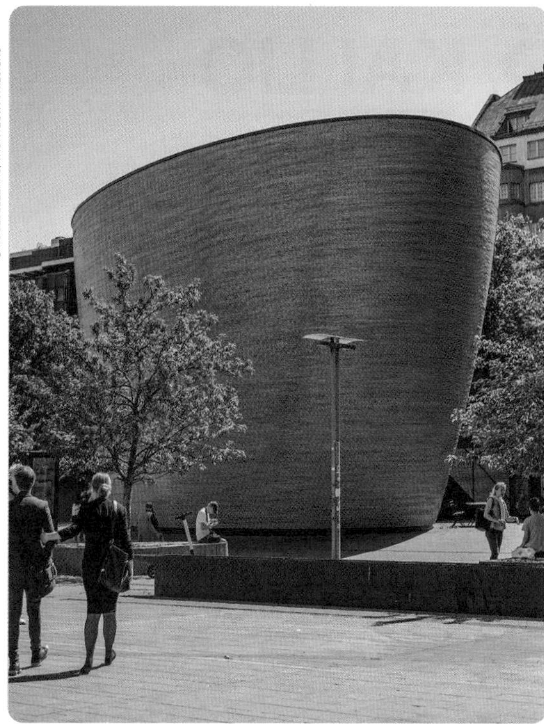

Kamppi Chapel

a permanent space for Tove Jansson's work, as well as a cinema complex. Today, Tennispalatsi is also one of the prime examples of the functionalist style in Helsinki.

## Cinema Orion

BIG-SCREEN ARCHITECTURE

Rare is the opportunity to enjoy cinema classics in an art deco building, but it can be done in Kamppi's Orion, one of Helsinki's oldest cinemas, dating from 1928.

Tickets cost €9 to €11, and the programme consists of Finnish and acclaimed films from around the world – no modern Hollywood spectacles here, though.

### BEST ART GALLERIES IN KAMPPI & PUNAVUORI

**Galleria Huuto**
A collective of independent artists hosts acclaimed exhibitions, giving space for both emerging and established names.

**Galleria Rankka**
Around the block from Galleria Huuto, Rankka is famed for its interdisciplinary art events as well as for hosting exhibitions of new talents.

**Helsinki Contemporary**
Dubbed Helsinki's trendiest gallery, the Contemporary is easily visited on a stroll along Bulevardi.

**Galerie Forsblom**
International and Finnish contemporary art by established artists and sculptors is exhibited here.

### WHERE TO DRINK IN PUNAVUORI & KAMPPI

**Bar Mate**
Tall windows, highball cocktails and tasty bar snacks make a perfect combination in the loft-styled bar.

**Mini Bar**
Small-scale bar with a big selection of spirits, from gin, whisky and rum to mezcal, cachaça and shochu on Eerikinkatu.

**Ateljee Bar**
Torni Hotel's scenic bar boasts the best views over Helsinki – from the balcony and bathroom – but they come with high price tags on drinks.

# TÖÖLÖ, KALLIO & KAISANIEMI

## NEIGHBOURLY VIBES WITH BOHEMIAN UNDERTONES

Töölö and Kallio have very different reputations, with Töölö dubbed as a 'village in the city', housing many of Helsinki's elderly people, and Kallio famed for its bohemian atmosphere that draws in the city's creatives. But the two districts share some similarities – friendly neighbourhood feelings and collections of corner-shop bars and cafes. Töölö's vibe is very calm, and nature is never far away. Kallio is another story, with the former working-class district now a trendy area filled with small bars and restaurants. But you will find a bit of nature here, too, with Kaisaniemi Bay – separated from Töölö Bay only by train tracks – stretching across Kallio's southern borders. Here, packed into a small patch of land, a flourishing park and a botanic garden forms a tranquil urban oasis, all hidden behind Helsinki Central railway station.

### TOP TIP

HSL city bikes dot Helsinki from the beginning of April till the end of October. Download its app and set out cycling around Töölönlahti, a 4.9km-long bay located behind Helsinki Central railway station. Take a break at the summer cafe Sinisen huvilan kahvila, with views over the bay.

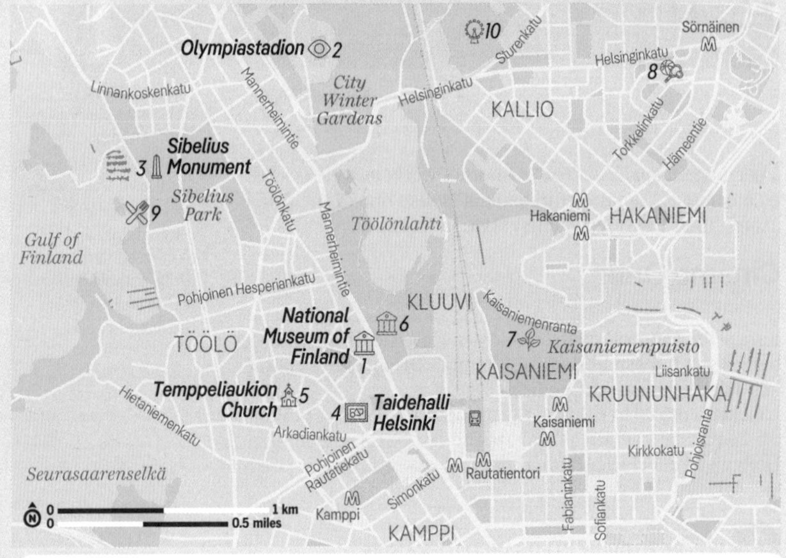


**HIGHLIGHTS**
**1** National Museum of Finland
**2** Olympiastadion
**3** Sibelius Monument
**4** Taidehalli Helsinki
**5** Temppeliaukion Church

**SIGHTS**
**6** Finlandia Hall
**7** Kaisaniemi Botanic Garden

**ACTIVITIES, COURSES & TOURS**
**8** Kotiharjun Sauna

**EATING**
**9** Cafe Regatta

**ENTERTAINMENT**
**10** Linnanmäki

## Cafe Regatta

CINNAMON BUNS AND KAYAKS

Cuteness – and cinnamon bun – overdose awaits at Cafe Regatta, a seaside Töölö cafe.

The red hut is unmistakable, and its freshly baked cinnamon buns are legendary.

In summer, it buzzes with activities: people enjoying cold drinks and coffees on its terrace, and others renting the cafe's kayaks, canoes or stand-up paddleboards to get another kind of viewpoint on the city.

In winter, there is an outdoor fire pit, giving warmth to people grilling sausages or sipping on hot chocolates around it.

TOP RIGHT:DMITRY NIKOLAEV/SHUTTERSTOCK ©, BOTTOM: MIKHAIL OLYKAINEN/SHUTTERSTOCK ©

National Museum of Finland

## National Museum of Finland

CASTLE FULL OF NATIONAL TREASURES

You can't mistake the granite Jugendstil building of the Kansallismuseo (National Museum of Finland) when seeing it on Mannerheimintie, opposite Alvar Aalto's Finlandia Hall.

The castle-meets-medieval-church construction, partly designed by Eliel Saarinen, holds a collection of Finnish cultural history from the Stone Age to modern times, and represents the romantic nationalism style in Finnish architecture.

The museum was finished in 1910 and opened in 1916, and it features several collections, varying from Finno-Ugric artefacts and numismatics to nautical mementos and modern music. There is also a collection of some 40,000 items from around the globe, stretching from Alaska to Namibia.

Kaisaniemi Botanic Garden

## Kaisaniemi Botanic Garden

A TROPICAL BREEZE IN THE CITY

Kaisaniemi's small patch of greenery is just behind the train station, next to Töölö.

Hidden behind the trees is one of the city's most visited attractions, the botanic garden (Kaisaniemen kasvitieteellinen puutarha) with its glasshouses protecting more than 800 species.

Most magical of all is the Santa Cruz water lily (*Victoria cruziana*), the seeds of which survived the Continuation War (1941–44) bombings that destroyed most of the garden.

There is a lush Rainforest House with coffee bushes and a Palm House with delicate orchids.

A visit makes an enchanting outing for the whole family throughout the year.

Sibelius Park

## Sibelius Monument

SYMPHONIUS SCULPTURE

Rising atop a small cliff, and surrounded by the seaside Sibelius Park in Töölö, the metal tubes of the Sibelius Monument seem to form a symphony of their own. Made in 1967 by the Finnish sculptor Eila Hiltunen, who wanted to embody the spirit of Sibelius' music, the monument received controversial reviews but has since become a national landmark. Stroll also to the nearby *Ilmatar ja sotka*, an art deco-style statue by Aarre Aaltonen, depicting the birth of the world according to Finland's national epic, **Kalevala**.

## Olympic Stadium

LANDMARK TOWER AND STADIUM

Take an elevator to the top of the 72m-high tower to get a birds-eye view over Helsinki, or admire the functionalist-style Olympic Stadium (Olympiastadion) from ground level. Either way, this is one of the city's most famous landmarks. The tower is open daily and you can also book tours of the stadium (stadion.fi), which include a visit to the sports museum Tahto and entrance to the tower. The stadium was originally intended to be the host venue for the 1940 Olympic Games, but the Games were postponed until 1952 due to the outbreak of WWII.

Finlandia Hall

TOP LEFT: ESTEA/SHUTTERSTOCK ©, LEFT: JREMES84/SHUTTERSTOCK ©

## Finlandia Hall

ALVAR AALTO'S MAGNUM OPUS

You can't mistake the white Finlandia-talo (Finlandia Hall) when seeing it rise along Töölönlahti's shoreline. When Alvar Aalto was commissioned by the City of Helsinki to create new plans for the city centre in 1959, the architect wanted to highlight Finland's independency, and designed a striking concert and congress hall almost opposite the Parliament House. The aim was to create a cultural zone matching CL Engel's Senate Square. Unfortunately, only Finlandia Hall ever materialised from these plans. The building was opened in 1971 and every detail is carefully planned – with the architect Elissa Aalto, Alvar Aalto's second wife, and interior designer Pirkko Söderman leaving their mark in the interiors. Finlandia Hall is under renovation till 2024, but its facade is still worth seeing.

RIGHT: JOAQUIN OSSORIO CASTILLO/SHUTTERSTOCK ©

Temppeliaukion Church

## Temppeliaukion Church

A ROCK-SOLID SIGHT

The circular Temppeliaukion kirkko (Temppeliaukion Church) is the antithesis of what people normally expect from church architecture. This church doesn't have spires reaching to the skies; instead, it is carved inside a rock.

And it pays to think outside the box because this church, also known as the Rock Church, has been one of Helsinki's favourite sights since 1969.

The construction was postponed during WWII, but finally, in the 1960s, the project kicked off again, with new designs from the architect brothers Timo and Tuomo Suomalainen.

The interior is excavated directly into the rock and the dome is supported by a skylight, providing plenty of natural light to the space. There are also no bells, though a recording of bells is played on loudspeakers.

The church is open daily to visitors, except when a service is being held – check the church website for service times before visiting.

There are also a handful of nice bakeries and cafes nearby in which to soak in Töölö's quaint neighbourhood feel.

### TAIDEHALLI

Just around the corner from Temppeliaukion Church is Taidehalli (Art Hall). It is unmistakable due to its pink exterior and photogenic lines.

Taidehalli has changing exhibitions, mainly of contemporary Finnish art, design and architecture, from the likes of Aino and Alvar Aalto and Paul Osipow.

The building itself is a prime example of the 1920s Nordic classicism.

If you are a budding Picasso, bring your pen, as Taidehalli organises life-drawing Croquis Nights every Tuesday, with limited attendance.

The museum is closed on Mondays.

### SILENT WORSHIP

To find another of Helsinki's unusual churches, be sure to visit the **Kamppi Chapel of Silence** (p64).

## WHY I LOVE TÖÖLÖ

**Paula Hotti**, writer

I might be biased in my love of Töölö, as this was the Helsinki neighbourhood I called home when I first moved here as a student.

Even though Töölö is well connected to the university with buses and trams, I would usually walk, especially in spring, when I could witness the elderly shop owners brushing the sidewalks and well-to-do ladies walking their little dogs.

Maybe time has added some gloss to these village-like images of the Töölö of my youth, but it can't be just my fancy because the neighbourhood is generally known as a village inside a city.

And this is why I still love Töölö as a recent returnee: for its warm neighbourly feel, but with the conveniences of a capital city.

## MORE IN TÖÖLÖ, KALLIO & KAISANIEMI

### Venture to Vallila

OLD AND NEW FINDS

Step north of Kallio to Vallila, an old working-class neighbourhood on the rise. For decades, Vallila's big draw was its **Puu-Vallila** district. Here, colourful wooden villas line quiet streets and it's hard to believe you're still in Helsinki.

The best spot to rest is **Pikku-Vallila**, a quirky corner restaurant. But apart from its cosy quietness, Vallila has recently got an upgrade to its rougher, and a touch rowdier, areas too. A cluster of bars and restaurants, as well as a hotel, are located in red-brick buildings known as Konepaja, the workshops for the Finnish railroad company VR's train carriages.

**Konepaja** is quickly becoming a favourite Helsinki hangout. There are also some of the city's newest rooftop bars, **Loi Loi** and **Alexis** – the latter is part of **Folks Hotel**, which combines a fab location with reasonable prices.

### Linnanmäki Amusement Park

FUN FOR THE FAMILY

Perched on top of a cliff adjoining Kallio, Linnanmäki has been Helsinki's centre of fun since the 1950s, and is now Finland's oldest and most popular amusement park.

The seemingly rickety wooden roller-coaster has provided sturdy rides for the daring ones since 1951, when it was Europe's tallest roller-coaster. There are 42 other rides in Linnanmäki as well as views over Helsinki from the park's hilltop location. Note also the colourful carousel dating from the end of the 19th century.

### Hietaniemi

OUTDOORS IN EVERY SEASON

South of Sibelius park, Hietaniemi peninsula is home to the popular summertime beach of Hietaranta, with beach volleyball courts and a cafe. The whole west side of Töölö makes a fabulous place for seaside strolls, cycling trips or kayaking tours.

There are also a few historic sites, such as the tranquil Hietaniemi Cemetery and Lapinlahti's former mental institution, now a creative hub with cafes, bakeries, art and events. There is also a Mental Museum sharing insight into the institution's history.

In winter, the sea is frozen and the peninsula is a popular place for walks and taking in the natural beauty.

## WHERE TO STAY IN TÖÖLÖ AND KALLIO

**Hotel Helka**
Friendly staff and relaxed atmosphere, plus rooms decorated in Finnish design and a homey bar in the lobby. **€€**

**Hotel Folks**
This trendy hotel in Vallila is the best base for exploring the bohemian neighbourhoods surrounding it. **€€**

**Töölö Towers**
Simply furnished apartments, from twin studios to penthouses, surrounded by Töölö's sights. **€€**

LEFT: MICHELE URSI/SHUTTERSTOCK © BOTTOM RIGHT: JONAS TUFVESSON/SHUTTERSTOCK ©

Kotiharjun Sauna

## Kotiharjun Sauna

HELSINKI'S OLDEST PUBLIC SAUNA

Dating from 1928, Kotiharjun Sauna is Helsinki's oldest public sauna, with a wood-burning stove providing gentle steams. The sauna is in Kallio and has an endearing feel to it.

Men and women bathe separately, but you can also rent a private sauna at a reasonable price. Towels, seat covers (*pefletti*) and anything else you might need for the sauna can be rented or bought on spot.

To top up the experience, the sauna also sells sauna *vihtas*, or bath brooms. Whack yourself with the *vihta* a few times and you will soon understand the point of it, with the practice not only cleaning your skin but also speeding up your blood flow and metabolism.

### BEST CAFES IN TÖÖLÖ & KALLIO

**Way Bakery**
Local favourite with fab brekkies, tasty pasta lunches and dinners, and moreish wines. €

**Cafetoria Café & Shop**
A Latin-Nordic cafe and roastery dedicated to bringing forth the best coffee aromas, located near Temppeliaukion Church. €

**Flät 14**
Build your own three-, five- or seven-piece breakfast menu from dishes such as cold smoked reindeer mousse and rice porridge – available from 9am to 4pm. €€

**Sinisen huvilan kahvila**
A summertime cafe located in an 1896 villa on the shores of Töölö bay. €

Coffee and a pastry

### WHERE TO EAT IN TÖÖLÖ

**Ateljé Finne**
In the sculptor Gunnar Finne's old studio, with Finne's artwork adding a nice touch to the dining experience. **€€**

**Aino**
Traditional Finnish food with a modern take in a charming restaurant – try the sea buckthorn crème brûlée. **€€**

**Finnjävel Sali & Salonki**
Elevating traditional Finnish ingredients to a contemporary level, the Michelin-starred restaurant is in Taidehalli. **€€€**

**Ruissalo Island, Turku (p78)**

## THE MAIN AREAS

**TURKU**
Modern harbour city. p78

**FASTA ÅLAND**
Scandinavian island escape. p88

**HANKO (HANGO)**
Historic seaside retreat. p100

**PORVOO**
Quaint medieval p109

# TURKU, THE SOUTH COAST & ÅLAND ARCHIPELAGO

## SCANDI SOUTHERN CHARM

Sweeping beaches and merry ferry adventures: seaside living is easy across tiny villages, yet a rugged history of seafaring and battle remains

The Åland Islands and Finland's southern coast are a vibrant beadwork of characterful little harbour towns with a lot of history. The Swedish and Russian empires fought for centuries over the area's ports, and today they're commandeered by daunting castles and fortresses that seem at odds with the sparkling sunshine and sailing boats.

Charming, history-steeped coastal points offer summer cruises, guest-harbour facilities, and charter boats to discover your own island. Inland, *bruk* (ironworks) villages such as Porvoo, Finland's second-oldest town, offer an insight into the area's industrial and trading past.

Anchoring the country's southwest is Finland's former capital, Turku, a striking seafaring city with cutting-edge galleries, museums and restaurants.

Turku is Finland's gateway to the glorious Åland archipelago, an interesting geopolitical anomaly that has more islands than it does inhabitants; though technically part of Finland, it is politically autonomous and Swedish speaking.

Åland is the sunniest spot in northern Europe, and its sweeping white-sand beaches and flat, scenic cycling routes attract crowds of holidaymakers during summer.

Yet outside the capital, Mariehamn, a sleepy haze hangs over the islands' tiny villages; finding your own remote beach among the 6500 skerries (rocky islets) is surprisingly easy.

A lattice of bridges and free cable ferries connects the central islands, while larger car ferries run abroad to Sweden and the archipelago's outer reaches.

LEFT: IGOR GROCHEV/SHUTTERSTOCK ©; RIGHT: HIVAKA/SHUTTERSTOCK ©

# Find Your Way

It's possible to see much of the region by public transport, but having your own vehicle is easiest. Trains are useful to reach larger towns, such as Turku and Hanko (Hango); otherwise bus routes are more frequent.

### Turku, p78

Finland's oldest city is also a contemporary juggernaut. Explore a cityscape delightfully blending old and new, from medieval masonry to experimental art.

### Fasta Åland, p88

Peaceful forests, scenic drives and fruit gardens galore in northern Europe's sunniest spot. Humming local life mixed with atmospheric seclusion will surely fill your cup.

### Hanko (Hango), p100

Seaside Nordic life at its prime. Discover war history and empire-style architecture in a charming port town full of friendly folks and fascinating stories.



LEFT: JAMO IMAGES/SHUTTERSTOCK ©, RIGHT: SERGEI AFANASEV/SHUTTERSTOCK ©

### CAR

Rent a vehicle at Helsinki Airport and explore all the way to Åland with ease. On the islands, car rentals are limited and more expensive. Expect to shell out for parking in centres such as Turku and Mariehamn.

### BUS

Buses run east and west from Helsinki, stopping in all towns and villages along the southern coast. The Turku archipelago is well served by buses from Turku, as is all of Fasta Åland from Mariehamn.

### FERRY

Jump on a ferry to get from Turku to Åland, or to Sweden – joining the Finnish holidaymakers indulging in a bit of karaoke on board. Island-hopping routes around Åland connect remote shores with the mainland.

ITÄ-SUOMEN
Sääksmäki
Vääksy
Heinola
Kuolimoj
Tuulos
Vuohijarvi
ETELÄ-SUOMEN
Lappeenranta
Hämeenlinna
Lahti
Pyhäjärvi
Kivljani
Taavetti
Kouvola
ETELÄ- SUOMEN
Porvoonjoki
Riihimäki
Anjalankoski
RUSSIA
Mäntsälä
Valkmusa National Park
Vaalimaa
Karkkila
Hyvinkää
Hamina
Kerava
Forsby
Loviisa
Kotka
Hiidenvesi
Vantaa
Porvoo
Kuutsalo
Kirkonmaa
Tammio
Kaunissaari
Nuuksio
Vantaa
Lohja
Espoo
HELSINKI
Eastern Gulf of Finland National Park
Ingå
Porkkala
Porkkalanselkä
Suursaari
Gulf of Finland
Prangli
Aegna
TALLINN
RUSSIA
ESTONIA

**Porvoo, p109**

Porvoo's Old Town is a must-see – and only 52km from Helsinki. Wine, dine and wander around historic wooden houses and cobblestone streets.

# Plan Your Time

Leave time to linger along the southern seaside. Discover the deserted beaches and harbours around fortresses and other sights. Chock-full artisan and antique shops also demand unhurried exploration.

LEENA ROBINSON/SHUTTERSTOCK ©

**Turun Linna (Turku Castle; p80)**

## If You Only Do One Thing

- Head straight for **Turku** (p78) to see its famed castle and cathedral; then peruse downtown's shops and galleries. For lunch, slurp soup at the **market hall** (p81). Stroll (or e-scooter) the 3km harbour stretch to Turku's main highlight, its **medieval castle** (p80). Head back, cross the river with the **Föri** (p78) and slip into the **Old Turku museum** (p79) for a couple of hours of ruin spotting. Watch the sun go down with craft beers and Finnish fare on a riverside terrace – and if you've still got energy, carry on for more drinks at a live-music pub or karaoke bar.

### Seasonal Highlights

Summer is the south's favourite season, when festivals and harbour hoopla abound. From October to April, main attractions – beaches, castles – close, but can be strolled around.

**MARCH**

Hot bebop and smoking sax hits Turku at several venues during its annual **jazz festival**.

**JUNE**

Turku's lively **Medieval Market** features historic reenactments and costumes by the cathedral and old square.

**JULY**

Join in **Hanko Regatta** carnival atmosphere – and discover Finnish metal at the thousands-strong **Ruisrock** rock fest in Turku.

FROM LEFT: GEOFF GOLDSWAIN, BELIKOVA OKSANA, JANUS ORLOV/SHUTTERSTOCK ©

## Three Days to Travel Around

● Wander around in Porvoo's **Old Town** (p110) and stock up on handmade sweets for a road trip to Hanko (Hango) and Turku. First stop is Hanko (Hango) to enjoy seaside relaxation – a **spa afternoon** (p101) or a quick wade at the **bathing house** (p102). Enjoy a cosy pub evening rubbing shoulders with locals before travelling to Turku the following morning. Leaving Hanko (Hango), don't miss the wartime relics at **Rintama Museo** (p102). In Turku, shop at boutiques and dine riverside between fascinating visits to the **castle** (p80) and **cathedral** (p81). A leisurely lunch at the **market hall** (p81) is an indulgent finale.

## If You Have More Time

● How low can you go? Finland's deepest southern parts offer lesser-known spots to unwind. **Fasta Åland** (p88), a six-hour ferry journey from **Turku** (p78), is an extraordinary place to unwind. Escape into lush forests and fruit orchards, discovering historic ruins and hidden harbours, between impeccable surf 'n' turf meals. Should nature call for getting even further off the grid, skip off to Åland's southernmost islands, such as **Föglö** (p97) and **Kökar** (p97), where untouched crags and countryside fulfil playful pirate fantasies. Or consider island-hopping on two wheels with a cycling adventure across Åland or Turku's Archipelago Trail.

**AUGUST**

East of Porvoo, the week-long **Hamina Tattoo** sees marching bands in a military music festival every even-numbered year.

**SEPTEMBER**

Feast on Åland's bounty during the **Skördefesten (Harvest Festival)** with open farms and special restaurant menus.

**NOVEMBER**

Åland restaurants, such as Smakbyn, hold **Christmas buffets** from late November, with fish delicacies, meatballs and more.

**DECEMBER**

Traditional **Christmas markets** light up the holidays. Porvoo's Town Hall Sq is a Finnish favourite.

FROM LEFT: CLAUDINE VAN MASSENHOVE, AD OCULOS, EMILY LUXTON, IGOR GROCHEV/SHUTTERSTOCK ©

# TURKU

Turku is Finland's second city – or first, by some accounts, as it was the capital until 1812. The majestic Turun Linna (Turku Castle) and ancient Gothic wonder, Turun Tuomiokirkko (Turku Cathedral) – both dating from the 13th century – are testaments to the city's storied past.

Contemporary Turku is even more enticing, challenging Helsinki's cultural pre-eminence with cutting-edge art galleries, summer music festivals and innovative restaurants. University students keep cafes and clubs buzzing, while designer boutiques and secondhand shops offer limitless scope for browsing beauty and buried treasure.

Through the age-old network of atmospheric streets and squares, the Aurajoki (Aura River) meanders picturesquely out to sea. For nature lovers, Turku is the gateway to the glorious Turku archipelago. As one of the country's main ports of entry (many visitors arrive by ferry from Sweden and Åland), it's a fabulous launching paid to exploring the Finnish mainland.

Turku
Helsinki

## TOP TIP

You'll get a kick out of hopping on the Föri – all day, the free mini-ferry conveniently shuttles walkers and bikers across the Aura in two minutes flat. Chugging since 1904, the orange commuter is Finland's oldest daily transport. Find it a few blocks southwest of the Martinsilta.

ROBSON90/SHUTTERSTOCK ©

**Aurajoki (Aura River; p81)**

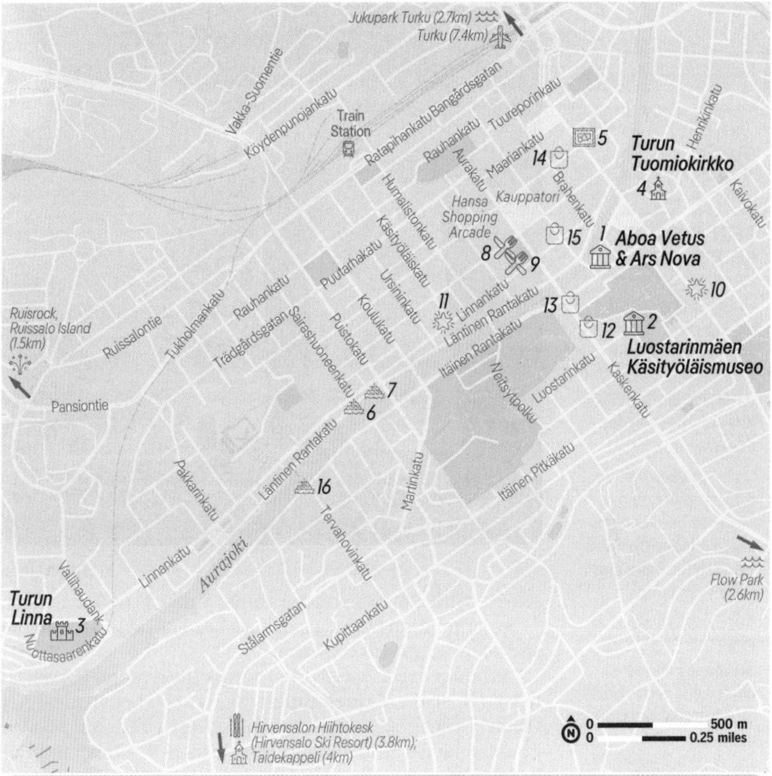

**HIGHLIGHTS**
**1** Aboa Vetus & Ars Nova
**2** Luostarinmäen Käsityöläismuseo
**3** Turun Linna
**4** Turun Tuomiokirkko

**SIGHTS**
**5** Auran Galleria
**see 5** B-Galleria

**ACTIVITIES, COURSES & TOURS**
**6** MS Rudolfina
**see 6** Rosita
**7** SS Ukkopekka

**EATING**
**see 9** Kalaliike S Wallin
**8** Kauppahalli
**see 9** Piece of Cake
**9** Sininen Juna Aschan Café

**ENTERTAINMENT**
**10** Karaoke CocoLoco
**11** Karaokebar Pelimies

**SHOPPING**
**12** Ateljee Agami
**13** Boutique Minne
**14** Butik Lilian
**15** Saarni

**TRANSPORT**
**16** Föri Ferry

## Medieval Masterpieces

ART MEETS ARCHAEOLOGY

In Turku, chase darkness and light through two incredible architectural marvels. The riverside **Aboa Vetus (Old Turku) museum** draws visitors underground to Turku's medieval

### WHERE TO EAT & DRINK BY THE RIVER

**Smör**
Organic, locally sourced dishes lit by flickering candles in a vaulted cellar. €€€

**Blanko**
Hip venue with great lunch specials and the best Sunday brunch in town. €€

**Kakolanruusu**
Seasonal modern fare and open-fire cooking in a former prison warehouse. €€€

### BEST ANTIQUE SHOPS

**Osto- ja Myyntiliike KJ Simolin**
Treasure shop with vases and ceramic tchotchkes – fight through the crowded doorway.

**Osto- ja Myyntiliike Kalustepalvelu**
Squeeze between tiny aisles piled with grand wooden furniture and statement lamps.

**Antiikkiliike Wanha Elias**
All shapes and sizes of miscellaneous bric-a-brac collected from estates.

**Wanhan Talon Tavarat**
Everything and anything – especially vintage kitchenware and decorations made of glass and porcelain.

**Art+Design**
Turku's most colourful antiques shop. Deals in 20th-century antiques, clothing and accessories.

EVAZA/SHUTTERSTOCK ©

Turun Linna

streets with imposing stone ruins. Some 37,000 artefacts, from ceramics to buried gold, have been unearthed from the site below (digs still continue).

A brighter experience is 7km across the river on Hirvensalo island, at the **Taidekappeli** (St Henry's Ecumenical Art Chapel). The neogothic brick chapel covers a medieval wooden granary named after Finland's first bishop. Its timber interior looks more like a Burning Man installation than a worship place, curving into a hypnotic Reuleaux triangle framing the altar in light. From outside, gaze at the strange, spectacular copper-clad structure – shaped like a tipped-up ship's bow, and bathed in sun on its rocky perch.

## Feudal Fortress

FINLAND'S LARGEST CASTLE

Founded in 1280 at the mouth of the Aurajoki, the gargantuan **Turun Linna** is easily Finland's biggest castle. It's free for visitors to roam the annexes of its stony outdoor courtyard, but admission to the museum inside is worthwhile too. The labyrinthine layout features dungeons, banquet halls and the castle's impressive Old Bailey.

Swedish count Per Brahe ruled Finland from the castle in the 17th century, while Sweden's deposed King Eric XIV was

### WHERE TO EAT & DRINK BY THE RIVER

**Kakola Brewing Company**
Easy-to-drink craft beers, served on a riverside terrace, ideal for long summer nights.'

**Surf Shack**
Laid-back SoCal vibes meet Scandinavia finesse: DJs, cocktails and vegan soft serve.

**Tintå**
Riverside wine bar with a cosy exposed-brick interior and terrace overlooking the water.

imprisoned in its round tower in the late 16th century. Today most Finns recognise the castle's distinctive architecture as the logo for Turun Sinappi (Turku Mustard).

## Fixture of Faith

'MOTHER CHURCH' FOR LUTHERAN FINNS

Consecrated in 1300, **Turku Cathedral** was rebuilt many times after damaging fires, but still looks majestic. It's a lively place, with a small museum of medieval paraphernalia, free summer organ concerts and some English-language services. Tune into Finland's YLE1 Radio at noon to hear the church's distinctive hourly bell – it's a patriotic reminder of the Continuation War, when Finns prayed together for victory.

## Finnish Food Tour

EAT YOUR HEART OUT

Turku's fabulous kauppahalli (market hall) is easily its cosiest, most atmospheric lunch spot. The historic covered market, built in 1896, is where locals of all ages gather for bites and coffee-break chatter across rich wood counters and tables. Vendors sell local delicacies, including artisan cheeses, meats, seafood and baked goods, but there's also multicultural cuisine and a vegan kitchen too.

Operating since 1887, the **Kalaliike S Wallin** fish counter serves the perfect hearty salmon soup – with cream or without. Meanwhile, cafes such as Sininen Juna Aschan, set in an old railway carriage, and **Piece of Cake** dole out sky-high desserts and seriously good espresso.

## Contemporary Art Corner

FED BY CREATIVE PASSION

Savour Turku's artistic streak at the adjacent **Auran Galleria** and **B-Galleria**. Hugging the corner of Yliopistonkatu and Aninkaistenkatu, Auran is a family-run gallery, operating for over 30 years. Monthly changing exhibitions from international artists are spread across two levels. Even if you don't have a few thousand euros to drop on a painting or sculpture, the mother-daughter owners are always happy to show visitors around.

Next door, the artist-run, nonprofit B-Galleria showcases young up-and-comers. Remove your shoes at the door and get up close to experimental installations. In the backroom studio, artists tinker away at sketches and graphic designs.

### ONCE UPON A CAPITAL

Åbo (Turku's original Swedish name), once Sweden's second-largest town, comes from a settlement (*bo*) on a river (*å*). When the Russians took over, the city, still deeply connected to Sweden, lost its capital status to Helsinki and became a commerce hub. The name Turku is an archaic Russian word for 'marketplace'. Today, the Aurajoki, lined with terrace restaurants and cultural sights, is Turku's hub for local life. These riverbanks, though, have been inhabited over millennia. Archaeological finds date back to the Stone Age, but Turku was founded with a Catholic settlement in 1229. In the 14th century, a new church and the Turku Castle saw the city consecrated as an administrative and spiritual base.

### WHERE TO DRINK IN STYLE

**Panimoravintola Koulu**
Former school turned elegant brewpub and beer garden with seasonal brews.

**Cosmic Comic Café**
Manga-lovers' dream pub. Comic paper walls, huge collection and craft beer.

**Uusi Apteekki**
Rest your pint on dispensing drawers turned tables in a historic former pharmacy.

**BEST LIVE MUSIC VENUES**

**Tiirikkala**
Cool cocktail bar in a wooden house; jazz and blues head up the weekend live-music programme.

**Bar Ö**
Bar with cosy living-room vibes, DJs and live bands.

**Dynamo**
Local DJs vie with national bands at this central venue. Great outdoor terrace.

**Concert Hall**
Home of Turku Philharmonic Orchestra, playing since 1790, when the Musical Society of Turku was founded.

**Venus**
Nightlife complex with live music, dance grooves and karaoke.

## Historical Handicrafts

ARTISANSHIP OVER THE AGES

Handiwork is a centuries-old tradition in Turku. Don't miss rambling around **Luostarinmäen Käsityöläismuseo**, a national treasure weaving together the past and present of local craftwork since 1940. This open-air handicrafts museum comprises stocky 19th-century wooden workshops and houses, situated along tiny lanes and grassy yards. In the workshops, there are 30 artisans (among them a silversmith, a watchmaker, a baker, a potter, a shoemaker and a printer) plying their trades in period costume. All the buildings are, surprisingly, in their original locations – spared by the Great Fire of 1827, which destroyed much of Turku.

## Designer Party Duds

FEELING FANCY, FINNISH STYLE

There's no better place to search for special-occasion wear than Turku. The city is a hot spot for Finnish designer formalwear. Come on a mission for 'dress-to-impress' attire, with sustainable fashions ranging from vintage to handmade.

**Ateljee Agami** is a sewing boutique-atelier with a 'slow fashion' philosophy: upcycling, natural fabrics and hand-production in Turku. The master sewer Harriet is passionate about early-20th-century designs, and particularly evening wear. Since the atelier aims for zero waste, drop in and see what beautiful leftover textiles or retro buttons are kicking around. **Boutique Minne** specialises in vintage designs for theatre and elegance. It's worth a check for Gatsby-esque hats and accessories. **Butik Lilian** also carries gently worn evening gowns seeking a second coming. Meanwhile, for suits and ties, **Saarni**, a self-described 'gentlemen's boutique', is packed with dapper finery.

**GRAND COVERED MARKETS**

Turku's market hall is Finland's second oldest, built in 1896 three years after **Helsinki's Vanha Kauppahalli** (p51). Both were designed by architect Gustaf Nyström.

## Enter the Moshpit

PEDAL TO THE METAL

Finland's summer rock festival, Ruisrock, is a 100,000 person-strong, once-in-a-lifetime affair. Gigantic stages and pyrotechnics galore take over Turku's Ruissalo Island for a single weekend every year.

Essentially Finland's Woodstock, it's the oldest Finnish rock festival and the second oldest in Europe, held since 1970. Many a rock god has gone head-to-head with the Ruisrock masses, including Bowie, Bob Dylan, Ozzy Osbourne, Oasis

**WHERE TO BUY VINYL**

**8raita**
One of Finland's best record shops – big selection and well-organised genres.

**Levykauppa Äx Oy**
Run by rock aficionados, all your head-banging prayers are answered here.

**Round Sound Records**
Secondhand vinyl, spanning genres. Not much rock, but a good jazz section.

and The Clash. What's fascinating is also taking in Finland's famous metal bands on home turf – and especially, their fandom crowd-surfing and moshing up a sweat. Don't expect a sea of black band T-shirts, though. The festival gear here is colourful and vibrant, plus meadows and beach stages provide uplifting scenery. Swimming, camping and activities such as yoga are all part of rocking out here.

## Killer Karaoke

FIVE MINUTES OF FAME

A little-known fact about Finland? Karaoke is a favourite pastime. A few mics, a machine and a screen are typical staples of pub culture. Finns, a normally reserved folk, perform with a stage presence that would impress reality show judges – and pub-goers young and old alike adore it. Cheering for all and tipping the karaoke host is good etiquette. **Karaoke CocoLoco** and **Karaokebar Pelimies** are two of Turku's best bars for all-night croon sessions. Many pubs host weekly karaoke nights.

## Cool Cruises

COME SAIL AWAY

Archipelago cruises are popular in the summer, with most boats departing from the quay at Martinsilta. Embarking on a sail from Turku is essentially a rite of passage. Cruises, while tending to be a little touristy, are still an enriching experience – sit back, sip wine and marvel at the sights.

**MS Rudolfina** provides lunch and dinner harbour cruises overlooking Turku Castle, Pikisaar Island and Ruissalo Island, while evening cruises show off Naantali Harbour and the Kultaranta (president's summer residence). Meanwhile, the historic **SS Ukkopekka** makes twice-daily cruises to Naantali, as well as evening dinners with dancing on Loistokari's island pier. The **Rosita** runs a one-hour cruise out to Vepsä Island and occasional day-long adventures to the lighthouse island of Bengtskär.

## Amusement Park Adventures

SWING, SLIDE AND PLAY

Get your heart rate pumping at two of Finland's favourite adventure spots. Turku is home to **Jukupark**, Finland's biggest waterpark, a wet wonderland of meandering slides, sprinklers,and pirate-themed play areas. Meanwhile, at **FlowPark**, little ones can play on swaying bridges, swings, jumps and cable slides. Apparatuses reach heights of up to 20m on a state-of-the-art rope course but there's also a low-rope course.

### UNUSUAL ACCOMMODATION

**Hotel Kakola**
Former prison transformed with plush, warm Scandinavian design – including a 'jailhouse chic' cell room. €€€

**Bridgettine Sisters' Guesthouse**
Run by nuns, this Catholic convent's guest wing is a haven with austere, spotless rooms. €

**Laivahostel Borea**
The SS *Bore*, a passenger ship turned hostel, docks outside the Forum Marinum museum. €

**Ruissalo Camping**
On Ruissalo Island, this campground has grassy sites, great cabins, saunas and Turku's closest beaches. €

**Park Hotel**
Art nouveau building overlooking a hilly park. Characterful rooms, classical music and a lobby parrot. €€

### GETTING AROUND

Downtown Turku is easily explored on foot. Bikes and ride-sharing scooters are also popular. Airport service is limited; usually it's cheaper to reach Turku from Helsinki by car or Stockholm by ferry.

# Beyond Turku

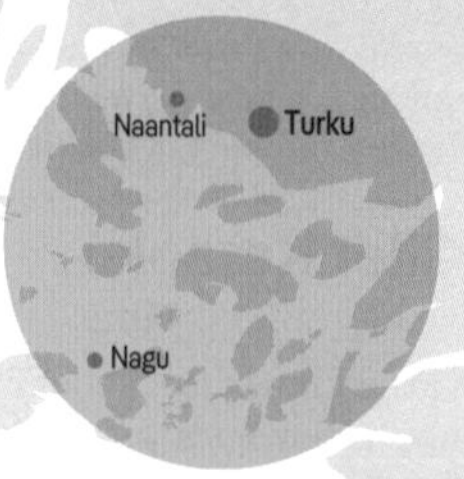


**Dance with Moomins, relax in saunas or savour forest solitude just a ferry ride away from Turku.**

Turku is a stepping stone to sea-salt retreats and wild islands elsewhere along the coast, to Åland, Sweden and beyond. For example, an awesome 20,000 islands and skerries make up the Turku archipelago, one of Finland's most spectacular natural attractions – just a hop, a skip and a ferry ride or two away. These shores offer no big-ticket sights, just quiet settlements, abundant birdlife and ever-changing views of sea and land.

The most effortless summer daytrip from Turku is the charming spa town Naantali (Swedish: Nådendal) only 15km east. From June to August, Moominworld (Muumimaailma) keeps Naantali very busy. Out of season, it's a misty ghost town – although locals work hard behind the scenes running Finland's third-busiest port.

### TOP TIP

In summer the mini-train Minijuna Aikataulu does a handy circuit between Naantali Spa and the harbour.

Naantali (p83)

INSPIRED BY MAPS/SHUTTERSTOCK ©

JAMO IMAGES/SHUTTERSTOCK ©

Muumimaailma

## Meet the Moomins

FUN FOR THE FAMILY

Beloved throughout Finland and beyond, the Moomins are a famous eccentric family of nature-loving, white-snouted, hippo-like trolls. Grab squishy hugs from them at **Muumimaailma (Moominworld)**. The no-rides amusement park, a 15km-drive from Turku, delights kids with hands-on activities across interactive playrooms.

Bump into costumed characters rambling through the Moominhouse and the Groke's Cave, and stir up an invention in Snork's Workshop. Other Muumimaailma highlights include a swimming beach and Emma's Theatre; the two-day ticket is also good for **Väski Adventure Island**. At Väski, older adventure-seekers will get their thrills on an island that features rock climbing, gold panning, zip lining and rope obstacle courses. Free shuttle boats depart every 30 minutes from Naantali near the bridge to Muumimaailma.

### THE STORY BEHIND THE MOOMINS STORY

Characters Moominpappa, Moominmamma and their timid child, Moomintroll, are based closely on creator Tove Jansson's bohemian upbringing with her artist parents. Others include the eternal wanderer Snufkin; the eerie Hattifatteners, who grow from seeds and are drawn to electrical storms; and the icy Groke, who leaves a frozen trail wherever she drifts.

Jansson, once a satirist lampooning Hitler and Stalin, first published the wholesome Moomin drawings in her political cartoons. She wrote the first of her nine children's books, *The Moomins and the Great Flood*, during WWII, followed by several cartoon books. Her comic strips debuted in the *London Evening News* in 1954, before being syndicated worldwide. Adaptations include a popular Japanese cartoon series, film and album.

### WHERE TO SHOP IN NAANTALI

**Moomin Shop**
Your one-stop shop in the Old Town for all things Moomin-related.

**Wanha Naantali Kauppa**
Old-fashioned Finnish sweets, knick-knacks and more silly souvenirs.

**Unikeko**
Home decor shop with local decorations made from fish skin and deer bone.

**ISLAND-HOPPING**

The five largest inhabited islands of the Turku archipelago, like most of the southern coast, are primarily Swedish speaking.

**Pargas** (Finnish: Parainen): The de facto 'capital' of the archipelago with interesting sights.

**Nagu** (Finnish: Nauvo): Shoreside harbour huts sell designer sailor-wear and smoked salmon; walking trails reveal birdlife.

**Korpo** (Finnish: Korppoo): Pristine forests and hidden beaches.

**Houtskär** (Finnish: Houtskari): Short on sights, yet tranquil.

**Iniö**: A tiny population and mighty sea landscapes. Of 1000 islets, only 10 are liveable.

## A Dandy Old Town

HISTORIC WOODEN HOUSES

Naantali's photogenic **Old Town,** easily reached by bus or a 15km drive from Turku, is a picturesque mix of harbour views and cobblestone streets. Centuries-old wooden houses are now home to handicraft shops, art galleries, antiques shops and cafes.

At **Naantali's museum,** trace the town's history from its convent roots. Housed in three wooden Old Town buildings dating from the 18th century, artefacts and exhibits cast light on disappearing trades such as needle making and goldsmithing.

## Spa, Ooh La La

AWESOME SAUNA LIFE

Naantali, 15km east of Turku by bus or car, has a spa tradition that began in 1723 with the discovery of the Viluluoto Spring and its therapeutic properties. Naantali's reputation as an illustrious resort town peaked in the 19th century.

Today, the top-class spa hotel **Naantali Spa (Naantalin Kylpylä)** is one of Finland's finest. Non-guests can also access its impressive facilities, including several pools, traditional Finnish saunas, and Turkish and Roman baths. Its massage and beauty treatments are popular – booking ahead in summer is a must.

Besides the upmarket spa complex, a large variety of rooms include spacious, contemporary digs, Moomin-themed family suites and luxurious apartments with private balconies. Two great restaurants are also well frequented by locals.

More sauna options in Naantali range from shoestring budget choices to splurge occasions. At **Hotel Bridget Inn**, spoil yourself with a luxurious suite featuring its own private sauna and terrace. On the other side of the spectrum, **Naantali's campground** offers good budget facilities and a beachside sauna. Cabins range from basic to more comfortable, with bathrooms, kitchens and even some with private saunas too.

**MORE MOOMIN MANIA**

Up for more Moomin madness? Check out Tampere's **Muumimuseo** (p120), an experiential art museum, where drawings, figurines and dioramas bring the quirky world of Tove Jansson into new dimensions.

## Medieval Monastery

ANCIENT GEMS UNEARTHED

Discover Naantali's origins as a monastic town with a visit to **Naantalin Kirkko** (Naantali Convent Church). Medieval

**WHERE TO DINE IN NAANTALI**

**Peculiar Café**
Stop by for a slice of pie in this cute house adorned with Moomins memorabilia. €

**Uusi Kilta**
Naantali's best restaurant has a sun-drenched terrace and superb seafood. €€

**Merisali**
In a restored spa pavilion, savour buffets, a pier-side terrace and live music. €€

Naantali, a 20-minute drive from Turku by car or 30 minutes by bus, grew up around the Catholic Convent of the Order of St Birgitta, which was dissolved after the 1527 Reformation.

Towering above the harbour, the massive 1462 church is all that remains. Archaeological digs have unearthed some 2000 pieces of jewellery, coins and relics now in the Naantali Museum. At 8pm on summer evenings, hear a trumpeter play vespers (evensong) from the belfry. There are also regular organ concerts.

## Off the Beaten Track

NATURE LOVER'S PILGRIMAGE

A popular way to experience the Turku archipelago is to cycle (or drive) the **Archipelago Trail**, a 230km circular route that starts and ends in Turku. Twelve bridges and nine ferries connect tiny, diverse islands, each with their own laid-back flair. Cycling across smooth country roads provides glimpses of fields and farms, bridges and beaches, villages and sea. Stop for rest and recuperation in the villages or welcoming guesthouses, and pick wild strawberries and swim off secluded skerries along the way.

From mid-May to August, the entire route can be completed from Turku by hopping between the main islands and islets, linked by eight ferries and a dozen bridges. The further you travel, the more forward planning is required, as ferries run less frequently between the outer islands. Use Ferry.fi to plan your route.

## R&R in Nagu

ARCHIPELAGO LIVING AT ITS BEST

Starving after all that pedalling? Take a breather in Nagu, the archipelago's highlight for relaxation.

A mandatory stop on the Archipelago Trail, cycle to this quaint town (or take a 1¼-hour bus with ferry crossing from Turku) to spend a few days gorging on fresh seafood, and invigorating with frigid dips and glorious sunsets.

Appealing guesthouses have comfy beds and saunas, but the meals will surely be the highlight. Lovely restaurants include **Köpmans** with its famous pike burger, plus local farmers and fishers selling fruit, vegetables and freshly smoked salmon from their kiosks. Pack a picnic and hit the road.

### LIVELY FESTIVALS

Naantali, a typically sleepy town, is fittingly home to a festival inspired by being tired. **National Sleepyhead Day** (27 July) is certainly not a bore, though. According to tradition, the last family member asleep on the previous night is woken up with a bucket of water. The city of Naantali takes it a step further by selecting a celeb 'Sleepyhead of the Year' to get tossed into the sea at 7am. From there, the carnival atmosphere doesn't stop until night, with a parade, cake bake-off, games and live music. Naantali's other big event is its two-week **summer music festival**. First-rate classical music and worldwide performers have been hosted here for over 30 years.

### GETTING AROUND

SS *Ukkopekka* sails between Turku and Naantali in summer, arriving at the passenger quay on the south side of the harbour.

Frequent, free public ferries connect the Turku archipelago. Meanwhile, the MS *Eivor* shuttles to the archipelago's more obscure islands.

# FASTA ÅLAND

Fasta Åland Helsinki

The core of the Åland archipelago is a dozen or so larger islands that are connected by bridges. Known as Fasta Åland (Ahvenanmaa in Finnish), this 'mainland' comprises 70% of the archipelago's land area – including its only town. It's also home to 90% of Åland's population. Fasta Åland offers more historical sites, cultural attractions and recreational activities than any other island – and receives the vast majority of tourists.

Åland's capital, Mariehamn, is on the mainland's southern side. Named by Alexander II after the Empress Maria, its broad streets lined with linden trees, recalling its Russian heritage, play home to a handful of shops, pubs and restaurants. It's the busiest spot in Åland – though still very laid-back. On long scenic drives, you'll find that Fasta often feels like a remote island. It's easy to find quiet stretches, surrounded by nature and sea, but still within striking distance of the capital.

### TOP TIP

Mariehamn contains the bulk of Åland's lodgings. Business and tourist hotels, as well as campgrounds and guesthouses, cover a wide range of prices and styles. As throughout the islands, rates are highest between mid-June and the end of August, and especially in July. Booking ahead is recommended, especially for weekends.

IGOR GROCHEV/SHUTTERSTOCK ©

**Mariehamn**

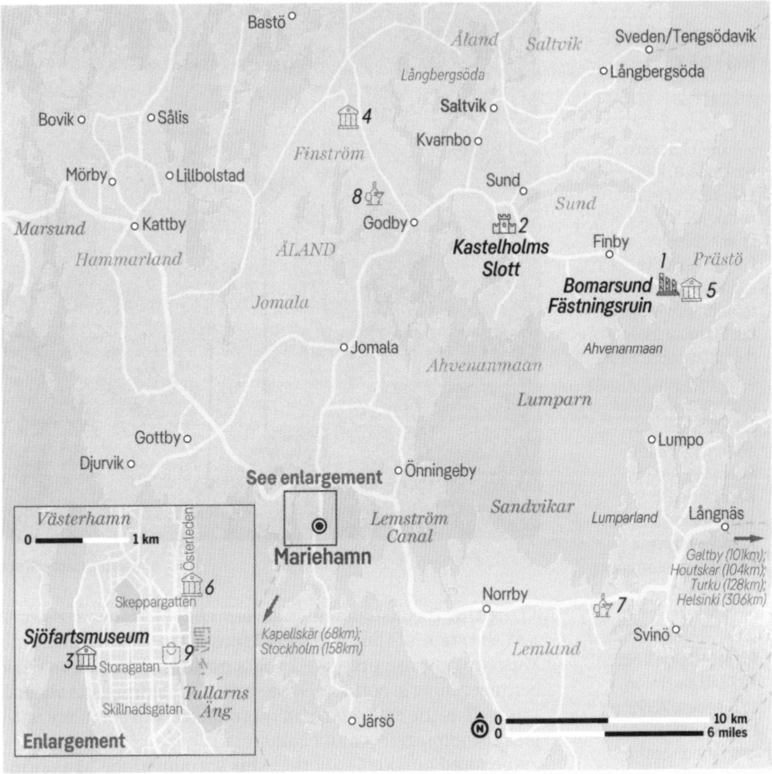

**HIGHLIGHTS**
**1** Bomarsund Fästningsruin
**2** Kastelholms Slott
**3** Sjöfartsmuseum

**SIGHTS**
**4** Ålands Fotografiska Museum
**5** Bomarsund Museum
**see 2** Fängelsemuseet Vita Björn
**see 2** Jan Karlsgårdens Friluftsmuseum
**see 3** Museumship Pommern
**6** Sjökvarteret

**EATING**
**see 6** Pub Niska
**see 2** Smakbyn

**DRINKING & NIGHTLIFE**
**see 9** Ålands Slöjd & Konsthantverk
**7** Amalia's Limonadfabrik
**8** Stallhagen Brewery

**SHOPPING**
**see 6** Guldviva
**see 9** Labelled
**see 6** Salt
**see 9** Torggatan 15
**9** Viktor Crafts & Designs

## Maritime History

AWAKEN YOUR INNER PIRATE

The atmospheric maritime quarter **Sjökvarteret** is a must-visit. Wander along the quay, lined with traditional schooners, and perhaps see boats under construction as well

### WHERE TO STAY IN ÅLAND

**HavsVidden**
At the island's far-northern tip, cliff-perched resort overlooking the Gulf of Bothnia. €€€

**Susannes B&B**
Homely feels in Hammarland. Charming rooms in a 19th-century house. €€

**Kvarnbo Pensionat**
Gorgeously decorated historic guesthouse with idyllic countryside in Saltvik. €€

### ÅLAND'S UNIQUE HISTORY

Åland is an autonomous state with its own parliament, flag, stamps and web suffix: 'dot ax'. Locals speak Swedish, not Finnish, and the islands' 'special relationship' with the EU means it is demilitarised, can sell duty-free and make its own gambling laws. Swedish-owned during the Middle Ages, the islands were ceded to Russia with Finland in 1809. Åland became Russia's westernmost outpost until the empire's defeat in 1856. Residents called for secession from Finland and return to Sweden. In 1921 a League of Nations convention crafted unique cultural and linguistic rights, and neutral political status here.

Locals may tell you they feel neither Swedish nor Finnish. Despite this, the islands are a popular holiday destination for Swedes and Finns alike.

THOMAS COLLETT/SHUTTERSTOCK ©

Kastelholms Slott

as the tiny reconstructed seafarers' chapel at the pier's end.

At the state-of-the-art **Sjöfartsmuseum** (Åland Maritime Museum), peruse preserved boats exploring Åland's marine heritage. Ships in bottles, sea chests and accoutrements abound – as well as the centrepiece, a reproduced ship complete with mast, saloon, galley and cabins.

Anchored outside is another star specimen, the **Museum-ship Pommern**. The beautifully preserved four-masted merchant barque was built in 1903 in Glasgow.

## Medieval Stroll

ROLLING GREENS AND GRAND SIGHTS

A sunny afternoon is well spent in Sund. Here, a marvellous trio of historic Åland landmarks, some of Finland's oldest, are set within short grassy strolls from each other.

The striking **Kastelholms Slott** is a Swedish-built medieval castle on a picturesque inlet. The keep towers are 15m high in parts, with walls of 3m-thick red granite. Exhibits showcase archaeological finds, including a medieval silver-coin hoard.

Make your way to **Fängelsemuseet Vita Björn**, a prison for 200 years, now a bite-sized museum with cells and an inmates'

### WHERE TO SHOP FOR ARTISAN GOODS

**Jussis Keramik**
Watch glass-blowers turn out brightly coloured ceramics and glassware in this workshop.

**Little BBQ's Junk Art**
Johan 'Joppan' Karlsson turns junk – old tools, appliances – into unique interior design.

**Mercedes Chocolaterie**
Mercedes makes exquisite pralines using cacao from her Venezuelan homeland and local ingredients (eg Åland nettle).

yard on display. Continuing south, the **Jan Karlsgårdens** open-air museum contains an impressive field of traditional 18th- and 19th-century Ålandic buildings and towering windmills.

## Artisan Souvenirs

INSPIRED BY ÅLAND'S OUTDOORS

Åland's natural environment, with its sea and sky, granite and forests, inspires many artists and artisans. Leave time to browse shops specialising in locally made products.

At the northern end of Österhamn in Mariehamn, it's easy to while away a couple of hours at Sjökvarteret. Here at the atmospheric quay, explore shops such as **Guldviva**, which specialises in brooches, cufflinks and necklaces influenced by the islands' flora and fauna. **Salt** is an excellent craft shop displaying local work, including textiles, ceramics, silverware and jewellery. The red-brown timber shed also stocks Finnish delicacies, such as sea-buckthorn jam.

Not far away, Torggatan 15 is a charming old wooden house packed with creative treasures. There's a handful of shops tucked into the various rooms - each one enticing in its own way. You never know what you'll find in **Viktor Crafts & Designs** among shelves stocking the works of 20 local artisans. The design studio and boutique **Labelled** sells clothing made from recycled fabrics, and the artists association **Ålands Slöjd & Konsthantverk** runs an upstairs gallery rotating exhibits of its members' work. Nobody leaves Torggatan 15 without at least one shopping bag in hand.

## Nerdy Nostalgia

EXTRAORDINARY CAMERA COLLECTION

Don't miss traipsing around the **Ålands Fotografiska Museum**'s gigantic collection of audiovisual equipment from the ages - perhaps the world's most comprehensive collection of camera gear.

This delightful museum, spread across the rooms and halls of a former school, is an unexpected Åland discovery. Peruse cabinets packed with over 16,000 pieces of AV paraphernalia, capturing the camera's history from the 1830s to today. What makes the collection so unique is it comprises not just vintage shutters, but video and sound-recording equipment rounded up around the world - vinyl players, TV and darkroom technology, eight-tracks, Walkmans and much more.

Displayed among the old pharmacy shelves, the photojournalism and the art are also nostalgic Mickey Mouse and Spice

### I LIVE HERE: FAVOURITE PHOTOGRAPHIC LOCATIONS

**Olle Strömberg**, who runs Ålands Fotografiska Museum, has been a shutterbug since age 10 - you can even see his first camera, Gevabox, on display (cameramuseum.com). These are his favourite spots for taking photos.

**Sankt Mikael Kyrka**
I like taking photos inside, especially of the murals, but also the special facade.

**Prästgårdsnäset**
A wonderful nature reserve. Easy to walk around in.

**Viking Market**
Such a genuine event with lots of interesting people!

**Hermas museigård**
Pictures and picnics: farm museum in Enklinge with buildings from the 1500s.

**Museumship Pommern**
Sailing ship harboured at the Åland Maritime Museum. She's so good-looking!

### WHERE TO CAMP IN ÅLAND

**Degersands Resort**
On Åland's most beautiful beach, well-furnished cottages and a traditional smoke sauna. €€

**Sandösunds Camping**
Idyllic campground with stylish townhouse rooms and well-kept beachside log cabins plus a 'floating sauna'. €

**Gröna Uddens Camping**
Campsite by the seaside, with spruce cabins, a safe swimming beach, minigolf and bike hire. €

Girls Polaroids and disposables, antique rolls of film, and chemicals for processing and making flash powder.

Lovingly run by husband-and-wife team Olle and Benita Strömberg, the exhibitions are curated from the couple's private collection of AV curios gone awry. Some setups are deeply personal; for example, a corner dedicated to the photographer who nurtured the collector's early passion for photography (featuring his cameras and the first photo of baby Olle in the 1950s). The living-room-like cafe is the perfect spot to chat with the couple about their treasures over coffee and cake.

### ISLAND FEASTS

**Kvarter 5**
Nordic cuisine with a sophisticated twist. Local ingredients, such as reindeer; everything made from scratch. €€€

**Indigo**
Contemporary menu in historic building and buzzing courtyard. Specials include Åland beef with homemade fries. €€

**ÅSS Paviljongen**
Marina views and creatively prepared local seafare: cod, perch, smoked shrimp and more. €€€

**Ångbåts Bryggan**
Semi-swanky harbourside place where the grill gets a workout. Live music and gorgeous sea views. €€€

**Kallas SkärGård**
Seasonally changing menu spiked with produce from the next-door farm plus wild berries and mushrooms. €€€

## Gastronomic Hot Spot

TOUR AND TASTE

Fasta Åland has an exciting dining scene that shows off the islands' freshest ingredients, from seafood to forest harvest, and the talent of its most creative chefs.

Get a crash course in Åland's special produce at **Smakbyn**, a 'taste village' with a farm shop, cookery courses, a bakery and a distillery. The centrepiece is the airy open-kitchen restaurant, where cooks work magic with seasonal organic produce and serve Åland staples, such as homemade *svartbröd* (the local dark bread that takes four days to make). The menu is always different but usually features delicious local perch fillets and the beloved open-faced steak sandwiches.

## Ålandic Treat

NOT YOUR AVERAGE PANCAKE

In celebration of Åland's 100-year anniversary in 2022, residents voted **Ålandspannkaka** (Åland pancake) the islands' dish of the century. Oven-baked, yet served either hot or cold, this isn't a pancake as you might imagine. It's a spongy treat, served like a pie slice, made with semolina and a hint of cardamom. Standard toppings include stewed prunes or raspberry jam and whipped cream (called *snömos* or 'snow mash' in Åland). It's available either as a dessert or as a sweet afternoon snack at most Åland cafes and restaurants. On Åland's Autonomy Day (9 June), pancakes are also festively served in Mariehamn's main square.

## Archipelago Pizza

FRESH FROM THE OVEN

Star chef Michael 'Micke' Björklund of Smakbyn is the brains behind **Pub Niska** and its delicious *plåtbröd* (Åland-style pizza). Toppings are diverse and delicious, including cold-smoked

### WHERE TO DINE WITH A VIEW

**Bodegan**
Pretty pierside restaurant with delectable Nordic grills, from salmon to tenderloin. €€

**Soltuna Restaurang**
Åland's highest restaurant – impeccable views but also tasty food and friendly service. €€

**Nautical**
Sea-inspired dishes, such as pan-fried Åland perch with caraway foam; served on the harbour. €€

## WALKING TOUR: EXPLORING THE BOMARSUND RUINS

This 4.2km walk is well signposted and mostly trailed, revealing mossy fields, rocky crags and breathtaking seascapes in sweet solitude (good shoes are a must). The entire route should take about two hours if you want to time hitting viewpoints Djävulsberget and Notvikstornet at sundown. Before you go, download Coastal Past, a GPS-navigated tour app.

The hike takes you around the series of ruins telling the dramatic story of 19th-century Russian rule and demise during the Åland War, starting off at the centrepiece **1 Bomarsund**, the best-preserved ruin. Cross and walk along the main road to take in exhibits at the **2 Bomarsund Visitor Centre**. Continue down the signposted route where piles of rubble indicate **3 former barracks and planned civic buildings**. This was once Skarpans, Åland's first town, where a busy postal route was set along residences, a school and armed food storage for around 2000 Russian soldiers and their families. Open the wooden gates and walk on the grass among the ruins – be careful, as rain can make their platforms slippery. Follow the trail back to the road, cross and pass by the little wooden hut where buses stop (the cutest bus stop ever) and turn right to follow the trail to show-stopping **4 Brännklinstornet**. Once you've passed it, the app will show a rocky ascent ahead to **5 Djävulsberget (Devil's Mountain)**. This is extremely difficult, so you're best to go all the way back out of the trail, turn left towards Bomarsund and left into the trail, a comparatively much easier path scaling the viewpoint. Go back down and head back to Bomarsund. The trail passing it northwards leads to **6 Notvikstornet** and can be driven if you're tired.

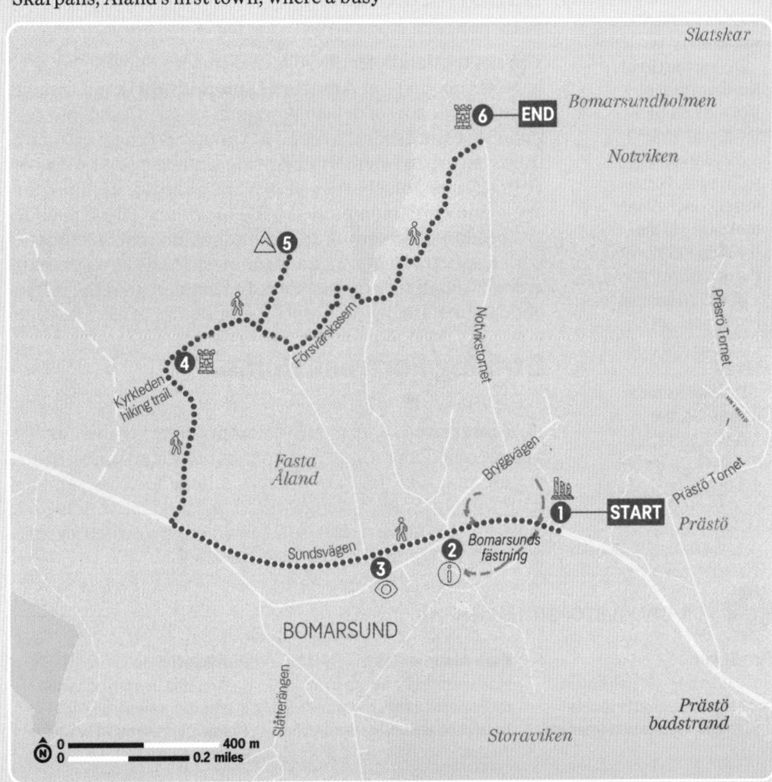

salmon and horseradish cream and, in true locavore spirit, Åland dairy cheese. Wander over to the maritime quarter to try one of these crispy creations. The interior feels like the inside of a ship, but the place to be is the glorious sunny terrace.

### WARTIME BASTIONS

More than 100 Bronze and Iron Age *fornminne* (burial sites) have been discovered across the Åland archipelago, attesting to over 6000 years of human habitation. Though all are clearly signposted, most are in fairly nondescript fields. The discovery of fortress ruins confirms that the archipelago was an important harbour and trading centre protected by the Vikings via maritime warfare.

During the Great Northern War of 1700–21 (dubbed the 'Great Wrath'), most Ålanders fled to Sweden. Further Russian incursions took place in the 1740s and 1809, with the Invasion of Åland, a 1918 WWI campaign, as the final act of militarisation ever here.

Despite its many fortresses, the Åland archipelago has been peaceful, politically neutral and demilitarised ever since.

## Brew Life

ISLAND MICROBREWERIES AND GASTROPUBS

Craft beer in Åland captures the remote essence of the archipelago, from swishy lagers reminiscent of forest greens and sea breeze to brews inspired by Viking traditions.

Beer lovers will feel right at ease at Åland's illustrious **Stallhagen Brewery** in Finström. It's perhaps the prettiest gastropub you will ever lay eyes on, a fabulous brewery overlooking an idyllic lake and horse paddocks. Sample unique, well-priced beer flights and rib-sticking food while musical jam sessions strike up on the terrace. Beers range from basic (pale ale or Baltic porter) to berry (blueberry ale or raspberry stout).

Opened in 2016, **Open Water Brewery** is a more recent addition known for hearty lagers, meads and ales adorned with bearded, nautical-inspired labels. Grab a pour from the makeshift wooden bar and ask the lads for a tour.

## Bubbly Elixirs

SNAP, CRACKLE, SODA POP

Thanks to Åland's fertile soils and smooth climate, big fruit harvests abound – at **Amalia's Limonadfabrik** in Lemland, taste the rainbow of delicious organic spoils infused into artisanal sparkling sodas. Around 10 variations range seasonally, from rhubarb to elderberry in spring, cranberry and strawberry in summer, blueberries or blackcurrants for autumn, and apple and cinnamon mulled wine in winter. The lemonades are produced according to traditional, no-frills techniques with few ingredients. Taste them in cocktails at restaurants around Åland, such as Smakbyn. In Lemland, tour the factory and manufacturing rooms before indulging in fizzy tastings.

## Striking Fortress Ruins

REMAINS OF RUSSIAN RULE

In **Bomarsund**, a former Russian military fortress, its battletorn relics offer a startling contrast to Åland's present-day demilitarisation. Bomarsund was a huge fortress complex, built from brick and strengthened with distinctive octagonal blocks, containing a garrison town, and protected by ramparts and a planned 15 fortified towers.

### PUB-CRAWL STOPS IN MARIEHAMN

**Pub Ettan**
Cosy dive bar specialising in honest pours, chatty locals and the islands' latest opening hours.

**Park Ålandia Pub**
Mariehamn's favourite living-room bar in a family-owned hotel. Local Stallhagen brews on tap.

**Pub Bastun**
Cult-status live music venue in a former sauna. Hosting Nordic underground bands since the 1970s.

NADEZDA SLOBODINSKAYA/SHUTTERSTOCK ©

**Bomarsund fortress ruins**

Following the war of 1808–09, Russia began building this major military structure as its westernmost defence against the Swedes. The fortress was incomplete, in 1854, during the Crimean War, when the French-British naval force bombarded it heavily from sea. Within four days the Russians were forced to surrender it.

In the **Huvudfästet** (main fort), only three of the defensive towers were completed. Today, they are an impressive sight, particularly Brännklint tower, its walls scarred by cannon and rifle fire. The overgrown foundations of the garrison town **Nya Skarpans**, as well as the Notvikstornet viewpoint, its seaward-facing canons and sniper perches, are also atmospheric.

Across the bridge, **Prästö** became Bomarsund's island of the dead, with a military hospital and separate Greek Orthodox, Jewish, Muslim and Christian graveyards for prisoners of war. The epic construction drew masons, artisans and soldiers from across the Russian Empire. Just after the bridge lies a nice bathing spot, as well as the small **Bomarsund Museum** displaying excavation bits. Further on, a 5.5-km walk via the Coastal Past app reveals those gravesites, the former Russian telegraph station and garrison hospital, and beautiful shorelines.

## THE APPLE OF FINLAND'S EYE

A mild climate, lots of sunshine and long autumns mean apple orchards thrive here. About 270 hectares are cultivated by 40-plus Ålandic apple producers, and the majority of apples (and also pears) in Finnish supermarkets are grown on the islands.

Apple season usually starts at the end of May, and by mid-August producers pick the early bloomers, with harvest typically lasting until October. From August to January, apple juice is a beloved local nectar. **Grannas Äppel** presses a variety of apples, from Lobo to Amarosa, into delicious, preservative-free juice. At the **Öfvergårds** farm, take an 'apple safari' tour with juice tastings. The farm shop stocks delicious souvenirs, such as pickled apple shoots and apple mulled wine.

## GETTING AROUND

Hire a car to explore your way around the island. Car rentals are limited and more expensive than in Turku; consider taking wheels over with you. Bicycles and mopeds are also available for hire on the islands.

# Beyond Fasta Åland

## The six municipalities beyond Fasta encompass the remote, harder-to-reach areas of the archipelago. Tiny islands even outnumber inhabitants.

If you're feeling that Fasta Åland is too mainstream, then you're due for a trip to the remote outer islands of the archipelago. These tiny granite islets stretch out across the Archipelago Sea between Fasta and Finland. Strewn with silver-birch forests and connected by ferries (and the occasional bridge), the islands are criss-crossed by winding roads, cycling routes and walking trails – as well as many, many waterways. So no matter your transport mode, the outer isles are ripe for exploration.

The thousands of islets in the outer archipelago fall into two geographic groups, served by two different ferry lines. The northern archipelago includes Kumlinge, Lappo, Brändö and Jurmo. The southern archipelago includes Föglö, Sottunga and Kökar.

### TOP TIP

Some free public ferries connect islands. Fuel is limited, so fill up before hitting the outer archipelago.

Åland archipelago

TSUGULIEV/SHUTTERSTOCK ©

VOVANTARAKAN/SHUTTERSTOCK ©

Sankta Anna Kyrka

## Rock Steady & Righteous

MEDIEVAL STONEWORK SANCTUARIES

These islands, each around a two-hour ferry from Fasta Åland, have long been populated – as sparsely as that may be. The islands' appealingly barren landscape once attracted Bronze Age seal hunters and Hanseatic traders. Archaeologists have uncovered early settlements at Otterböte. Little remains of their time here now, save for a trio of gloriously well-preserved medieval stone churches.

Hidden away a 2km path north of Kumlinge village, don't miss the **Sankta Anna Kyrka** (St Anne's Church), an attractive, multicoloured fieldstone church. The interior contains incredible 500-year-old Franciscan-style paintings. The shrine to Mary on the altarpiece and the baptismal font likely date from the mid-13th century. Brändö's landmark church is a whitewashed beauty that dates to 1898.

Meanwhile in Kyrkvägen (Föglö), the **Sankta Maria Magdalena Kyrka** was first built in the 14th century, but only the nave remains of this original building. Most of the structure was rebuilt in 1860, which explains the neogothic detailing.

### BEST ARCHIPELAGO ISLANDS TO VISIT

**Brändö**
Northernmost municipality of the Åland archipelago, known for its approximately 1180 islands outnumbering approximately 500 inhabitants.

**Föglö**
With more than 500 residents, the largest outer-island municipality with more civil servants than farmers.

**Kökar**
Dangling off the archipelago's southern end, a rocky island with a lovely desolate air.

**Kumlinge**
Kumlinge is little visited but much beloved for its peaceful forests and low-traffic walking trails.

**Vårdö**
So-called 'guardian island'; on its highest mountain, ancient bonfires once warned other islands of danger.

### WHERE TO DINE ON SEAFOOD

**Restaurant Seagram**
Famed seafood buffet in Degerby – a smorgasbord of grilled and smoked fish, and prawns. €€€

**Restaurang Galeasen**
Classic island fare, such as grilled whitefish and fried perch, overlooking Lappo's Guest Harbour. €€

**Glada Laxen**
On Bärö, slurp on lobster claws in an old coastguard station set by the marina. €€€

The church is on an island south of Degerby, connected by a bridge and a scenic road. During a 1967 restoration, workers found an old crucifix containing a bone and a parchment, leading folks to believe it was a relic of Mary Magdalene herself.

**Sankta Anne Kyrka** sits on the ruins of a medieval Franciscan monastery on the island of Hamnö, just west of Kökar. The monks' chapel and ruined walls make for a pensive evening stroll. Inside, look for the unusual votive, a Turkish pirate ship.

### JURMO'S HIGHLAND COWS

Tiny Jurmo is home to certain shaggy-haired inhabitants: Highland cows. The long-horned animals hailing from Scotland have been grazing fields around the island since 2002. Organic steaks are a speciality of **Café Kvarnen** near the pier – sold raw for cabin cookouts or grilled and seasoned with island herbs. The meat is said to have a less fatty texture and even be slightly gamey. Come into contact with one of these gentle beasts, and you may not be able to stomach eating them, though. Many will receive head scratches and slices of apple as treats. Touching their horns is always a big no.

## Catch a Craving

FRESHWATER ANGLING

Hankering for fresh fish? The conservation island of Björkör, close to Degerby Harbour, offers some of Åland's best angling for salmon and perch. **Coja Fishing** can take you there and help organise an overnight cabin, where you can cook your fresh catch to perfection.

## Sailors' Selection

PRESERVING MARITIME HISTORY

Feast your eyes on restored Åland sailing boats – and then, take one out on the water yourself.

At the **Archipelago Museum** in Lappo, a two-hour ferry from Fasta Åland, marvel at an impressive collection of historic wooden sea craft of all sizes and functions. There are rowing boats, fishing boats and one of the last remaining examples of a *storbåt* (launch).

The **Storbåt Tacksamheten** is a grand, red-sailed wooden beauty holding port in nearby Nagu since 2017. Though it has been crafted according to traditional methods and materials, modern, sustainable touches include solar energy panels. Sailing season is from May to October.

## Take the Kumlinge 'Eight'

CIRCLE AROUND THE COAST

Kumlinge, a 2½-hour drive (including ferry transport) from Fasta Åland, is one of Åland archipelago's least-frequented islands with some of the most gorgeous walking trails. Get a load of commanding sea and forest panoramas on the so-called **Kumlinge åttan** ('eight'): an infinity loop-shaped route through the island's heart.

The 12.5km trail covers all the main historical sights with ample signposts and calming solitude – climb rocks, gaze out to sea and spot wildlife, probably without ever meeting any

### WHERE TO STAY IN A GUESTHOUSE

**Pellas Gästhem**
A former Brändö schoolhouse, delighting guests with activities ranging from picnicking to fishing. €€

**Gästhem Enigheten**
Creaky-floored rooms in Föglö with old stoves and period furniture. €€

**Hotel Gullvivan**
Modest hotel with fantastic sea views from every room. On Björnholma island, north of Brändö. €€

HIVAKA/SHUTTERSTOCK ©

Kumlinge

other visitors (let alone any of the island's 300 or so residents).

Most trekkers start the trail at the quaint, medieval Sankta Anna Kyrka, which leads through town up to the Kumlinge Apotek, an old-fashioned, richly interiored pharmacy that's still in business today.

Meanwhile, at Hotel Svala, you can see a former 'cottage hospital' turned cute boutique hotel. Look out for the village's maypole, which locals festoon with bright flowers during Midsummer celebrations.

Along the way, pass by bucolic countryside homes and, as you get deeper into green woodland, keep your eyes peeled for birdlife and wildlife. Crane, roe deer, fox and elk all make their home here.

Reaching the jagged coastline, it's easy to see why Kumlinge has been historically called 'the rocky passage'. Take the chance to climb rocks and enjoy a picnic on the sea bay.

## BEST CAMPGROUNDS WITH SAUNAS

**Brändö Stugby**
Splendidly located campground; cabins with kitchens and campsites. Hire a rowing boat to explore the seascape. €

**Fisketorpet**
Relax in a red cottage/pitch a tent overlooking the water. Kayaks, bikes, paddleboats for rent. €

**Sandvik Camping**
Sheltered sites, kitchen and laundry facilities, plus BBQ, shop, bikes and a good swimming beach. €

**Hasslebo Gästhem**
Outside Kumlinge village, eco-sensible campground with bio-toilets, solar power and organic breakfasts. €

**Isakssons Stugby**
Cottages with fully equipped kitchens. Specialises in organising fishing trips. €

## GETTING AROUND

The core group of islands – Brändö, Torsholma, Åva and Jurmo – are connected by bridges and free ferries, with a signposted bike route traversing them as well. If you prefer to travel by boat, the winding waterways are brilliant for kayaking and sailing.

# HANKO (HANGO)

## On a long, sandy peninsula, Hanko (Swedish: Hango) grew up as a well-to-do Russian spa town in the late 19th century.

During this period entrepreneurs and industrialists built opulent seaside villas, with fabulous Victorian and art-nouveau architectural detailing. Many of these beauties have a new life after their noble beginnings as cosy B&Bs and restaurants.

With over 30km of beaches, swimming and sunbathing are two of the town's chief attractions. There are several attractive sandy strands – and no shortage of beautiful deserted ones for long walks in solitude.

Hanko's (Hango's) a good jumping-off point for the southern archipelago. Or you can stay on dry land and relish the fruits of the sea at the town's many excellent restaurants. Whatever you do, get to know the town's friendly locals – they love crowding around pub fireplaces to drink, and often partake in karaoke sessions.

### TOP TIP

Hanko's (Hango's) accommodation is limited, so booking ahead is essential – the tourist office provides a list of private accommodation. Home shares via Airbnb and other platforms may be preferred to downtown accommodation. B&Bs in Hanko's (Hango's) Russian Empire–era villas often do not have en-suite bathrooms (back in the day, everyone washed at the spa!).

TSUGULIEV/SHUTTERSTOCK ©

**Hanko (Hango)**

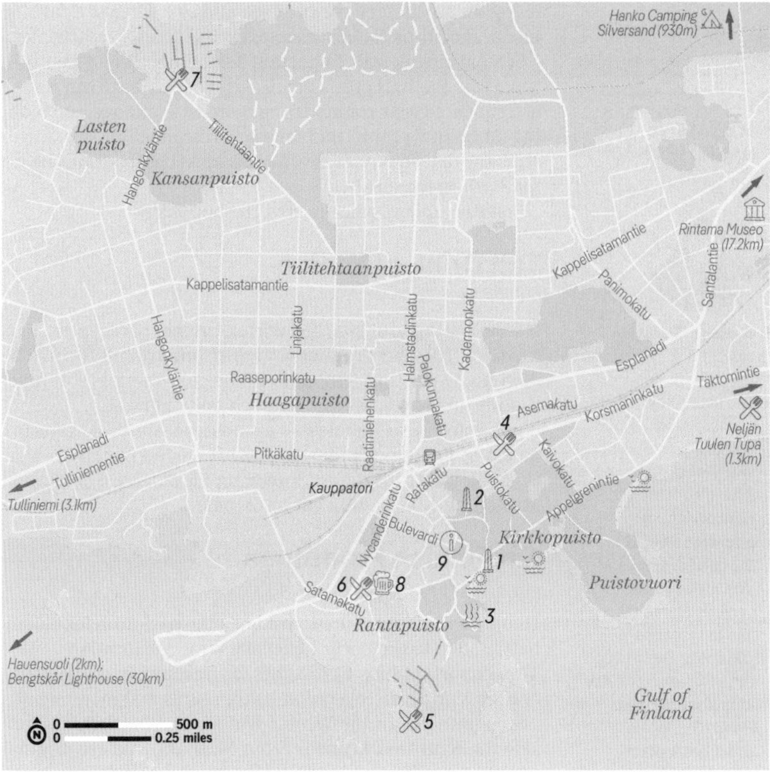

**SIGHTS**
**1** Monument of Liberty
**2** Water Tower

**ACTIVITIES, COURSES & TOURS**
**3** Regatta Spa

**EATING**
**4** B&B Korsman
**5** Hangon Portti
**6** Origo
**7** På Kroken

**DRINKING & NIGHTLIFE**
**8** Hanko Brewing Company

**INFORMATION**
**9** Tourist Office

## Energising Baths

TAKE THE PLUNGE

In the 19th century, Hanko (Hango) was a popular spa town for Russian nobility. Today, the **Regatta Spa** is the best-known throwback to this period. The gorgeously modern facility features a massive glass-enclosed pool for soaking while

### WHERE TO STAY IN CENTRAL HANKO (HANGO)

**Villa Maija**
Flawlessly restored rooms in a 19th-century villa packed with character; some with wonderful sea views. **€€€**

**Villa Aurora**
Lovingly restored villa with cute rooms and lovely common areas plus a knowledgeable tour-guide owner. **€€**

**Hotel Bulevard**
Converted from a police station (with some rooms in former cells); no-frills, budget-friendly stay downtown. **€€**

enjoying 270-degree views of sea and sky. There's a full spa menu, including facials, massages and beauty treatments.

Sea bathing is still important to the port town's culture too. Near the harbour, a small red wooden **bathing house** is frequented year-round. It's customary to change into bathing (or birthday) suits and take a refreshing dunk, usually to start the day. In winter, a water pump keeps a hole in the ice for lionhearted locals.

Visit the tourist office to rent the house key.

**WHY I LOVE HANKO (HANGO)**

**Barbara Woolsey**, writer

The locals say, 'You can leave Hanko, but Hanko never leaves you.' As I write this, it hasn't left me yet. Hanko (Hango), population 8000, is the perfect small town in many ways – empty, secluded beaches and landscapes juxtaposed with lively pubs fuelled by chatty locals and karaoke. Hanko (Hango) is a rare great place, where people say hello on the street. It's no wonder so many Helsinki dwellers nested here during the pandemic – some never left and opened great shops and restaurants. This revival makes it a wonderful time to visit.

## Tall Drink of Water

VIEW FROM THE TOP

Hanko's (Hango's) soaring **water tower**, perched on Vartiovuori Hill, is a prominent sight from around town. The 48m-high structure, Finland's first water tower, is still functioning and is responsible for such tasty tap water.

The tower also doubles as an observation deck, offering amazing panoramas. Zip up the lift (listen closely to hear sloshing water inside) for sweeping views across town and crystalline seas leading out to Estonia.

## On Finnish Frontlines

REMEMBERING HANKO'S (HANGO'S) HISTORY

Hanko's (Hango's) shores have been the backdrop for bloody battles, due to the port's beneficial strategic location. This important history of fights for freedom, and finally liberation, can be discovered at its museums and monuments.

Step onto one of the Winter War's worst battlefronts outside the **Rintama Museo** (Front Museum) and see original trenches, bunkers and artillery guns left behind.

Indoors, the permanent exhibition 'Hanko in Foreign Hands' tells the whole story. Afterwards, it's worth driving 5km further east to **Skogby**, where there are also still earth-covered bunkers in the forests near the road.

Back in town, where the Bulevardi (boulevard) meets the beach is the **Monument of Liberty**. The statue depicts two lions, Hanko's (Hango's) present-day protectors named Conrad and Aurora, who commemorate the landing of liberating German forces in 1918. The monument was taken down after WWII but re-erected in 1960 with new text simply stating 'For our liberty'.

**WHERE TO HOBNOB WITH LOCALS**

**Pub Grönan**
Lively pub in a former military warehouse where revellers bop to live bands and DJs.

**Wallis**
Hanko's (Hango's) favourite karaoke bar. Sip a drink on the waterfront terrace and sing with locals.

**Nöjen Vin & Öl**
Rub shoulders with the afternoon crowd of locals warming up by the fire.

TSUGULIEV/SHUTTERSTOCK ©

Bengtskär Lighthouse

## Brewed by the Sea

MARITIME CRAFT BEER

Kick back and relax at a brewpub inspired by the Scandinavian aesthetic and the seaside. In a restored red-and-white warehouse, the **Hanko Brewing Company** is one of the village's best places to stare out to sea. Light lagers and ales are perfect for long laid-back summer afternoons on the harbour-front terrace. Posters and bags with cool graphic designs inspired by Hanko's (Hango's) maritime history make for great souvenirs.

## Finland's Tallest Beacon

FOLLOW THE LIGHT

On a clear Hanko (Hango) evening, you may be able to see **Bengtskär Lighthouse** casting light across the waves – and there's certainly nothing quite like climbing inside of it.

Take a short ferry to the island and climb the 252 steps to the top. Towering 52m above the waves 25km offshore from Hanko (Hango), the Nordic countries' tallest lighthouse was

### HARBOUR HISTORY

As the southernmost town in Finland, Hanko (Hango) was a strategic anchorage well before its founding as a town in 1874. It was also a point of emigration: between 1881 and 1931 about 250,000 Finns left for the USA, Canada and Australia via these docks.

At the end of the Winter War, the March 1940 peace treaty with Russia required the ceding of Hanko (Hango) as a naval base. Its inhabitants evacuated as the Russians moved in with a garrison of 30,000 and constructed a huge network of fortifications. Hanko (Hango) was isolated from the Russian frontlines and eventually abandoned in December 1941. Citizens returned to see their damaged town the following spring. Learn more at the Rintama Museo.

### WHERE TO ENJOY A COFFEE BREAK

**Alan's Café**
Enjoy house-baked treats, such as cinnamon buns, in an old wooden villa or its courtyard.

**Park Café**
Clapboard cottage restored to Victorian grandeur. Perfect for a summertime coffee with occasional live music.

**Nöjen Vin & Öl**
Living-room bar with cosy fire, chatty locals and upstairs karaoke bar that's packed on weekends.

built in 1906 to protect ships from the perilous archipelago waters. It was damaged extensively during the Continuation War by the departing Red Army but has been refurbished. There are historical exhibits downstairs and fabulous views from the top. Consider also spending the night as the lighthouse contains simple but panoramic accommodation.

### REGATTA EXTRAVAGANZA

Every July, **Hanko's Regatta** transforms these quiet shores into some of Finland's busiest. For several days up to the event, the town and its harbour becomes overrun with impressive yachts and thousands of spectators. More than 200 boats compete, and a high-spirited party atmosphere includes live bands and big terrace parties.

Hanko (Hango) at its liveliest is mighty intoxicating, but locals will probably tell you they are just as happy every year when the madness is over. If you plan to attend the regatta, reserve accommodation and restaurants several months in advance. Consider also staying outside of Hanko (Hango) - for example in Raseborg - to also get some distance from the event.

## Age-old Graffiti Tags

ARCHIPELAGO ETCHINGS

Visit **Hauensuoli**, or Pike's Gut, a narrow strait between Tullisaari and Kobben, to see how sailors from countries around the Baltic Sea once waited out storms. At the protected natural harbour, sailors killed time by carving their initials or tales of bravery into the rocks, earning the area the nickname 'Guestbook of the Archipelago'. Some 600 carvings dating back to the 17th century remain.

## British-Finnish Fusion

DELECTABLE SLOW FOOD

At **B&B Korsman**, savour Sunday dinner perfection. Indulgent buffets are inspired by the chef-owner's Glaswegian roots and passion for Finnish produce: Yorkshire puddings, lamb entrecôte and mushroom risotto, plus salads with his self-pickled vegetables.

## Pescatarian's Paradise

CATCHES OF THE DAY

With 130km of coastline, it's no wonder that seafood is a Hanko (Hango) highlight. Several fine restaurants are clustered near **East Harbour** such as **Origo**, distinguishing itself with geothermal heating, local, organic ingredients and a seasonal gourmet menu. Braised pork cheek cooked overnight is a treat, as is the salmon soup with dark bread.

Go on a foodie pilgrimage to **Hangon Portti**, a two-minute ferry journey from the East Harbour pier. This little whitewashed, wicker-furnished cottage is perched on a rugged granite island. Sailor's meatballs (with mashed potatoes and lingonberry jam), a smoked-and-glazed-pork 'captain's burger' with potato salad, and archipelago tapas are among the dishes.

Meanwhile, **På Kroken**'s yacht-shaped buffet teems with options from its smokehouse, as well as boat-fresh lobster and shellfish. The adjoining cafe serves cheaper dishes, including fabulous salmon soup with dark archipelago bread. Stock up on picnic fare at its fish shop.

### GETTING AROUND

Hanko (Hango) is easily reached from Helsinki by train. The two-hour journey departs several times daily and includes a changeover (though direct routes are planned for late 2023). Buses also run several times daily. Rent a bicycle to visit surrounding swimming spots, the busy beach at Silversand, and other nearby natural wonders.

## MARVELLOUS HANKO (HANGO) VILLAS WALKING TOUR

Through the heart of Hanko (Hango), embark on this architectural walking tour. It shows off the port town's turn-of-the-century heyday, from villas to industrial bulwarks. At Hanko's (Hango's) western harbour, don't miss the 4000-sq-metre rubble building, a former **1 butter warehouse**, and landmark of national romanticism. Here, trainloads of butter (once Hanko's main winter export) were stored and shipped around the region. **2 Hotel Regatta** is an art nouveau vision in mustard. Heading away from the shore, the **3 Lignell Building**, once a Jugendstil (art nouveau) landmark, was so badly damaged in WWII its facade was fully replastered. Until the 1990s, it served as a coastal artillery.

Head to **4 Appelgrenintie**, the villa strip. Take in the grand 19th-century properties according to their names: Villa Elisabeth (No 5), Villa Maija (No 7) and Villa Frenckell (No 8), in their varying stages of upkeep. Continue to the **5 Casino**, a gorgeous Jugendstil (Art Nouveau) restaurant and a last memory of Hanko's (Hango's) spa days. Don't miss going inside to gaze at the drippy chandeliers and rich wood furniture. The restaurant only operates seasonally, but these days there are also antique and designer vintage pop-ups.

Continue up Appelgrenintie to the former **6 Finnish-English Biscuit Factory** which, from 1916, was Hanko's (Hango's) favourite brand until production was suspended from wartime. Heading north to shore, the **7 textile mill of the Kudeneule Oy factory,** producing tricots and hosiery, is one of architect Viljo Revell's most revered works of industrial architecture. Pine forests are viewed through floor-to-ceiling windows.

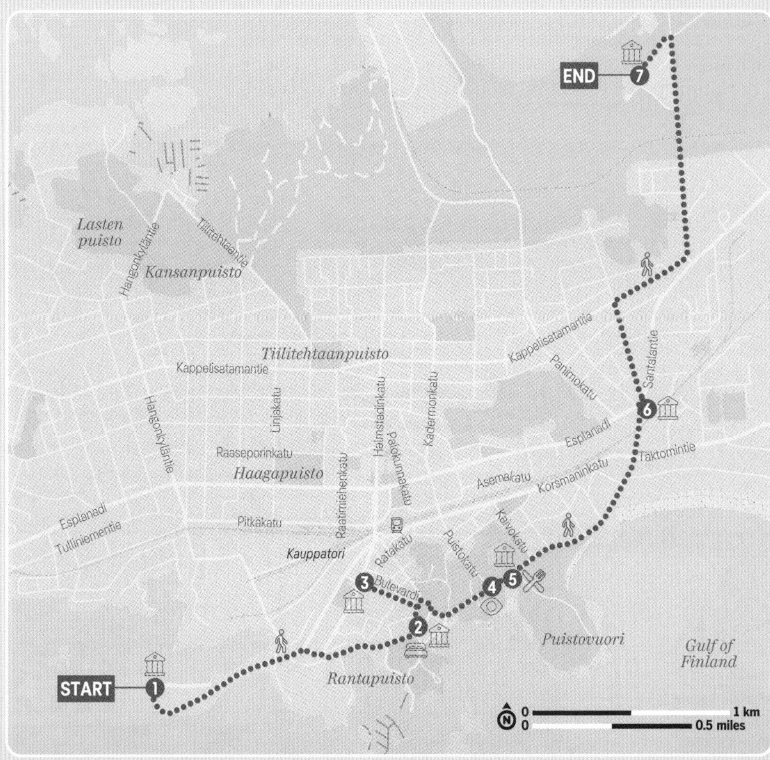

# Beyond Hanko (Hango)

## Cruise along the coast and discover a string of tiny villages and their treasures, from medieval buildings to modern artisanship.

Midway between Turku and Helsinki, 55km from Hanko (Hango), Fiskars is a charming factory village turned Finnish creative hub. Brick neoclassical buildings house studios, galleries and showrooms for cutting-edge design. More than 100 artisans, designers and artists live and/or work here, and there's lots to stroll about and discover.

Nearby Raseborg is home to the seaside resort of one of Finland's oldest towns. It's an ideal base for exploring Ekenäs Archipelago National Park by boat or kayak, as well as the evocative ruins of Raseborg Castle. In 2009 Ekenäs merged with the nearby towns of Karis and Pohja under the official name of the municipality Raseborg, though all names are still used.

### TOP TIP

Most people visit Fiskars on a day trip, but it's worth staying overnight – especially if Hanko (Hango) is booked out.

**Raseborg**

TSUGULIEV/SHUTTERSTOCK ©

SEREGA_TM/SHUTTERSTOCK ©

Raseborg Castle

## Holding Court in Raseborg

LEAVE NO STONE UNTURNED

Step back 500 years to explore what remains of one of Finland's most impressive medieval castles. Looming on a high rock overlooking a grassy sward, the late-14th-century **Raseborg Castle**, a 35km drive from Hanko (Hango), was strategically crucial in the 15th century, when it protected the trading town of Tuna and exiled king of Sweden Karl Knutsson Bonde held his court here. The castle was abandoned in 1558 and lay deserted for more than 300 years. Nowadays the crumbling fortress is ripe for solo exploration, but you can also sign up for a tour with Slottsknekten (slottsknekten.fi).

## Archipelago Adventures

CRUISING A NATIONAL PARK

**Ekenäs Archipelago National Park**, a 30-minute drive from Hanko (Hango), is where endless blue panoramas abound. Almost 90% of the 52 sq km park is water, so to explore the 1300 islands you'll need to take a tour from the harbour,

### ONCE UPON A FISHING VILLAGE

Midway between Turku and Helsinki, the seaside resort of **Ekenäs** (Finnish: Tammisaari) is one of Finland's oldest towns. In 1546 King Gustav Vasa founded the seaside village as a trading port to rival Tallinn in Estonia. The names of the streets in the **Gamla Stan** (Old Town) still reflect the crafts that were practised there. The enchanting area is filled with 18th-century wooden buildings named after types of fish – a legacy of the area's fishing-village beginnings. The Gamla Stan still exhibits its origins as an artisan trade centre; its narrow streets bear the names of their industries, such as Hattmakaregatan (Hatters' St) and Linvävaregatan (Linen Weavers' St). Today most of the Old Town is residential.

### WHERE TO DINE IN RASEBORG

**Café Gamla Stan**
Enjoy fresh juice and pie in a shady apple orchard or the cafe's cosy cottage. **€**

**Restaurant GH Fyren**
Pierside restaurant with an alluring terrace and sea views. Local dishes include fried perch with gnocchi and sea bird. **€€**

**YLP!**
The first zero-waste pizzeria in Finland and Scandinavia, using only ingredients from local producers. **€€**

such as an archipelago cruise with Saariston Laivaristeilyt or a kayaking tour with Paddlingsfabriken. Chartering your own boat is also popular.

The most frequented island is **Älgö**, with a 2km nature trail that takes in the island's observation tower. There's an old fisher's home that's been converted to include a sauna and campsite facilities.

On the islands of Fladalandet and Modermagan, you can camp in the park overnight. However, many other islands are off limits to visitors, particularly the ecologically fragile outer islands. For information on the park and campground bookings, visit Naturum Visitor Centre in Ekenäs.

### FINLAND'S LARGEST ISLAND

**Kimito** (Finnish: Kemiö) is a sprawling coastal island located 65km southeast of Turku. Numerous inlets and waterways weave their way through the forested isle, which is dotted with seaside villages. Take your time exploring the island, as there are fascinating sights along the way, including a historic church in Dragsfjärd and an art-filled manor house in Kimito.

But the main attraction is further south. You guessed it: more islands. Kimito is the main jumping-off point for **Archipelago National Park**, a scattering of spectacular islands that stretches south and west into the sea. Attractions include Finland's tallest lighthouse, a century-old fortress island and a recreated Viking village. Cruises depart from Kasnäs, the harbour on the southern extreme of Kimito island.

## Uncovering Creativity

AWESOME SOUVENIRS

Souvenir hunting is a real treat around **Fiskars**, a former industrial town turned creative hub. Fiskars' *bruk* (ironworks) began in 1649 with a single furnace and went on to make millions of horse ploughs. In 1822 Turku apothecary Johan Jacob Julin bought the factory and the company boomed, producing a huge range of farming and household items, including its iconic orange-handled scissors (since 1967).

Take a day trip to Fiskars, a charming factory village where brick buildings are home to studios and showrooms for cutting-edge design.

Today more than 100 artisans, designers and artists live and work in repurposed buildings. Stroll through the picturesque centre and discover Finnish designs inside the craft shops, studios and galleries transforming neoclassical buildings. Free town maps from the tourist office detail Fiskars' historic buildings and the shops contained within.

In the clock-tower building, visit the **Onoma** design shop, which carries sharp, stylish arts, crafts and homewares produced by members of the Fiskars Cooperative of Artisans, Designers and Artists. Meanwhile, at **Fiskars Shop**, you can buy the Fiskars company's distinctive scissors (and other handy stuff). It also has a small exhibition on the firm's history.

Boutique **Vanja Sea & Friends** sells adorable knits for children. **Kuura Cider** sells Champagne-style apple cider and sweet apple liqueur.

### GETTING AROUND

The northern and southern archipelagos are served by the archipelago's system of ferry lines. Scheduled connections between islands, and to and from Fasta Åland, happen a few times daily.

# PORVOO

Finland's second-oldest town is a popular day or weekend trip from Helsinki. Porvoo (Swedish: Borgå) officially became a town in 1380, but even before that it was an important trading post. Its historic Old Town includes oft-photographed riverside warehouses that once stored goods bound for destinations across Europe. Away from the river, the cobblestone streets are lined with charming wooden houses of every colour. Birthplace of national poet Johan Runeberg, the town is peppered with signs commemorating his whereabouts on various occasions.

Porvoo is home to a fantastic dining scene and a burgeoning arts movement. You could call it the cafe and confection capital of Finland, with a history of chocolate production still represented and a range of fabulous, atmospheric cafes along the riverfront. During the day these streets are buzzing with visitors, but spend a weeknight to have the place more or less to yourself.

## TOP TIP

It's possible (and pleasant) to arrive in Porvoo on a cruise from Helsinki. The noble old steamship *JL Runeberg* cruises from Helsinki's kauppatori to Porvoo's passenger harbour in summer and makes an excellent day trip, with various lunch options available. It's 3½ hours each way, so you may prefer to return by bus.

FINN STOCK/SHUTTERSTOCK ©

**Porvoo**

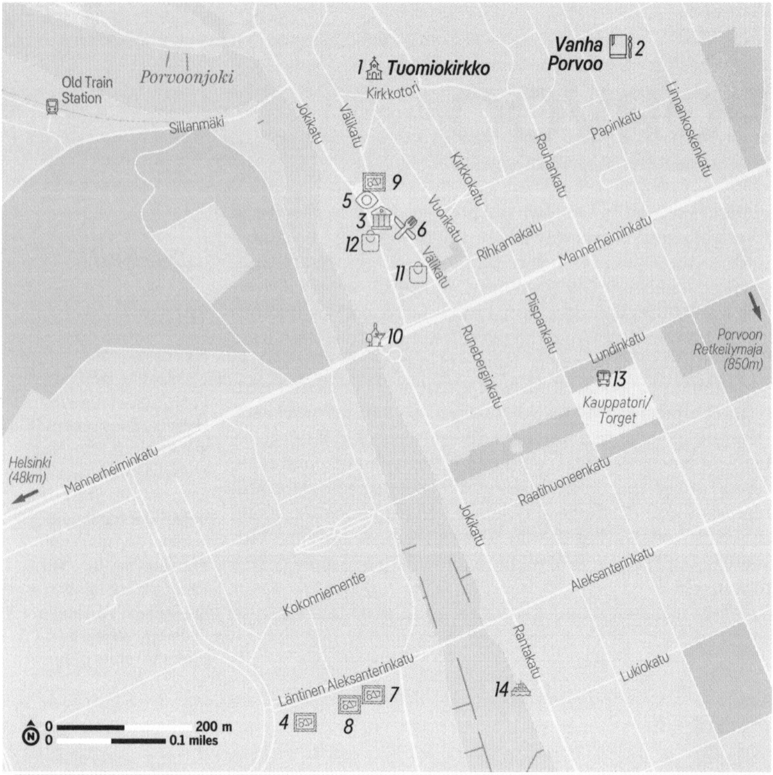

**TOP SIGHTS**
**1** Tuomiokirkko
**2** Vanha Porvoo

**SIGHTS**
**3** Porvoon Museo
**4** Taidetehdas
**5** Town Hall Square

**EATING**
**see 6** Cafe Postres
**6** Helmi Tea & Coffee House

**DRINKING & NIGHTLIFE**
**see 9** Cafe Fanny
**7** Galleria Fikka
**8** Gallery Kulma
**9** Gallery Vanha Kappalaisentalo
**10** Porvoon Paahtimo

**SHOPPING**
**11** Brunberg
**12** PetriS Chocolate Room

**TRANSPORT**
**13** Bus Station
**14** Passenger Harbour

## Charming Old Town

SAUNTERING COBBLED STREETS

**Vanha Porvoo** is one of Finland's most enticing old quarters, an entrancing tangle of cobbled alleys and wooden warehouses. Once a vibrant port and market, Porvoo now has craft boutiques, galleries, souvenir stores and antique shops lining the

### WHERE TO STAY IN PORVOO

**Hotel Runo**
Modern boutique hotel in historic art nouveau building, with art exhibits and an attic spa. **€€€**

**Hotelli Onni**
Opposite the cathedral, this gold-coloured wooden building is perfectly placed. Each room is unique. **€€€**

**Hotelli Pariisin Ville**
Plush place combining modern luxury, heritage atmosphere. Some rooms have mini saunas and courtyard views. **€€€**

main roads. The rust-red storehouses along the Porvoonjoki are remarkable: cross the old bridge for the best photos. The relatively less-touristed area is east of the cathedral; Itäinen Pitkäkatu is one of the nicest streets. In the Old Town, visit Porvoo's museum on the beautiful cobbled **Town Hall Square**. The town-hall building (**Vanha Raatihuoneentori**) houses most of the collection, with a clutter of artefacts relating to the town's history.

## Capital of Sweets

HOME TO FINLAND'S SWEET TOOTH

Specialising in handmade chocolates and liquorice delights. **Brunberg**'s factory shop is a favourite for its chocolate truffles and *pusu* (kisses) made of chocolate and whipped cream. At **PetriS Chocolate Room**, the handmade pralines, fruit-flavoured sweets and a rainbow array of macarons are divine.

Another local speciality is Runeberg torte: an almond-rum cake supposedly the favourite breakfast of Finnish poet JL Runeberg. Traditionally it's a treat eaten on his birthday (5 February), but sample it any time at **Helmi Tea & Coffee House**. The **Vanhan Porvoon Glassikko** ice-cream factory serves unusual flavours like rose and brown butter with pine seed.

## Cathedral Calling

RAVISHING ARCHITECTURAL RESTORATION

Porvoo's stone-and-timber **Tuomiokirkko** (cathedral) sits atop a hill overlooking the Old Town. The church is a personification of *sisu* (the Finnish tradition of keeping tough). The church has been vandalised by fire numerous times since the 16th century, most recently in 2006. Admire the renovation work across the ornate pulpit and tiered galleries, magnificent exterior and freestanding bell tower. The cathedral is an important stop for Finnish pilgrims; this is where Tsar Alexander I convened the first Diet of Finland in 1809, giving Finland religious freedom.

## Gallery Gallivanting

CAPTIVATING ART CIRCUIT

Porvoo's blossoming gallery scene ranges from classical to contemporary. Leading the movement is **Porvoo Art Hall** (Taidetehdas), a tractor factory turned sprawling modern-art space. Exhibitions from Finnish artists change every month at **Galleria Fikka**, a space focused on media and installation art curated by the Porvoo Artists' Association, and **Gallery Kulma** showcasing painted works. In the Old Town, make a stop at **Gallery Vanha Kappalaisentalo**; a tiny, wooden house featuring masterworks going back to the 18th century.

### BEST PLACES TO DINE IN PORVOO

**Bosgård**
Serious foodies should head to this farm restaurant for organic Charolais steaks and burgers. €€€

**Fryysarinranta**
Local delicacies, including Porvoo snails, in one of Old Town's red wooden warehouses. €€

**SicaPelle**
Modern seasonal tasting menus with a fusion twist – for example, dashi scallops. €€€

**Café Cabriole**
Gratifying lunch buffet and cakes galore in impressive art-nouveau digs. €€

**Zum Beispiel**
Spacious, light filled cafe serving up modern international fare, from salads to pastas. €€

### GETTING AROUND

Buses travel between Porvoo bus station and Helsinki's Kamppi every 30 minutes or so. You can also consider a cruise trip from Porvoo's passenger harbour.

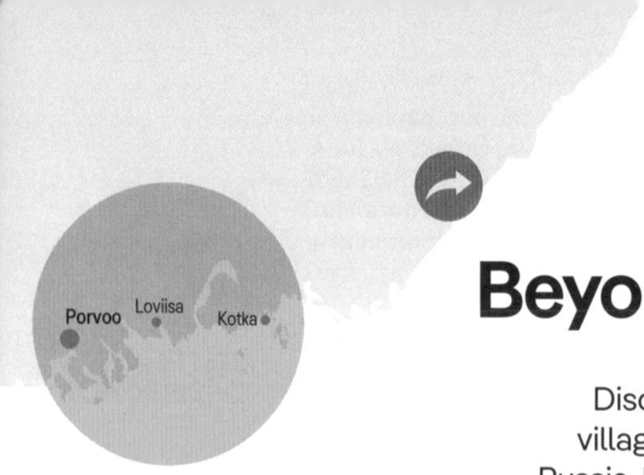

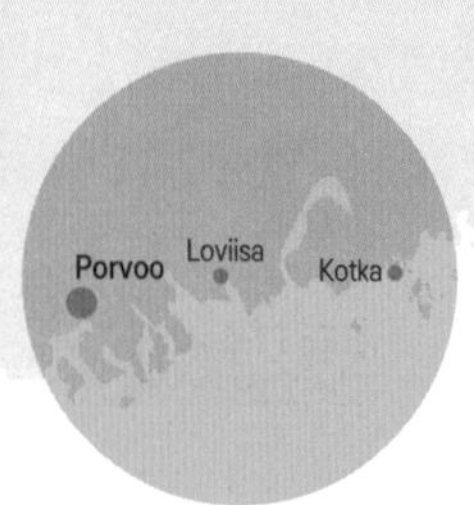


# Beyond Porvoo

Discover quiet yet charming villages leading eastwards to Russia. Historic seafaring routes are revealed on sailing trips

### TOP TIP

In mid-July, celebrate Kotka's seafaring heritage at the Maritime Festival with regatta, concerts, markets and a huge wooden-boat show.

Porvoo is a gateway to Finland's historic east. About 130km east of Helsinki, Kotka is Finland's only city on an island. In Kotka's early days, the Kymijoki provided a critical transport route for logging and rich waters for fishing, developing the city into one of Finland's most important industrial ports. Kotka is home to several superb sea-focused attractions, most notably the Merikeskus Vellamo. The archipelago islands, with their quaint villages and salty breezes, make for appealing day trips. On dry land, parks and public art aim to conjure up touristic appeal. But this hard-working port can't shake its inherent grittiness – lending to an appealing authenticity.

**Merikeskus Vellamo**

ELENANOEVA/SHUTTERSTOCK ©

ELENANOEVA/SHUTTERSTOCK ©

Langinkoski Imperial Fishing Lodge

## Southeastern Shores

KOTKA'S SEAFARING ROOTS

Head to **Kotka**, an hour's drive or 1½-hour bus ride from Porvoo, for sea-focused attractions celebrating the local swashbuckling history. Get up close and personal with icebreakers and shipwrecks at the **Merikeskus Vellamo** (Maritime Centre). The tanker-sized, wave-shaped museum recounts Finland's seafaring life. The headline attraction is the *Tarmo*, the world's third-oldest icebreaker (1907), which ploughed Finnish waters until it was retired in 1970.

Situated 5km north of Kotka amid the salmon-rich Kymijoki's rapids, the rustic wooden **Langinkoski Imperial Fishing Lodge** was built in 1889 for Tsar Alexander III. Most of the furniture is original, and rooms look much as they did when he was a frequent summertime visitor – quite impressive, considering this is today the only preserved building outside Russia owned by the emperor. Walk downstream and discover his memorial fishing stone, as well as the area's gorgeous riverside forest setting (now a 28-hectare nature reserve with walking trails).

### MUSICAL DISCOVERY

Hamina, located just 40km from the Russian border (95km drive east from Porvoo), has long been a military town. Today, it is one of the best places in the world to discover military music at its semiannual **Hamina Tattoo**.

The week-long festival sees professional soldiers, otherwise known as field musicians, performing ceremonial tunes. The event is organised by the Finnish Defence Forces, yet rock and jazz shows, as well as visiting bands (from Scottish bagpipes to Caribbean steel-pan performers) provide diverse flair.

The main highlight is a parade through Hamina's picturesque town square. Concerts are held in Kesäpuisto Park and on 'Tattoo St' (Fredrikinkatu), and at the especially evocative ruins of the 18th-century fortress Hamina Bastion.

### GETTING AROUND

Frequent train and bus services connect villages to Helsinki and Porvoo.

## THE MAIN AREAS

**TAMPERE**
City life with industrial undertones. **p120**

**SAIMAA LAKELAND**
Lakes, seals and scenic roads. **p129**

**JYVÄSKYLÄ**
Alvar Aalto's architecture. **p139**

# TAMPERE, THE LAKELAND & KARELIA

## URBAN DISCOVERIES AND NATURE EXPERIENCES

Fairy-tale forests, glittering lakes and creative cities define Finland's central region.

LEFT: NBLX/SHUTTERSTOCK ©; RIGHT: RICHARD WESTLUND/SHUTTERSTOCK ©

Karelia's hearty feasts and riveting wildlife, Saimaa Lakeland's serene labyrinths of lakes and islets, Tampere's buzzing city life and Alvar Aalto's world-class architecture in Jyväskylä are just some of the highlights to be discovered in this central area, stretching from Karelia on Finland's eastern border to the country's third-largest-city, Tampere, with the Lakeland in between.

Today, the scenes around Saimaa's waterways, where, until the end of the 20th century, Finland's 'green gold' – logged trees – used to float with the romanticised log drivers on top, are dominated by summer cottages and little boats moored beside lakeside hotels and city docks.

Tampere's edgy city scene has industrial roots, too. Located by the city-centre rapids of Tammerkoski, the Finlayson cotton mill and linen factory drew the working classes into the city in the 19th century, creating wooden-house districts to home them. Now, these quaint neighbourhoods host museums, cafes and plentiful scenes of the cosy Finnish lifestyle.

In the eastern region of Karelia, the sparsely populated land feels like a true wilderness, even though during WWII more than 400,000 Russian Karelians crossed the border here into Finland, accompanied by a hearty culinary culture. Little by little, their tasty meals spread all over Finland, and now delicacies such as Karelian pies and stews are enjoyed everywhere.

**HÄMEENLINNA**
Castle and nature reserve. **p146**

**KOLI NATIONAL PARK**
Nature trails and Karelian feasts. **p152**

# Find Your Way

Finland has over 100,000 lakes, and most of them are located in the Lakeland and its surroundings. We have picked itineraries, cities and nature trails to showcase the area's history, culture and culinary finds.

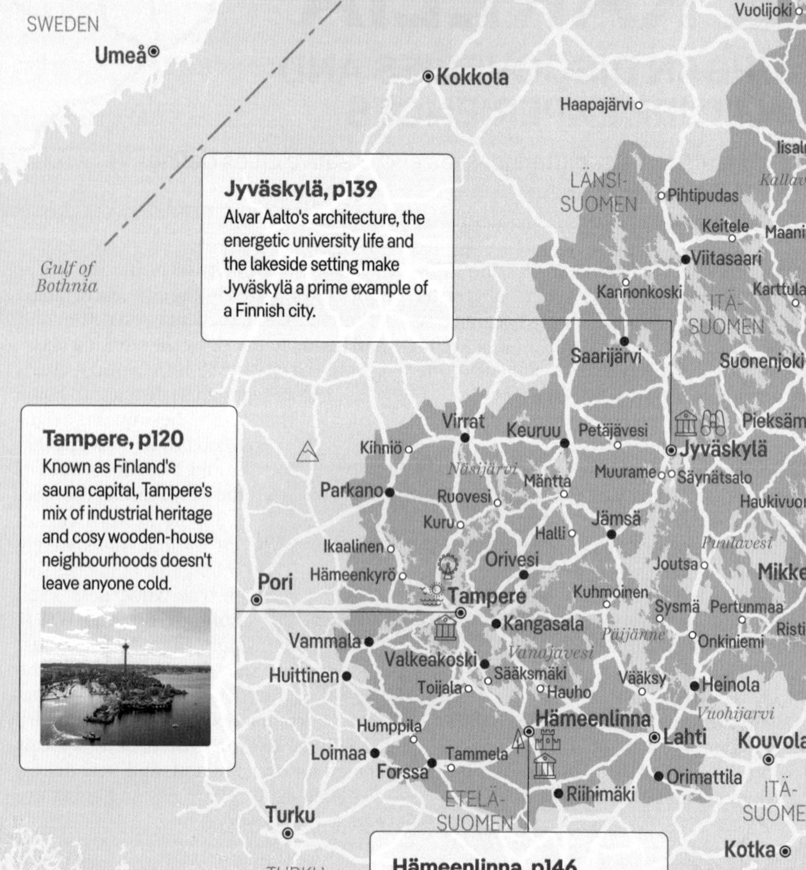


**Jyväskylä, p139**
Alvar Aalto's architecture, the energetic university life and the lakeside setting make Jyväskylä a prime example of a Finnish city.

**Tampere, p120**
Known as Finland's sauna capital, Tampere's mix of industrial heritage and cosy wooden-house neighbourhoods doesn't leave anyone cold.

**Hämeenlinna, p146**
Boasting a medieval castle and a nature reserve, Hämeenlinna is a perfect stop between Helsinki and Tampere.

LEFT: RALAND/SHUTTERSTOCK ©, RIGHT: O.KEMPPAINEN/SHUTTERSTOCK ©

### Koli National Park, p152

With its bare hilltops rising on the shores of Pielinen, which is dotted with forest-covered islets, Koli National Park is like a miniature Lapland.

### CAR

Hitting the road by car is the best way to explore the area, especially if you wish to experience the wildlife and nature trails in the more remote foodie spots of Karelia and Lakeland.

### BUS

If you don't have a car, bus is the next best bet to reach remote places such as Koli and Kuhmo. Matkahuolto operates throughout Finland and various local bus services operate regionally. Red, two-storey Onnibussi is a low-fare option for shuttling between cities.

### TRAIN

The region's main cities, Tampere, Jyväskylä and Savonlinna, are easy to reach from Helsinki by train. Trains to Tampere take just under two hours, with almost 50 departures per day. Trains depart for Jyväskylä almost every hour and take around 3 ½ hours. Trains to Savonlinna take more than four hours, with about five daily departures.

### Saimaa Lakeland, p129

It's all about nature, with Saimaa's lakes and islands making a picturesque setting for cottage life, cycling tours, hikes and water sports.

# Plan Your Time

City life, soothing lakes and vast wilderness intermingle in the area around Tampere, the Lakeland and Karelia. Sample the distinctive cuisines, take a plunge in the refreshing lake waters and spot some wildlife.

FINN STOCK/SHUTTERSTOCK ©

Tampere (p120)

## If You Do Only One Thing

- Head straight to **Tampere** (p120) and its central Tammerkoski channel, where the former **Finlayson** (p121) linen factory stands by the rapids. The red-brick building is now a creative hub with museums, galleries and restaurants.

- Next, pop over to the world's only **Moomin Museum**(p123) to explore the world of Tove Jansson and her famous characters before heading to **Pyynikki** (p125) neighbourhood and its hill with a viewing tower. Rest your legs and enjoy freshly fried doughnuts and coffee in the tower's cafe. Finish the day with a sauna in Finland's oldest public sauna, **Rajaportin** (p125).

### Seasonal Highlights

Cold winter months are for snow sports. Summer is ideal for exploring lakeside cities, while autumn is perfect for hiking.

**JANUARY**

Marvel at **Koli's tykkylumi**: the snow-laden branches of the fir trees create an otherworldly sight on the slopes.

**FEBRUARY**

Enjoy cream-filled buns and sledge rides on **Shrove Tuesday**, or hot drinks and cinnamon buns (*korvapuusti*) on any day.

**MAY**

The best time to try to spot one of the world's most endangered seals, the **Saimaa ringed seal**.

FROM LEFT: WIRESTOCK CREATORS, LARS KASTILAN, PASCAL VOSICKI/SHUTTERSTOCK ©

## Three Days to Travel Around

- After a day in **Tampere** (p120), dive deep into the Lakeland, heading to Mikkeli and its quaint manor houses with hotels, restaurants and shops, stopping to admire **Jyväskylä's Alvar Aalto architecture** (p140) along the way.

- From Mikkeli, continue on the A62, taking a lunch break at **Sahanlahti** (p130) and learning about its history as a sawmill community. Then continue to **Savonlinna** (p130) to visit its medieval **castle** (p130), famed as a dramatic setting for the fabulous Opera Festival. Drive on to nearby **Punkaharju** (p134) to see the scenic ridge winding across the lake.

## If You Have More Time

- Start in Helsinki and head east towards Koli National Park, with a stop en route at **Lappeenranta** (p133) to explore its fortress and a night in Puumala's **Sahanlahti** (p130), located on Saimaa's shores. Continue to **Koli National Park** (p152) to explore nature trails and Finland's archetypal national landscape with barren clifftops and lakeside scenes.

- Drive further north for the chance to spot **Kuhmo's wildlife** (p155) – sightings of bears, wolves and wolverines are possible. From Kuhmo, start driving back towards Helsinki, stopping to enjoy Alvar Allto's architecture in **Jyvaskyla** (p139) and thriving city life in **Tampere** (p120) along the way.

**JUNE**

Temperatures rise above 20°C and **markets** fill with berries and vegetables. Kuopio is famous for its summery market life.

**JULY**

Spend a night in one of Kuhmo's **wildlife huts** as the sun stays below the horizon for only a couple of hours a night.

**OCTOBER**

Autumn foliage reaches central Finland. Beautiful, and mosquito-free, time for **hikes**.

**DECEMBER**

The **Christmas market** in Tampere opens. Vendors arrive from all over Finland to sell Yuletide foods, drinks and crafts.

FROM LEFT: RNDMS, IMAGEBROKER.COM, MARGARITA HINTUKAINEN, TAMPERE PHOTOGRAPHY/SHUTTERSTOCK ©

# TAMPERE

If the world's only Moomin Museum isn't reason enough to visit Tampere, there's plenty more to explore, from the red-bricked, city-centre Finlayson museum and restaurant hub lining the powerful rapids of Tammerkoski, to the pretty wooden-house neighbourhood with a historic public sauna – it's the perfect warm welcome to the city.

Tampere's wooden houses and red-brick buildings hide an industrial past set in motion in 1820 when the Scot James Finlayson set up a linen factory here. By the beginning of the 20th century, one-third of Tampere's inhabitants were factory workers. This set the tone for the working-class city's later development as a central stage in Finland's Civil War, when the bourgeois 'whites' fought against the working-class 'reds'.

Today, Tampere is the self-proclaimed sauna capital of the world, and the city's industrial heritage mixed with its creative energy provides many layers to explore.

### TOP TIP

You can explore Tampere on foot, but cycling is a good alternative outside the winter months. City bikes are dotted around the city from mid-April to the end of October, and can be rented through an app (Tampereen kaupunkipyörät). E-bikes are available in bike-rental stores.

AIMUR KYTT/SHUTTERSTOCK ©

**Vapriikki**

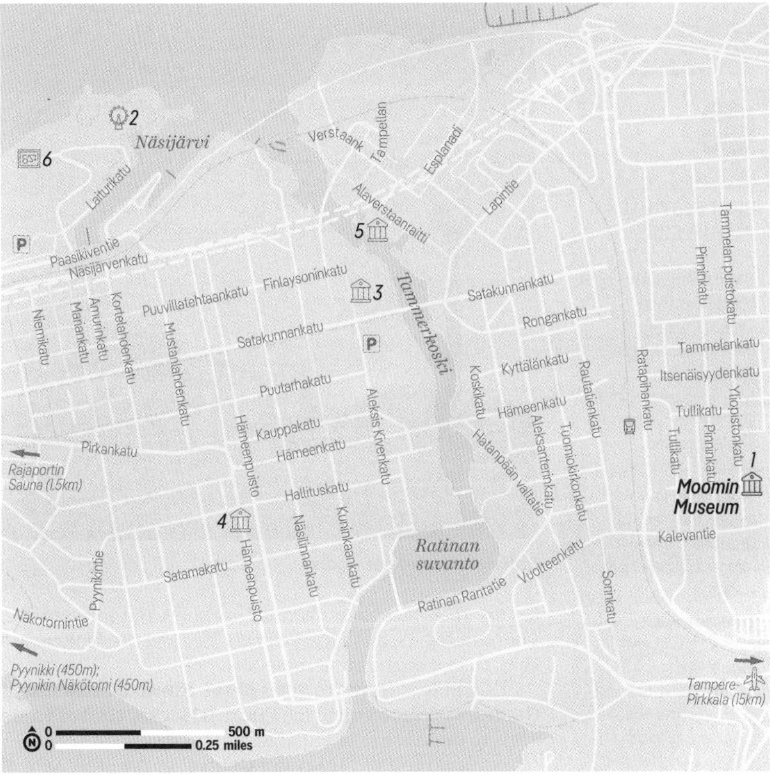

**HIGHLIGHTS**
**1** Moomin Museum
**2** Särkänniemi
**see 5** Vapriikki

**SIGHTS**
**see 3** Finlayson Centre
**see 5** Finnish Hockey Hall of Fame
**3** Finnish Labour Museum Wersta
**see 5** Finnish Museum of Games
**4** Lenin Museum
**5** Tampere Museum of Natural History

**DRINKING & NIGHTLIFE**
**6** Sara Hildén Art Museum

## History by the Rapids

THE WHITE-WATER CORE OF TAMPERE

The rapids of the Tammerkoski channel create a powerful backdrop to the city's main shopping street, Hämeenkatu. Visiting the industrial red-brick buildings lining the rapids, you will quickly get the gist of Tampere's past and present. Start from **Vapriikki**, a cluster of museums located in an old

### WHERE TO STAY IN TAMPERE

**Unity**
Convenient hub in Pyynikki with a gym and pizzeria-cum-brewery in the building. €€

**Solo Sokos Hotel Tampere**
For the best views in Tampere, head to the Finnish chain hotel's top-floor bar. €€€

**Dream Hostel & Hotel**
Best budget find. Choices range from a 16-bed dormitory to a studio with a sauna. €

## BEST FESTIVALS IN TAMPERE

**Sauna Open Air Metal Festival**
One of the largest metal music festivals in the Nordic countries takes place in early July, hosting big names and talented newcomers.

**Tammerfest**
In late July, tens of thousands arrive to hear popular Finnish bands.

**Tamperrada**
Finland's biggest foodie event is a multiday competition in September, when local restaurants offer small bites and *pintxos*, with a fixed price around the city.

**Saari Blues**
At the end of August, Viikinsaari transforms into a stage for blues and roots music performed by talented Finnish artists.

TAMPERE PHOTOGRAPHY/SHUTTERSTOCK ©

**Särkänniemi amusement park**

factory that once manufactured turbines and locomotives. The building itself is a marvellous sight, and inside there are more than a dozen small museums.

Kids will love the retro vibes of the **Finnish Museum of Games**, whereas a visit to the **Finnish Hockey Hall of Fame** helps to make sense of Finland's wintry obsession.

Next, head to the **Finlayson Centre** on the other side of the rapids. There are restaurants, cinemas and shops in the area and guided tours to the rooftop of the former factory, where you can see Tampere from another perspective. Check out also the Finnish Labour Museum Werstas and the Sulzer steam engine still in its original place.

Werstas also operates the world's only Lenin Museum near Hämeenpuisto. The museum is located on the spot where the Russian Social Democratic Labour Party held underground meetings at the beginning of the 20th century, and where Lenin and Stalin met for the first time in 1905.

It's a five-minute stroll from the Finlayson Centre to **Tallipiha**, where old stables now house a nostalgic cluster of little shops and cafes, charming in any season, but especially beautiful at Christmas time.

## WHERE TO STAY IN TAMPERE

**Lillan Boutique Hotel & Kök**
Charming and chic, this boutique hotel with a restaurant is located in a 100-year-old villa. **€€€**

**Lapland Hotels Tampere**
A breeze of Lapland in the city centre, this Finnish chain hotel has stylish rooms with splashes of northern influences. **€€€**

**Omena-hotelli Tampere**
Finnish budget chain hotel with self check-in, located in the city centre. **€€**

## Magical Moomins

SEE TOVE JANSSON'S BELOVED ARTWORK

You don't need to have kids to be enchanted by the Moomins. The characters were created by Finnish-Swedish artist Tove Jansson in the 1930s, and they have since conquered the world in comic strips, books, TV shows and as toys.

The world's only **Moomin Museum**, and one of two Moomin -themed attractions in Finland, is framed around Tove Jansson's drawings, which line the walls of the two-storey exhibition space.

Much-loved quotes from the books are sprinkled around the space, reminding us of the characters' philosophical natures. The lighting is dim and the atmosphere magical, especially downstairs where small crystal-like threads hang from the ceiling.

There are also miniature scenes from the books on display, crafted by Jansson's partner, the graphic artist Tuulikki Pietilä. Photography is only allowed in a dedicated part of the museum. Closed on Mondays.

**Muumimaailma** (p84) in Naantali is an idyllic island where you can visit the Moomins' and their friends' houses and interact with the characters. The Moomins' homes are only open in summer, although you can visit the island all year.

### BEST PUBS & CLUBS IN TAMPERE

**Public House Huurre**
BBQ and pub-styled food from ribs to fish and chips, all washed down by its own brews under the Kaleva label. €€

**G Lab**
A music club in an industrial setting with drinks and snack food. €

**Ruby & Fellas**
An Irish pub that serves food and hosts karaoke every weekend at 10pm before live music kicks in at 11.30pm. €€

**Ravintola Telakka**
Behind the railway station, this bar has a summery outdoor terrace, restaurant and live music. €€

**Konttori**
Beer lovers gather in Konttori with more than 200 beers to choose from; ciders also available.

## Särkänniemi

FUN AND ART IN ONE PARK

Located by Näsijärvi's shore, Särkänniemi amusement park is easy to spot due to its 168m-high observation tower, **Näsinneula**. The tower has a viewing deck at 120m, as well as a slowly rotating restaurant.

Apart from the viewing tower, there are 32 different rides in the amusement park, including six roller-coasters.

Families with smaller children can visit the **Doghill Fairytale Farm**, with cute farm animals to pat and a colourful cluster of small wooden houses with figures based on the popular Finnish Koiramäki children's books.

Visit also Särkänniemi's **Sara Hildén art museum**, with a collection of more than 5000 works. Apart from modern masters such as Joan Miró and Paul Klee, there is also an impressive range of modern Finnish art.

The museum's collection is based on the collection of Sara Hildén, a fashion-trade businesswoman, who accumulated the art over decades of dedicated work. The museum is closed on Mondays, and will move to the city centre in 2026.

### WHERE TO EAT IN TAMPERE

**Pyynikin Brewhouse**
This brewhouse serves tasty food with craft brews and a terrace by Tammerkoski. €€€

**4 vuodenaikaa**
Enjoy French cuisine, wine and the bustling atmosphere of Tampere Market Hall. €

**Kajo**
A sustainable, fine-dining set menu includes seasonal ingredients from hay and cloudberries to Nordic kimchi. €€€

## BEST PUBLIC SAUNAS IN TAMPERE

**Kuuma sauna**
Modern city-centre sauna, open all year with the possibility to try ice-hole swimming.

**Rauhaniemen kansankylpylä**
Lovely lakeside bathing facility dates from the 1920s and heats up every day.

**Kaukajärven sauna**
The sauna's long platform makes it easy to dip into the lake – frozen or not – after a sauna.

**Kaupinojan sauna**
Open year-round, the lakeside sauna has a kiosk where you can buy Finnish sausages to grill over an open fire.

INSPIRED BY MAPS/SHUTTERSTOCK ©

**Kuuma sauna**

## Island Idyll

ESCAPE TO TRAILS AND BEACHES

Beyond its urban amusements, Tampere has some great nature escapes. One such is **Viikinsaari**. From mid-May to early September, the island can be reached on a 20-minute ferry ride departing from Laukontori in the city centre and operated by Suomen hopealinja (hopealinjat.fi).

The island is a protected area with short nature trails to explore. There are also little beaches dotted around on which to grab some sun, and you can take a dip in the lake.

The island has multiple possibilities for activities, including miniature golf and stand-up paddleboard (SUP), rowing boat and kayak rentals. Or try the Finnish game Mölkky, a simple version of bowling, played with wooden logs.

Take your own picnic basket (bringing alcohol to the island is not allowed) or enjoy a leisurely lunch at the island's summer restaurant, Viikinsaari.

## GETTING AROUND

Tampere trains depart from Helsinki's Central railway station about every 30 minutes, running from around 4am to 11pm. Buses also run regularly.

If you arrive by car, most hotels in Tampere have parking facilities, but they might charge extra. There are also plenty of parking garages and street-side parking around the city. Payment typically requires a credit card or an app, as instructed on the parking spaces. The city itself is easily explored on foot – with the help of public transport or city bikes if needed.

## SCENIC STROLL WITH A SAUNA

Explore the fringe of the city centre on this walk among art, views and some of the city's best baking. Start from the **1 Tampere Art Museum**, which contains Finland's second-largest art collection, including works from Finnish masters such as Helene Schjerfbeck and Akseli Gallen-Kallela. After checking out the museum, walk one block north to find a sight straight from 19th-century Tampere. This is the **2 Amuri Working Class Quarters**, consisting of wooden houses that host exhibitions on working-class lifestyles in Tampere between 1882 and 1973. After the museums, stop in Amuri's beloved neighbourhood cafe, **3 Amurin Helmi**, serving freshly baked goods from buns to bread rolls and oven pancakes (*pannukakku*) in a wooden-house setting beside the Working Class Quarters.

Walk southeast to **4 Pyynikki hill**, the tallest longitudinal esker in the world, rising 80m above the surface of Pyhäjärvi lake. Atop the hill, there's an elevator to the tip of the **5 Pyynikki Observation Tower** to take in the views over the forest-covered hillsides and city scenes.

From here, you will be able to see another iconic tower in Tampere – Näsinneula in Särkänniemi amusement park. At the foot of the tower, the **6 Pyynikin munkkikahvila** cafe is famed for its fresh doughnuts. Wind down from the hill climb by continuing northeast to one of Finland's most famous saunas, **7 Rajaportin sauna,** which has been heated up regularly in the photogenic Pispala neighbourhood since 1906. The sauna has separate changing and sauna facilities for men and women plus a common terrace on which to chat and cool down between *löyly* (the steam of sauna).

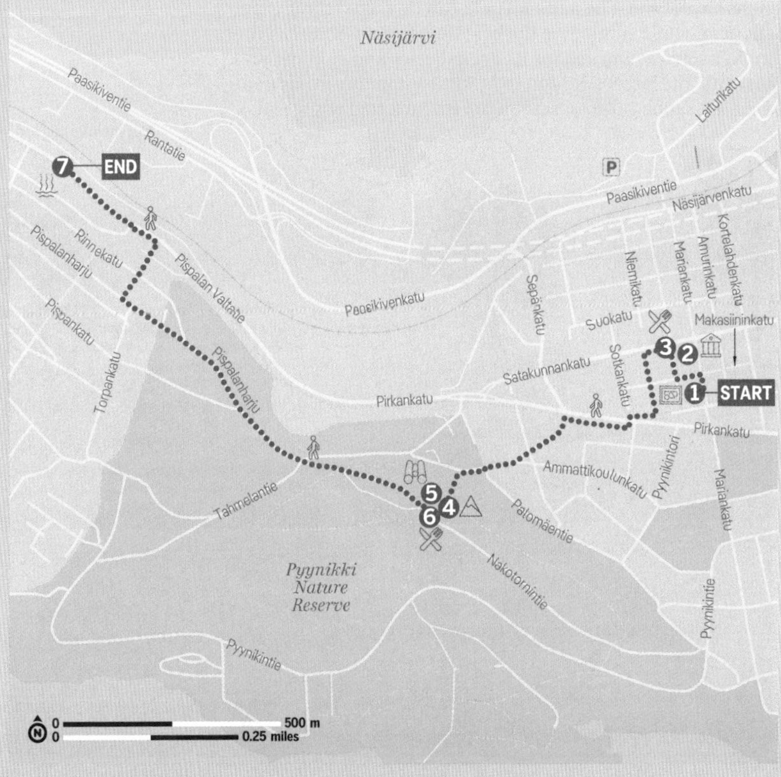

# Beyond Tampere

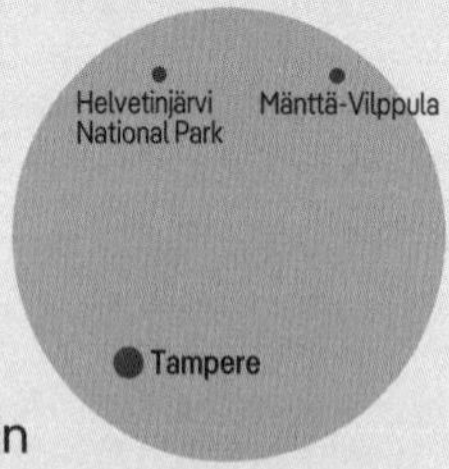

Helvetinjärvi National Park
Mänttä-Vilppula
Tampere

**Shake off Tampere's urban buzz with artsy finds in a small town or on a hike through a national park.**

Tampere is very much Pirkanmaa region's urban hub, but there are some great spots to explore beyond the city. Helvetinjärvi (Hell's Lake) National Park is famed for its namesake lake, edged by rocky cliffs, and Helvetinkolu, a 2m-wide, 40m-long canyon carved during the Ice Age. There are several walking trails, from a few hundred metres in length to an 11km hike that takes you from the top of the hills to the bottom of the gorges – the terrain is challenging but some sections have stairs. The national park can be visited throughout the year, while summer is the best time to visit Mänttä-Vilppula, a town renowned for its art galleries and summer arts festival. The latest addition to Mänttä-Vilppula's attractions is an art sauna – a good reason to visit on a cold winter's day.

## TOP TIP

A car is necessary when visiting Helvetinjärvi National Park, but there is a bus connection to Mänttä-Vilppula.

**Helvetinkolu gorge**

THE VISUAL EXPLORER/SHUTTERSTOCK ©

ILARI NACKEL/SHUTTERSTOCK ©

Serlachius Museum Gösta and Gustaf

## Mänttä-Vilppula

ART AND A DESIGN SAUNA

Dubbed an Art Town, Mänttä-Vilppula is a 75-minute drive northeast of Tampere. The Serlachius Museums run a daily shuttle from Tampere to the museums between June and August; outside that season, the bus runs from Tuesday to Sunday.

Mänttä-Vilppula's city centre first developed around the 19th-century wood industry, and its main sights are the **Serlachius Museum Gösta and Gustaf** – the former is dedicated to the arts, and the latter to history. The lakeside art museum's old section is inside a manor house, once the home of paper mill owner Göstä Serlachius. One of Finland's most influential art patrons, his collection of Finland's golden age art, as well as old European masters, forms the core of the museum and is one of the most important private fine-art collections in the Nordic countries.

The dedication of the Serlachius family to the arts is still commemorated today in an annual **contemporary-art**

### BEST SHOPPING IN MÄNTTÄ-VILPPULA

**Taito Shop**
Taito Shops, which are dotted across Finland's biggest cities, are dedicated to Finnish design and crafts, and their sweaters, posters, linen, tote bags and DIY equipment make great souvenirs.

**Myllyrannan uniikit putiikit**
Linen, natural products from Lapland, clothes and interior decorations can be found in this lakeside cluster of boutiques.

**Satumaista**
Mostly Scandinavian-styled items, from sleek mugs, plates and jars to candles and seasonal drinks, such as bottles of *glögi* (mulled wine).

### WHERE TO STAY IN MÄNTTÄ-VILPPULA

**Mäntylinnan huoneistomajoitus**
Experience Finnish lifestyle in apartments in a 1950s building furnished with vintage finds. €€

**Art Hotel Honkahovi**
Some rooms share a bathroom in this lakeside hotel built in functionalist style with windows looking over the lake. €€

**Mäntän Hovi**
The boutique hotel's slightly dated feel is compensated by some great architectural and design details. €€

festival taking place from around mid-June to the end of August. But visiting in wintertime doesn't leave anyone cold, either. Book a space to take the heat in the museum's award-winning **art sauna**, where the harmonious exterior hides a round sauna room as well as artsy details from designer sauna towels to the mosaics in the showers. Afterwards, you can enjoy a meal in the museum's restaurant.

## Helvetinjärvi National Park

HELLISHLY GOOD VIEWS

Take a 75-minute drive north from Tampere and you will arrive at a gate made from two trees turned upside down, their roots forming an arch above the road, and with a sign reading 'To Hell'. This is Helvetin portti (Hell's Gate), one of two entrances to Helvetinjärvi National Park. The gate can be found on Helvetinkoluntie 775 (Kankimäki parking lot) and there's another gate on the park's west side in Ruovesi. There are various hiking options in the park, with camping and toilet facilities dotted along the trails, especially on the park's northern side. Pitch your tent near Haukkajärvi beach and witness beautiful sunsets over the lake, or stay at Ruokejärvi camping site, closer to the park's main sights. You can also book the rustic Hiedanmaja cottage, available as accommodation from May to October.

At the moment, the only circular hike leads from Kankimäki to Helvetinjärvi's two main sights: Helvetinjärvi lake and Helvetinkolu gorge, formed some 200 million years ago when the bedrock split. The 4km trail includes stretches of duckboard across marshland, pathways through forests and a few sets of stairs that climb and descend. Entry into the gorge itself is blocked for safety reasons, but it can be admired from a viewing platform above.

Just outside the national park, **Siikaneva's** duckboard trails showcase Finland's marshy landscape. Here, you can also find **Ollinkivi**, a round glacial erratic that was one of Finland's first nature sights protected by environmental law.

### A BOOKSTORE WORTH SAVING

A rarity in rural Finland, the 120-year-old antiquarian **Vinhan kirjakauppa** bookshop makes a great pit stop for booky travellers in Ruovesi, a small village with about 4000 inhabitants. After being owned by the same family for four generations, the bookstore was close to being shut down, but was saved by two book-loving Finns, and it will open in 2023 freshly renovated. The lovely wooden building is on Ruovesi's main street.

### GETTING AROUND

The best way to reach Helvetinjärvi National Park is by car or camper van, for which there are specific parking lots. A bus from Tampere runs three times a day on school days, leaving you 10km from the park.

# SAIMAA LAKELAND

Saimaa's reputation is almost mythical in Finland. It seems like the labyrinth of lakes and islands has been here since the beginning of time, though it was created 11,000 years ago when the glaciers of the last Ice Age withdrew across Finland, carving and moving landmasses and leaving thousands of lakes behind. Around this time, a population of ringed seals separated from their pack in the Arctic Ocean and were left stranded in freshwater. These ringed seals are now endemic to Saimaa, and though they remain endangered, their numbers have risen from dozens to more than 400 in recent decades thanks to enthusiastic conservation campaigns.

The seals are a great attraction, but Finns also enjoy coming to Saimaa to bask in the summer sun, staying in their cottages lining the lakes' shores as the region's villages come to life with outdoor terraces and little festivals. Come in winter and the lakes are covered with ice and snow – as well as locals ice-hole fishing, skating and skiing.

**TOP TIP**

Contact local tourist offices for information about cycling trips around Saimaa Lakeland in summer. There are two popular circular routes, one covering 120km and the other, 60km. Both trips include ferry rides and ridges winding across the lakes. There are also hotels, restaurants, cafes and spots for swimming along the routes.

NIKIFOROV ALEXANDER/SHUTTERSTOCK ©

**Olavinlinna castle (p130)**

## BEST LOCAL FOOD & DRINK IN SAVONLINNA

**Saimaa's salmon soup**
Creamy salmon soup is an everyday lunch option in this cosy restaurant-cafe located on a cobblestoned street near the castle. €

**Lörtsy**
A deep-fried and flat meat pie is best enjoyed fresh from a stall in the market square. If you're a sweet tooth, or a vegetarian, try one filled with apple jam. €

**Waahto Brewery**
Ales to porters and coffee stout, as well as apple cider, served by the harbour. €

## Savour Savonlinna

SAIMAA'S KING OF THE CASTLE

Savonlinna, with its medieval castle and busy summertime harbour, is the jewel of Saimaa. Located on its own island, **Olavinlinna** castle dates from the 15th century when Sweden wanted to protect its eastern regions against the Novgorodians.

Olavinlinna now hosts an annual Opera Festival, started by the Finnish opera singer Aino Ackté in 1912.

The castle is dimly lit and its slightly claustrophobic corridors and staircases are fun to explore. Guided tours in English run hourly from June to August.

Neighbouring **Riihisaari** used to harbour Olavinlinna's war boats until Finland's border shifted further east in 1617, making the castle's defences obsolete: Riihisaari came to house grain-drying kilns, known as *'riihi'* in Finnish, and the name stuck.

Riihisaari holds Savonlinna Museum with various exhibitions, including History of Saimaa, featuring life-sized Saimaa ringed seals and some intriguing sailing and sea-life

### ON THE WAY TO KOLI

If you're heading to Koli National Park (p152) from Helsinki, **Lappeenranta** makes a good pit stop before you continue deeper into the Karelian landscape. Lappeenranta is the capital of South Karelia, whereas Koli is part of North Karelia.

## RURAL STAYS IN SAIMAA LAKELAND

**Tertti Manor**
Countryside getaway near Mikkeli with rooms in a renovated old barn within a manor-house setting. **€€**

**Hotel & Spa Resort Järvisydän**
The lakeside spa and the glass-walled suites are the draws here. **€€€**

**Sahanlahti Resort**
Lakeside hotel with an award-winning restaurant using local ingredients, as well as a buzzing harbour. **€€**

paraphernalia such as James Bond–like diving costumes from the 1950s.

**Linnankatu** is a cobblestoned street leading from the castle *(linna)* to Savonlinna's harbour. Grab lunch or coffee at **Kahvila Saima**, inside an old wooden villa and serving salmon soup and sweet treats.

Savonlinna's **kauppatori** (market square) and **satama** (harbour) sit side-by-side and are best experienced in summer when local delicacies such as fried vendace and *lörtsy* are sold at stalls. The harbour holds a handful of old ships now transformed into restaurants, and pleasure boats offering slow rides to various parts of Saimaa. Jump aboard and take in the beauty of Saimaa. Cruises vary from one to eight hours.

## Kolovesi & Linnansaari National Parks

AQUATIC NATIONAL PARKS

Kolovesi and Linnansaari national parks are located on islands on Lake Saimaa. In summer, Järvisydän Resort offers kayak and boat trips to Linnansaari, while another hub at which to start exploring both parks is Oravi village, which has various accommodation possibilities, including small cabins and tree tents on Linnansaari island itself, as well as apartments and lakeside glass houses in the village. From Oravi, you can also take a boat taxi to get to Linnansaari.

When the lake is frozen, Linnansaari can be reached from Oravi and Järvisydän on marked trails, but don't stray from the path as it is important to provide a peaceful breeding period for the Saimaa ringed seals.

Linnansaari's landscape is created by the slash-and-burn techniques used by the island's farmers since the 16th century. Eventually, new deciduous forests grew from the burnt land, and now, the light-filled leafy forests create a safe haven for species from beavers to white-backed woodpeckers. There are trails of various lengths crisscrossing Linnansaari, the highlight being a climb to Linnanvuori, a rocky cliff with views of Saimaa's blue horizon.

Kolovesi National Park can only be visited during summer. Paddling quietly between the islets and tall cliffs rising from Lake Saimaa reveals the area's landscape at its most magical. Keep an eye on the small rocks, as it's possible to spot a ringed seal or two resting on them. From Oravi, it takes one to two days to paddle to Kolovesi, with camping possibilities along the way.

### BEST BOAT TRIPS IN SAIMAA

**Saimaa Canoeing**
Self-guided kayak tours, with camping possibilities along the way (respecting the 'everyman's rights'), or using Saimaa Canoeing's private yet rustic lodgings dotted around the islands. Tours vary from a few hours of seal spotting to multiday expeditions.

**Slow-Boat Tours**
In summer, slow-boat tours are readily available in all bigger towns around Lake Saimaa.

**MS Aino**
This old steamboat slowly makes its way from Ristiina and Mikkeli to the prehistoric cave paintings at Astuvansalmi.

### WHERE TO STAY IN SAVONLINNA

**Lossiranta Lodge**
Simply furnished lakeside boutique hotel with spectacular views of the medieval Olavinlinna. €€

**Hotelli Punkaharju**
Stylishly Scandinavian decor, a restaurant using local produce and a beautiful setting on one of Saimaa's eskers. €€€

**Saima**
Charming wooden villa has six rooms with vintage furniture – the suite is spacious and one room has castle views. €€

## WHY I LOVE SAIMAA LAKELAND

**Paula Hotti**, writer

Growing up near Saimaa Lakeland, the best thing about local road trips with family were the stops for ice cream. It took me a couple of decades to appreciate what had always been there: a lakeland setting with its own archipelago, its endemic species of seal and manor houses putting up feasts of local produce.

But most of all, amid all the hecticness of modern life, the calming effect of sitting atop a cliff, looking at the lakes dotted with small islands covered in pines, is unparalleled. Lapland might offer its oohs and Helsinki its aahs, but here, sitting on the shores of Saimaa, nature wraps you in a reassuring calmness.

ELENANOEVA/SHUTTERSTOCK ©

Saimaa

## Seal Spotting

SEE THE ELUSIVE RINGED SEALS

Saimaa is home to one of the world's most endangered freshwater seals, the Saimaa ringed seal. These animals descend from ringed seals that were separated from the pack when the land rose after the last Ice Age, some 9500 years ago. Now, due to a tenacious protection campaign, there are about 400 seals living in Saimaa. The seals are typically under 1.5m and weigh 50–90kg.

The best time to spot the elusive creatures is from May to mid-June, when the seals climb on top of rocks to moult, but you can make sightings till September.

As Saimaa ringed seals are protected, it's advised to try to view them on a guided tour. The professional guides also know the best spots for sightings.

If you do venture out on your own, never go too close to the seals: the rule of thumb is to be at a distance at which you can see them with binoculars.

One of the best ways to take in the beauty of Saimaa, and spot the seals, is to take an eco-boat (lakelandgte.fi) ride, si-

### WHERE TO STAY IN LAPPEENRANTA

**Rakuuna**
The building used to house the city's dragoons, and the military theme still shows in the simply furnished rooms. **€€**

**Boutique Hotel Lähde**
Good value for money, this sustainable hotel features Smeg fridges in the rooms and is near the harbour. **€€**

**Original Sokos Hotel Lappee**
This Finnish chain hotel with a pool is located in a shopping mall, so shops, restaurants and cafes are close by. **€€€**

lently gliding between Saimaa's many islands for an intimate feel of the landscape.

An eco-boat trip from Puumala lasts 75 minutes and includes an informative narration given by the skipper. Binoculars – and coffee and buns – are available. In the end, you will hear a popular Finnish song telling the story of a lonely bachelor befriending a seal. The song made people fall in love with the seals and might have saved them from extinction, too.

## Lappeenranta

BARRACKS AND BORDERS

Lappeenranta's close proximity to the Russian border has shaped its history through the ages. In fact, the city is established on a fortress built here in the 1640s. Although Lappeenranta has since grown – it's now home to more than 70,000 inhabitants and a small harbour offering cruises to Saimaa Lakeland – the fortress is still the city's highlight, hosting a bundle of museums, from the Lappeenranta Museum of Art to the Cavalry Museum.

On and around the fortress, there are also craft and boutique shops, cafes and views over Saimaa and the city.

A day is enough to explore Lappeenranta's main sights and it can be covered on foot, resting at some of the city's many restaurants or coffee shops along the way.

You can also take advantage of the city's position as a gateway to Saimaa and enjoy a cruise on one of the slow boats operating from the harbour. The boats head to Saimaa's archipelago and all the way to Puumala and Savonlinna.

Alternatively, cruise along the ill-fated Saimaa channel connecting Finland's waterways to the Gulf of Finland via Russia. The 814km-long canal was built in the 1850s and has been an important waterway but today, since part of the canal is located in Russia, it has very little international cargo traffic.

### BEST CAFES IN LAPPEENRANTA

**Kahvila Majurska**
Located atop the fortress, Majurska's old-fashioned charms and cakes lure in a steady flow of people.

**Pulsan Asema**
If you have time, drive 20 minutes from the city centre to Pulsa, a former railway station turned cafe and design shop offering boutique B&B accommodation in summer.

**Satamatie 6**
Award-winning cafe and roastery, steaming up stellar flat whites as well as sweet and savoury treats by the fortress.

### GETTING AROUND

City-hopping between bigger hubs, such as Savonlinna and Lappeenranta, is possible by public transport. The bus from Lappeenranta to Savonlinna takes four hours and 40 minutes, with a change in Mikkeli, whereas the train curves close to the Russian border and takes just over five hours, with a change in Parikkala.

## ROAD TRIP AROUND SAIMAA LAKELAND

This circular road trip starts from **1 Savonlinna** (p130) and takes in many of Saimaa Lakeland's best spots for scenery, food and observing the local lifestyle.

From Savonlinna, take road 14 and then the 464 towards **2 Hotel & Spa Resort Järvisydän** (p131). Relax in the lakeside spa or join a kayaking tour to the nearby **3 Linnansaari National Park** (p131).

Next, continue towards Juva on roads 464, 467 and 14. The rural landscape hides an English tearoom with a Finnish twist, including rye-bread finger sandwiches and scones made of buttermilk. After a refreshing break at the **4 TeaHouse of Wehmais**, sampling its teas selected by Finland's first tea sommelier, continue to **5 Mikkeli** where you'll find hospitable manor houses. Nearby **6 Kenkävero** has a restaurant and boutique shops full of local designs, from jewellery to kitchenware. **7 Tertti Manor** (p130) serves food in its manor-house restaurant and cafe, and has upscale barn accommodation available.

Continue on road 62 towards Sahanlahti Resort and you will pass a winding ridge with views over rocky islets scattered around the lake. This is **8 Lietvesi Scenic Route**, part of the Saimaa Geo Park and picturesque evidence of the area's Ice Age shaping. This is just before **9 Pistohiekka beach**. Stop at the nearby **10 Sahanlahti Resort** (p130) for lunch – the restaurant has been awarded for its delicious use of local produce. If you have more time, spend the night and immerse yourself in Sahanlahti's history as a 19th-century sawmill community. Finally, head back past Savonlinna to Punkaharju and **11 Punkaharju ridge**, the most famous of Saimaa's eskers. Spend the night in Hotel Punkaharju and enjoy its yoga, sauna and forest bathing, as well as its award-winning food, before returning to Savonlinna.

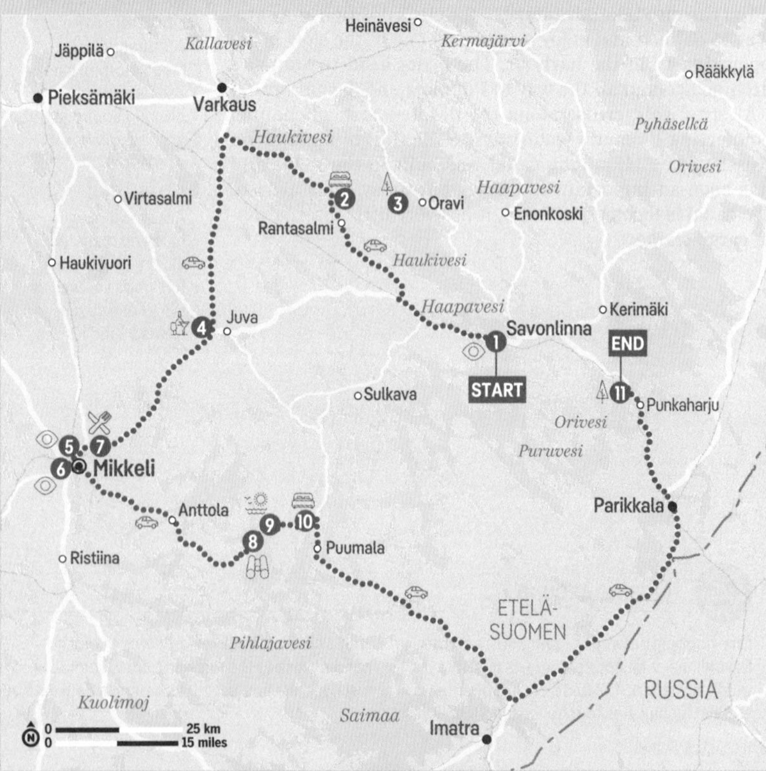

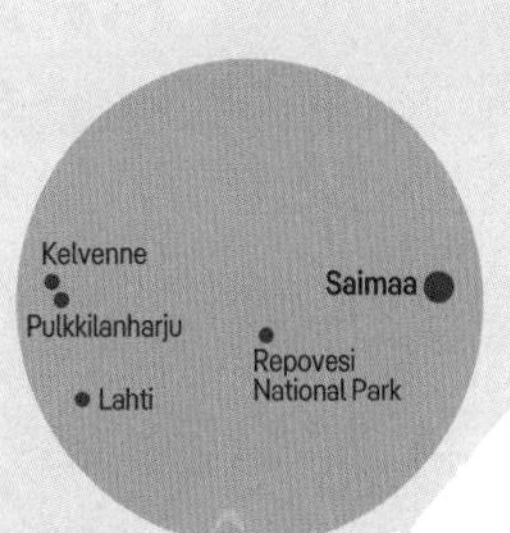

# Beyond Saimaa Lakeland

Explore Salpausselkä Geo Park's Ice Age marvels, or get curious over arts and sports in Lahti, Finland's leading green city.

### TOP TIP

Saimaa Lakeland is surrounded by the Karelian wilderness in the east and vast expanses of dense woodland in the north. Lahti, in the southwest, gives a taste of urban lifestyle among Finland's signature lakes and forests.

The strap of land between the Saimaa Lakeland and Helsinki makes a great area to explore in southern Finland. Like everywhere in the south, the landscape is dominated by forests and lakes: here, the main water is called Päijänne. Surrounded by the recently anointed Salpausselkä Geo Park, the region's main city Lahti is also unsurprisingly Finland's leading city in sustainability.

With three ski-jump towers and plenty of cross-country tracks, Lahti is also known for its winter sports. But it's not all about wintry fun here: in summer, there's an outdoor pool at the foot of the tallest tower, and the city centre has sights from a cute harbour to impressive museums to keep you busy.

ARTBBNV/SHUTTERSTOCK ©

Saimaa Lakeland

### BEST MUSEUMS IN LAHTI

**Lahti Ski Museum**
Located by the ski-jump towers, this museum details the history of skiing in Finland – the highlight is the 3D ski-jump simulator.

**Radio & TV Museum Mastola**
Nostalgic museum with a vast collection of old TVs and radios, located near the railway station.

**Finnish Motorcycle Museum**
Finland's only museum dedicated to motorcycles is located just outside the city centre (take bus 2); it's open from May to September and other months by advance booking.

**Museum of Visual Arts Malva**
A feast for the eyes and belly, this city-centre museum hosts various exhibitions and three modern restaurants.

KARAVANOV_LEV/SHUTTERSTOCK ©

Lahti ski jump

## Lahti

SKIING AND SUSTAINABILITY

Long known as a winter-sports centre, primarily for its ski jumping and cross-country skiing, a 2¾-hour drive from Savonlinna. The European Green Capital of 2021, the city has been reinventing itself, tackling sustainability issues with success and establishing a flashy new Museum of Visual Arts Malva.

To feel the importance of snow to the Finnish psyche, visit Lahti's three imposing **ski towers**, which are a 15-minute stroll from the city centre in Salpausselkä. If lucky, you might see jumpers floating in the air like feathers as they practise their craft. In summer, there's an **outdoor swimming pool** at the foot of the tallest tower, making it an extraordinary spot for a day out. Stroll around **Lahti harbour**, lined with cafes and restaurants, with boats barely bobbing on Päijänne's calm surface.

To understand more of the key elements of forests and wood in Finland, pop over to **Pro Puu**, a small gallery

### BEST HOTELS IN LAHTI

**Solo Sokos Hotel Seurahuone**
Awarded internationally for its sustainability, the city-centre hotel also has designer loft houses with kitchenettes. **€€€**

**GreenStar Hotel**
In a block of flats next to Lahti's railway station, this hotel's ecological ethos counters its lack of flashy design. **€€**

**Hostel Matkakoti Patria**
Small, budget-friendly single and double rooms with shared bathrooms near the railway station. **€**

showcasing Finnish wood design. Finally, head to the **Museum of Visual Arts Malva** in the city centre. After exploring the exhibitions, which vary from sculptures and painting to poster art and interior design, take a break in the modern cafe Kahiwa, the Malski bistro or the downstairs brewery restaurant Ant Brew. When you leave Malva, check the Alvar Aalto-designed church **Ristinkirkko**, directly opposite.

## Salpausselkä Geo Park

NEW GLOBAL PROTECTED AREA

A unique landscape shaped by ice and water, the Salpausselkä area near Lahti was granted Unesco Global Geo Park status in 2022, highlighting the region's internationally significant geological landscapes.

The two Salpausselkä ridges - terminal moraine formations left by the Ice Age some 12,000 years ago - run the length of southern Finland and are at their most stunning near Lahti. Altogether, the formation is almost 500km long, rising at times as high as 80m. There are plenty of nature activities here, ranging from marshland walks to bike tours (see visitlahti.fi for details), but the main sights are the **Kelvenne** esker island and **Pulkkilanharju** esker, both part of **Päijänne National Park**. Kelvenne island is located in the southern part of Päijänne and can only be accessed by boat, such as MS *Jenni Maria* from Padasjoki harbour, from the end of June till early August.

Pulkkilanharju is best reached by car – it's 40 minutes from Lahti. The esker is about 8km long and includes a small patch of Päijänne National Park. Apart from the photogenic esker and bridges connecting small islands, there's a cute canal-side town, **Vääksy**. Vääksy's channel was built in 1871 and today it's Finland's busiest canal. The area is dotted with lovely cafes and restaurants in which to spend an hour or two.

### BEST FOOD & DRINK IN VÄÄKSY

**Ranskalainen kyläkauppa**
French breakfasts, brunch and lunch in a charming pink house with a design boutique attached. €

**Kanavan panimo**
For thirsty travellers, Vääksy's craft brewery opens its terrace in June and July, and the brewery shop and pre-booked tours operate all year-round. €

**Kanavan helmi**
Artisanal ice creams, sumptuous doughnuts and other sweet treats by the idyllic Vääksy canal. €

## Repovesi National Park

HIGHS FOR ROCK CLIMBERS

Between the heartlands of Saimaa Lakeland and Lahti lies Repovesi National Park, a 2½-hour drive from Savonlinna and an hour's drive from Mikkeli. Repovesi is most famous for the vertical rock wall **Olhavanvuori**, rising 50m directly from a pond below. This is Finland's main destination for rock climbers, and a dramatic sight for everyone. It's also a good place for birdwatchers, as flocks of red-throated loons live by the

### BEST RESTAURANTS IN LAHTI

**Soppa Baari**
Lahti Market Hall's lunch find, with three daily-changing soup options, varying from meat and fish to vegetarian. €

**Gastropub Mylly**
All-day breakfasts, homey lunches and a touch-flashier dinner in gastropub style. €€

**Roux**
Fine-dining restaurant with several set menus (including vegan) as well as à la carte. €€€

## BEST TRAILS IN REPOVESI NATIONAL PARK

**Ketunlenkki**
Leaving from Lapinsalmi parking lot, the park's most popular route is a circular, 3.5km walk, and includes a water crossing by cable ferry and views from the Lapinsalmi bridge.

**Kakkurinkierros**
The 26km trail is the park's longest, taking two to four days to complete and passing the park's main sights.

**Korpinkierros**
This circular 4.3km trail shows Olhavanvuori cliff, rising from its pond, from all angles.

O.KEMPPAINEN/SHUTTERSTOCK ©

**Olhavanvuori (p137)**

cliff. The national park can be explored by foot, bike or kayak, which are available to hire at the park's service points – Olhavanvuori, however, is out of reach for cyclists. Another popular sight is the 55m-long Lapinsalmi suspension bridge.

Repovesi National Park is open all year-round but, as with many other forest walks, the pathways here are not maintained during winter months, though they get tramped by visitors. There are also many private cottages here, which are off-limits even under Finland's everyman's rights. Repovesi's Valkjärvi Group Camp cottage can be pre-booked from April to October (luontoon.fi).

The easiest way to get to Repovesi National Park is by car, but from mid-June to the end of October, bus 15 from Kouvola runs to the park on weekends. Alternatively, jump off the train in Mäntyharju and canoe, kayak or cycle the remaining 47km to Repovesi.

## GETTING AROUND

Lahti is less than an hour by train from Helsinki, with one or two departures every hour. To visit Lahti's surroundings, a car is the best option.

# JYVÄSKYLÄ

Jyväskylä is dubbed the Athens of Finland due to its university campus and thriving creative spirit. The city centre is concise and clustered around the main shopping street, Kauppakatu, which runs 2km from 'Yläkaupunki's' (Upper Town) university area to 'Alakaupunki' (Lower Town). Along the way, there are bars, restaurants, museums, galleries and shops, as well as architecture from Alvar Aalto and Kirkkopuisto (Church Park), the city centre's main area of greenery.

Ascend a block uphill from Kauppakatu and you'll find yourself at the foot of a city-centre hill, Harju, where the residents of the city go walking, running and occasionally partying. A view down towards the harbour shows Jyväskylä in another light: not only a studious academic hot spot with a youthful spirit, but also a calm lakeside city with an abundance of nature activities on offer.

**TOP TIP**

Jyväskylä's city centre is easily explored on foot in a day or two, but in nice weather consider also renting a bike and exploring around Jyväsjärvi, the lake at the centre of the city. It'll give you a glimpse into both urban life and the city's nature-driven lifestyle.



MARIS GRUNSKIS/SHUTTERSTOCK ©

**Alvar Aalto Museum (p140)**

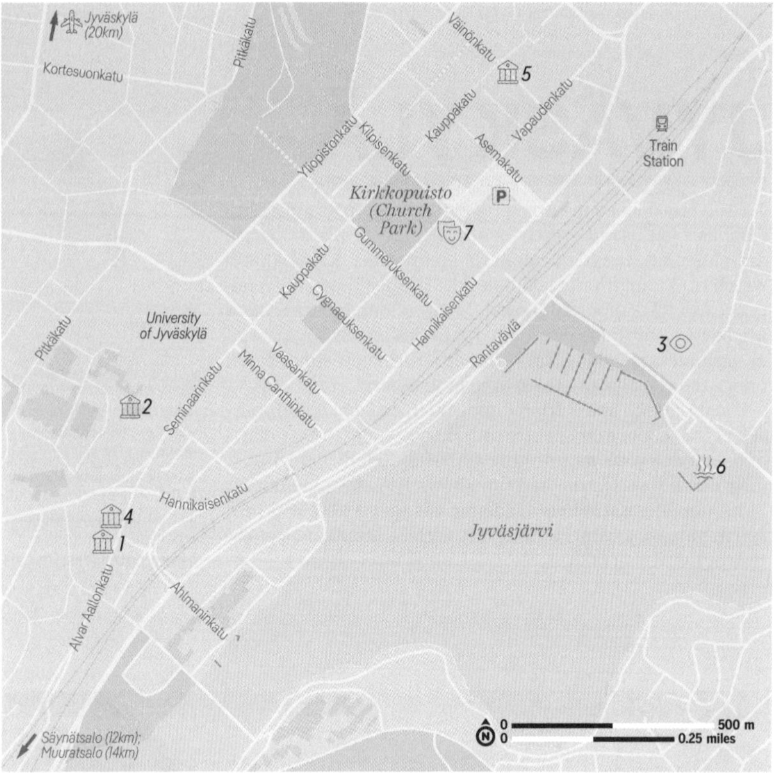

**HIGHLIGHTS**
**1** Alvar Aalto Museo
**2** Capitolium
**3** Lutakko
**4** Museum of Central Finland
**5** Workers' Club

**ACTIVITIES, COURSES & TOURS**
**6** Viilu

**ENTERTAINMENT**
**7** Jyväskylä City Theatre

## Alvar Aalto's Jyväskylä

ARCHITECTURE OVERLOAD

Jyväskylä has the largest number of Alvar Aalto–designed buildings of any city in the world. There are 29 in total, with the architect living and starting his career here, where he also married Aino Aalto, a designer and architect of her own standing. Get insight into Aalto's Jyväskylä at **Alvar Aalto Museum,** dedicated to architecture and design, and located inside a building designed by Aalto in the early 1970s. Next door, see

### WHERE TO STAY AND EAT IN JYVÄSKYLÄ

**Boutique Hotel Yöpuu**
Award-winning boutique hotel has rooms decorated with Finnish designs, and superb Finnish breakfast items. **€€**

**Hotelli Verso**
On the main shopping street, the interior is a touch worn out but the toiletries-packed sauna is a treat. **€€**

**Teeleidi**
The best tearoom in central Finland, set in an old villa between Alvar Aalto Museum and the university campus. **€**

the Aalto-designed Museum of Central Finland. Then, walk uphill to the university campus and pop inside the red-bricked **Capitolium**, built in 1955. From the campus area, which is dotted with Aalto's work from the 1950s, stroll down Kauppakatu to Kirkkopuisto and you'll recognise Aalto's style in the white **Jyväskylä City Theatre** facade on the opposite side of the park. Continue down Kauppakatu until you come to the corner of Väinönkatu, where Aalto's first significant public building, the Workers' Club, dating from 1924–25, stands.

Other Aalto highlights include the Muuratsalo Experimental House and Säynätsalo Town Hall, outside the city. Muuratsalo Experimental House can be visited by tour (alvaraalto.fi) from the beginning of June to mid-September. Säynätsalo Town Hall is open daily from June to September, with tours in English starting at noon. Outside those months, bookings can be made two days prior to your visit. There is also accommodation available inside Säynätsalo Town Hall. Visit Jyväskylä (visitjyvaskyla.fi), the city's tourism organisation, also organises Alvar Aalto tours.

Another intriguing set of Aalto's works is in Rovaniemi (p192). Big parts of the city were destroyed in the Wehrmacht retreat in 1944 and then rebuilt to a plan by Alvar Aalto, with its main streets in the shape of a reindeer head. Aalto's signature works here include a library and the city hall.

## Jyväskylä Harbour

FUN BY THE WATER

In recent years, Jyväskylä's harbour has gone through rapid modernisation. Sprinkled with cafes, cruises and a modern sauna, the waterside area is now a popular spot for locals and visitors. The harbour is easy to reach from the city centre: walk downhill, cross the train tracks and you'll find yourself by Jyväsjärvi's shores in a neighbourhood called **Lutakko**, mostly known for its namesake music venue.

The latest addition to the harbour is a modern sauna and restaurant, **Viilu**. There are three different types of mixed saunas, so bring your swimsuit – there are separate changing rooms for men and women. After, or in between, saunas, it is possible to cool off on the terrace, plunge into the lake or relax in a hot tub. The saunas heat up every day from 9am to 10pm.

If you prefer a more private and unique sauna setting, you can rent a **sauna float**, with Jyväskylä having many providers. Many **slow-boat tours** also depart from the harbour to cruise on the calm waters around Jyväskylä. Check out **Alvar Aalto's old boat**, permanently docked next to Viilu.

### I LIVE HERE: WHERE TO FIND LIVE MUSIC IN JYVÄSKYLÄ

**Ismo Puhakka**, a Jyväskylä-born-and-bred musician from the band Muuan Mies, shares his favourite gig venues.

**Vakiopaine**
Shabby and understated bar with Kaurismäki vibes, attracting both academia and workers, becomes a stage for poets, folk singers and bands in the evenings.

**Ylä-Ruth**
Another bohemian bar favoured by artists, journalists, musicians and underground artists.

**Lutakko & Musta kynnys**
The city's best live-music venues, with big-name bands from near and far performing.

**Poppari**
When done with their own gigs, the city's musicians gather here for wild jam sessions. If you know how to hold an instrument, you can climb onto the stage with the stars.

### GETTING AROUND

With its central location, Jyväskylä is easily reached by bus or train from Finland's major cities. There's also plenty of parking in the city centre should you arrive by car.

## VIEWS, VAULTS AND FEMINISTS WALKING TOUR

Apart from Alvar Aalto's architecture, there is plenty to see in Jyväskylä. Start from **1 Harju**, the 34m-high hill that rises just one block from the city's main shopping street, Kauppakatu. Climb the stone-walled stairs and take in the view over the city and the lake. The hill has a walking path around it and the slopes are covered with majestic pine trees. On top is the **2 Vesilinna observation tower** featuring a scenic cafe and restaurant as well as the small **3 Natural History Museum of Central Finland**.

After taking in the views, descend back to the city centre and visit **4 Jyväskylä Art Museum** and the neighbouring **5 Craft Museum of Finland**. The art museum showcases Finnish and local art on two floors. The museum is closed on Mondays, and admission is free on Fridays. In the Craft Museum, admire Finnish traditional costumes and learn about the world of crafts through smells, sounds and tastes. Both museums line **6 Kirkkopuisto** (Church Park). A red-brick church dating from 1880 stands in the middle of the park, and on one side a statue of the Finnish author and feminist Minna Canth keeps an eye on passersby. The park also has a glass-walled bistro and uplifting light installations during the Christmas season.

From here, it is a few blocks' walk to **7 Toivolan vanha piha**, an old-fashioned and lovely courtyard lined with wooden buildings containing little boutiques and craft workshops. Don't miss the charming **8 Museum Shop Sparvin**, located in Jyväskylä city centre's oldest building, dating from 1861. Finish your walk in the courtyard's Kahvila Valkoinen Puu, a cosy cafe set in a cellar with red-brick vaults.

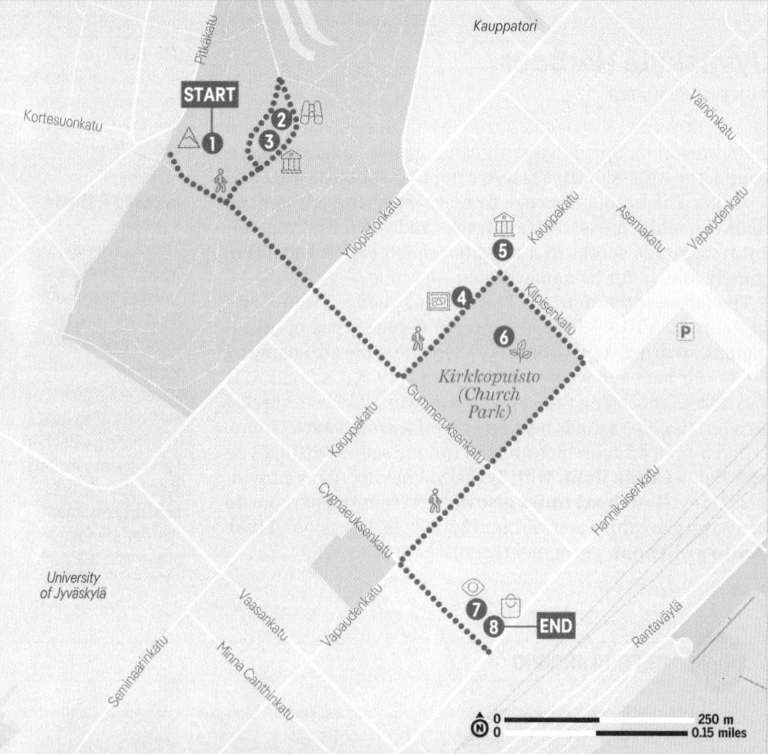

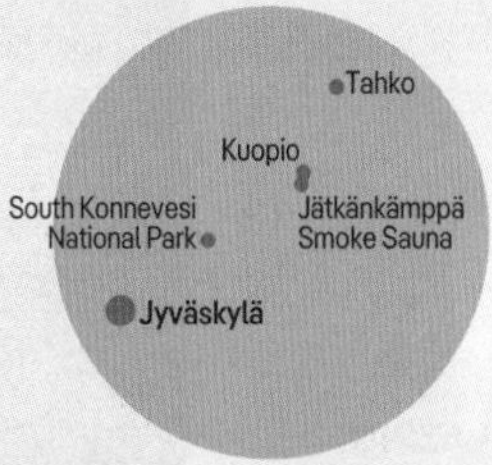

# Beyond Jyväskylä

Tahko
Kuopio
South Konnevesi National Park
Jätkänkämppä Smoke Sauna
Jyväskylä

For more city life, head northeast to Kuopio, the affable capital of Northern Savonia, renowned for its traditional cuisine.

Known for their distinctive dialect, the people of the Savonia region tend to have a cheeky twinkle in their eye. And no wonder – with Savonia's towns and cities located on lakeshores and surrounded by forests, the area oozes calm lifestyle. Kuopio is the capital of Northern Savonia, celebrated for its lively summer market square and year-round market hall selling traditional foods. Kuopio and Northern Savonia was the first area in Finland to receive the European Region of Gastronomy Award, which it received in 2020–21. Apart from foodie finds, Kuopio makes a great stop for a relaxing day or two in a beautiful lakeside setting.

RNDMS/SHUTTERSTOCK ©

**Kuopio market square (p144)**

SHEVCHENKO ANDREY/SHUTTERSTOCK ©

Minna Canth statue

### TRAILBLAZING FEMINIST

In Kuopion korttelimuseo, visit Minna Canth's salon. **Minna Canth** (1844–97) was Finland's first female writer and journalist writing in Finnish, as well as a pioneering feminist. Widowed at the age of 35 with seven children, Canth was an advocate for women's education and equality, causing a stir with her critical plays. Although an applauded celebrity of her time, she was also verbally attacked by those opposing her views. Canth is the first Finnish woman to be honoured with her own flag day: 19 March is Minna Canth Day and celebrates social equality.

## City Walk in Kuopio

A TASTE OF THE FOODIE CAPITAL

Kuopio is two hours' drive from Jyväskylä, and its **market square**, *'tori'*, is at its liveliest from June to August, with stalls selling traditional foods from the area, such as the famous *kalakukko* (rye-crusted bread with fish and pork baked inside) and berries from nearby farms.

The square's Jugendstil **Market Hall** caters to foodie cravings year-round.

From the *'tori'*, stroll three minutes to **Kuopio Art Museum**, focused on Finnish art. Almost next door rises an imposing Jugendstil mini-castle, dating from 1904 and housing **Kuopio Museum**, which includes both Kuopio Museum of Natural History and Kuopio Museum of Cultural History.

The museums line Snellmanninpuisto, where the 1816 **Kuopio Cathedral** is located. The area and the wooden-house quarters on the south side of the park are an integral part of Kuopio's cultural heritage.

### WHERE TO STAY IN KUOPIO

**Lapland Hotels Kuopio**
Centrally located hotel with a few touches of Lapland in the decor, as well as saunas for guests every evening. **€€**

**Spa Hotel Rauhalahti**
A popular spa on the shores of Kallavesi as well as the traditional Jätkänkämppä smoke sauna in the forest. **€€**

**Boutique Hotel Sawohouse**
Homey and budget-friendly boutique villa, 7km from the city centre, with an underground gig venue. **€€**

Here, **Kuopion korttelimuseo** tells the story of city living at the turn of the 19th century.

Jump on to buses 6, 7 or 9 at the '*tori*' to head to the **Puijo viewing tower** (with restaurant). The bus takes about five minutes, and you'll then need to climb uphill to the tower for about 15 minutes – the views from on top will reward the effort.

At the harbour, board a Roll's boat to enjoy the scenic lakeside setting of Kallavesi from June to late August, or drive an hour out of town to find **South Konnevesi National Park**, with its pine forest and ponds lined by rugged cliffs and scenic settings for a picnic.

In snowy months, visit **Tahko**, a 45-minute drive north of Kuopio, for a night in a cottage or spa hotel, or a day out on its slopes for downhill skiing or snowshoeing.

## Jätkänkämppä Smoke Sauna

SMOKING-HOT TRADITION

A traditional smoke sauna is an out-of-the-ordinary experience even for Finns. Jätkänkämppä sauna (Lumberjack's sauna) is one of the most lauded of these – it's located on the shore of Kallavesi in Kuopio, a 1¾-hour drive northeast of Jyväskylä.

Take bus 7 from Kuopio's market square and jump off at Spa Hotel Rauhalahti. There is a sign to the sauna, which is located a short walk away through the forest.

Pay for the sauna in the main building, where a buffet dinner, accompanied by traditional tunes from an accordion, is served. Booking ahead for the buffet is advised. Here, you can also buy cold drinks to take to the sauna and enjoy on the terrace outside with views towards the lake.

Remember to bring your swimsuit, as the sauna is mixed. Changing rooms are separate for men and women, and the receptionist will give you a towel. There are also special sauna towels on which to sit. Have a shower, step inside and relax.

It might take an acquired taste to enjoy the smokiness, but the experience is memorable: the scene inside, with people wrapped in a dim husk, is like something from an old Flemish painting.

### WHERE TO EAT IN KUOPIO

**Kahvila Kaneli**
A gramophone pouring out bossa nova tunes sets the mood in this cute restaurant-cafe with simple lunches and an abundance of juicy cakes and pies. €

**Muikkuravintola Sampo**
Smoked, rolled in rye flower, fried... the vendace comes in many forms in this restaurant dedicated to the small fish since 1931. €€

**Musta Lammas**
Although located in a cellar, this esteemed restaurant serves fine-dining plates inspired by the surrounding nature. €€€

### GETTING AROUND

Kuopio city centre can be explored on foot in a day, and city buses will take you to outlying sights such as the Jätkänkämppä smoke sauna.

# HÄMEENLINNA

Founded in 1639, Hämeenlinna is Finland's oldest inland city, and its main attraction is still its medieval castle. The city's origins actually go back to the late 11th or early 12th century, when a community settled here soon after Swedish nobleman Birger Jarl's crusade to Finland, establishing Swedish rule in Finland. In those days, Hämeenlinna was a crucial trading point passed by two important roads: the Hämeen Härkätie from coastal Turku to Hämeenlinna, and the Ylinen Viipurintie leading to what is now the Russian city of Viaborg. In 1777 Gustav III of Sweden changed the city's centre to its current location. After three-quarters of the city was razed by fire in 1831, the German architect CL Engel, who also created Helsinki's empirical look, designed Hämeenlinna's new appearance to match the growing bourgeois tastes – though not many of Engel's buildings now remain.

**TOP TIP**

For a picturesque stroll, take a peek at Eteläkatu in the city centre, where a row of charming villas date from the early 20th century.

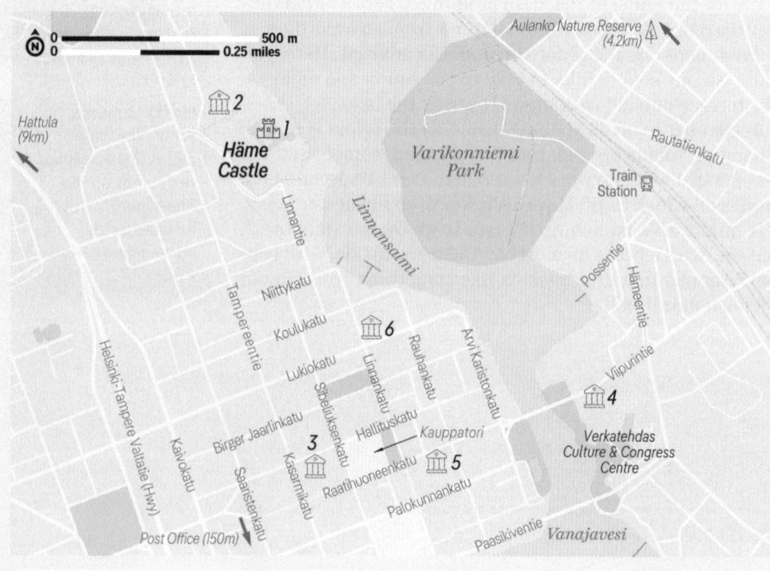


**HIGHLIGHTS**
**1** Häme Castle

**SIGHTS**
**2** Artillery, Engineer and Signals Museum of Finland
**3** Birthplace of Jean Sibelius
**4** Hämeenlinna Art Museum
**5** Hämeenlinna City Museum
**6** Palander's House

KARASEV VIKTOR/SHUTTERSTOCK ©

Häme Castle

## Häme Castle

CENTURIES OF HISTORY

A 20-minute stroll from Hämeenlinna's central railway station, the city's main sight, Häme Castle (Hämeen linna), rises on the shores of Vanajavesi lake.

The castle started as a single-storey stone camp, fortifying Swedish rule in the late 13th century. A few decades after a successful defence against a Novgorodian raid in 1311, the castle got a second storey, built from brick, and it is now one of three medieval brick buildings left in Finland.

Faced with disasters from fires to collapses and conquerors, Häme Castle also experienced grand times, particularly when the influential Lady Ingeborg was the castellan in the early 16th century.

The castle was briefly ruled by the Danes in the 1520s, and fell under Russian rule from 1713 to 1721, a period known as the Greater Wrath. When the Swedes returned to power, they

### BEST NATURE EXPERIENCES IN HÄMEENLINNA

**Paddling in Lake Vanajavesi**
See Häme Castle and Hämeenlinna National Urban Park, the first of its kind in Finland, from the waters by joining a kayaking tour.

**Ahvenisto open-air pool**
Built for the 1952 Olympic Games, the open-air Ahvenisto pool, located next to a sandy beach, is open from early June to mid-August.

**Katajistonranta Olympic sauna**
Also built for the Olympics, this lakeside sauna has a heated hot tub and possibilities for kayaking and SUPing if booked well in advance.

### WHERE TO STAY IN HÄMEENLINNA

**Matin ja Maijan Majatalo**
Quaint city-centre villa, with homey features, from wooden floorboards to a lobby with small library. €€

**Original Sokos Hotel Vaakuna**
Vaakuna's location near the railway station and on Vanajavesi shores is ideal for exploring Hämeenlinna. €€

**Hostelli Naurava Kulkuri**
Simply furnished hostel with shared bathrooms a 20-minute walk from the city centre. €

### JEAN SIBELIUS, NATIONAL COMPOSER

Born in Hämeenlinna in 1865, Jean Sibelius was raised in a female-dominated environment after his father died of typhoid when Sibelius was three years of age. In his childhood he received piano lessons from his aunt and, more importantly, his uncle gave him a violin, which Sibelius loved. Although the Sibelius family was Swedish speaking, Jean (known as Janne in his boyhood) also spoke Finnish and attended Hämeenlinna's Finnish-language Normal Lyceum, the first Finnish language 'Normal-Lycée' in Finland. Later, he would become one of the greatest influences in creating Finland's national identity as the country struggled to free itself from Russian rule. Today, Sibelius is celebrated all over the world but has a special status in Finland as the country's national composer.

extended the castle's defences and built a grand Crown bakery with six ovens to cater to its troops.

After many battles, Russia defeated Sweden for good, and Finland became part of the Russian Empire in 1809. CL Engel redesigned the castle as a prison in 1841 and, four decades later, Finland's only convict prison for women was established here. The castle's time as a prison ended in 1953, when the building's restoration started.

Now, Häme Castle exhibits its rich and ragged history, and the **Prison Museum** can be visited in the summer months.

Next door is the **Artillery, Engineer and Signals Museum of Finland**, which gives information on the wars in which Finland has fought over the centuries.

## Aulanko Nature Reserve

VIEWS FROM THE TOP

Aulanko Nature Reserve's history spans more than 10,000 years, to a time when the first people of Häme region were living in the area. But the resident who most shaped Aulanko was colonel Hugo Standertskjöld lived, who lived here in the late 19th and early 20th centuries, modifying Aulanko's landscape to create an English-style garden with artificial ponds, roads and leisure pavilions. He also planted foreign flowers and trees in the area.

Finland's government acquired the land in 1963, and in 1991 it became protected by the law. Now, there are several easy walking paths crisscrossing the park, the longest one stretching for 7km.

In winter, there are two cross-country skiing tracks (4.5km and 6.5km) that are lit up, as well as an unlit 10km track around Aulangonjärvi lake. But the main sight here is a 33m-high granite **viewing tower**. The view from the top looks over the dark forests and lakes, and the tower's interior features make climbing the stairs a joy.

Descend from the tower using the stone staircases. Here, you will be greeted by a family of bears in their cave – this is Karhuluola (Bear Cave), a sculpture carved by Robert Stigellin in 1906.

### WHERE TO EAT IN HÄMEENLINNA

**Cafe Marenki**
Furnished with old-fashioned wooden tables and chairs, this cute cafe serves hefty breakfasts to kick off the day. **€**

**Vanai Bistro & Bastu**
Finnish ingredients are used to dish up magical plates in the city's old barracks – there's a sauna on the premises too. **€€**

**Piparkakkutalo**
A classic in a quirky wooden building, 'Gingerbread House' serves home-style fine-dining dishes. **€€**

## City Museums

BIRTHPLACE OF A COMPOSER

Just around the corner from Hämeenlinna's central market square, an unassuming plaque decorates a yellow wooden building. This is the birthplace of Finland's most celebrated composer, Jean Sibelius (1865–1957), and now one component of Hämeenlinna's excellent collection of museums.

Sibelius lived his first 20 years in the building with his family, and it was in this home that the young boy started his career in music.

The **Birthplace of Jean Sibelius museum**, closed on Mondays, includes a beautiful music room with two pianos and a small bed chamber, believed to be the place where Sibelius was born – if you ask, the receptionist will play your favourite piece of Sibelius music from a CD during your visit.

Elsewhere in the city, the **Hämeenlinna Art Museum** features an art collection that was saved from Vyborg in the 1930s, and exhibits Finnish and foreign art in its two buildings.

**Hämeenlinna City Museum**, located in a striking city-centre Jugendstil building, drills into Hämeenlinna's history across two floors, while **Palander's House** is a fabulous example of a 19th-century bourgeois home and the accompanying lifestyle in Hämeenlinna.

Booking ahead for guided tours is advised – check opening times online, as they change every season.

### INSPIRATIONAL VIEWS

It's said that the Hämeenlinna-born composer Jean Sibelius got his inspiration for one of his masterpieces, *Finlandia*, while admiring the scene from Aulanko's viewing tower. If you pause for a moment and take in the view, you'll appreciate how this could be true.

### CREATING A FINNISH IDENTITY

Jean Sibelius was an integral part of Finland's artistic golden era, which lasted from 1890 to 1910, aiming to create a national identity for a country struggling to rid itself of Russian rule. For more, see page 246.

### GETTING AROUND

Hämeenlinna is located between Helsinki and Tampere, and can be easily reached from both cities by train, bus or car. The bus station is in the city centre, while the railway station is a short walk away. Parking is simple in Hämeenlinna.

# Beyond Hämeenlinna

## Hämeenlinna's surrounds are dotted with artsy finds, from world-class glass-blowing to fun naive art. Take a day and tour around.

Many people know the stern granite statues carrying spherical lamps in their hands that guard Helsinki's Central railway station, and even more will have seen the wavy Aalto vase, adorning many homes since the 1930s. The former are works by the sculptor Emil Wikström, and the latter was designed by the world-renowned architects and designers Aino and Alvar Aalto. Today, Wikström's home and *ateljé* (studio) can be visited near Hämeenlinna in Visavuori, and pioneering items of Finnish glass design can be seen and bought at Iittala Village, where you can also watch glass-blowers at work. Iittala Village's playful naive-art exhibition is another must-visit.

### TOP TIP

In summer, hop aboard a Hopealinja boat, slowly shuttling between Hämeenlinna and Tampere and stopping at Visavuori in between.

ESA RIUTTA/SHUTTERSTOCK ©

**Finnish design glassware**

## Iittala Village

COLOURFULLY NAIVE

Many know Finland for its design, especially glasswork, with much of the fame due to Iittala, 20 minutes' drive outside of Hämeenlinna, which has been making waves in the glassware world since 1881.

After kicking off the business with Swedish designers, Iittala started to produce glass and crystal items designed by Finns during the 1920s and '30s. Then, Aino and Alvar Aalto brought their functionalist style to Iittala, with such items as Aino Aalto glasses and the curvy Aalto vase. Later designers included Tapio Wirkkala, Timo Sarpaneva and Kaj Franck.

Today, you can visit the glass-blowing Iittala factory's viewing platform and witness the magic. Other spots to visit in Iittala Village include **Iittala Design Museum** (open June to August daily except Monday; otherwise open on weekends) and the colourful art at the **Iittala Centre of Naive Art**, creating a welcome contrast to Iittala's controlled lines.

There are many boutique shops in the area, including Iittala's classics in the **Iittala outlet**, ceramics at **Keramiikkapaja Anubis**, and bow ties made of leather recycled from old boxing gloves at **Naskali Leather**.

## Visavuori

SCULPTURES AND COMIC STRIPS

Visavuori in Valkeakoski, 25 minutes' drive from Hämeenlinna, was the art nouveau domicile of the sculptor Emil Wikström (1864–1942) and his grandson, the beloved Finnish cartoonist Kari Suomalainen (1920–99).

The national-romantic-style house was designed by Wikström himself, with art nouveau details inside. The house is also a prime example of Karelian building design.

In Wikström's old studio, you can see almost 100 of his works on display. Downstairs, there is a summer cafe. Suomalainen was a prolific political cartoonist, and his strips are exhibited in Kari's Pavilion.

From June to August, Visavuori is open daily; otherwise from Wednesday to Sunday.

### BEST EXPERIENCES NEAR HÄMEENLINNA

**Hattula Church**
A Gothic church from the late 15th century, famed for its impressive al secco wall paintings; open April to mid-August.

**Evo Hiking area**
A 40-minute drive northeast from Hämeenlinna, Evo makes a great family trip with fishing possibilities (see for permits luontoon.fi)

**Torronsuo National Park**
If you're exploring by car and interested in marshlands, head to Torronsuo, 60km southwest of Hämeenlinna.

### GETTING AROUND

Iittala Village and Visavuori can both be reached from Hämeenlinna by car, bus or train in about half an hour.

# KOLI NATIONAL PARK

Located on the shores of Pielinen, Finland's fourth-larges Koli National Park is the heart of the North Karelia re,

Koli's highest peak, 347m Ukko-Koli, is southern Finland's highest point. From the bare summit, the views sweep over forest-covered slopes to the shores of Pielinen, which is dotted with small islands. This is also Finland's best-known landscape, immortalised in Eero Järnefelt's paintings and inspiring his travel companion, the composer Jean Sibelius.

But you don't need to have an art degree to appreciate Koli's beauty. In winter, the national park is the southernmost point in Finland to witness the magic of crown snow-load, which transforms the foliage into a magical sight, heroically carrying the weight of snow. Winter is also the time to tackle Koli's slopes on skis or snowshoes.

The region's towns are sparsely scattered and offer few accommodation, restaurant and sightseeing options. Here, everything is about nature.

### TOP TIP

Koli Nature Centre Ukko is accessible by a funicular and there's car parking nearby. The centre has a little museum and maps of the area. Many walks begin from the centre, while others start from Koli village and Koli harbour. Longer trails also set out from nearby towns such as Lieksa.

HIVAKA/SHUTTERSTOCK ©

**Koli National Park**

## Hiking in Koli National Park

SOUTHERN FINLAND'S HIGHEST POINTS

Koli National Park has more than 60km of marked trails, ranging from an accessible (slightly tricky) 800m route to a multiday 60km hike.

A classic is the 1.4km **Huippujen kierros** trail, taking in Koli's most famous peaks, **Ukko-Koli**, **Akka-Koli** and **Paha-Koli**. Here, the mountaintops are bare, pale grey and white quartzite, and the views sweep over lake Pielinen and its islands. Twisted and barren tree trunks mix with lush pine trees.

Another good route along the peaks is the 7.5km **Mäkrän kierros**, which heads to pristine forests and glades and has a spot for a campfire. This route has some steep climbs but the views from 313m Mäkrä hill, rising 219m above Pielinen, make the effort worthwhile.

The longest hike winds around **Herajärvi** lake, covering 60km and taking four days. It can also be cut almost in half, making it a three-day, 35km walk. The Herajärvi route isn't open in winter, but the shorter and more popular routes have tramped trails, left behind by a stream of other hikers.

### BEST WINTER EXPERIENCES IN KOLI NATIONAL PARK

**Snowshoeing**
Tackle Koli's snowy slopes on snowshoes and admire the trees carrying the weight of snow on a self-guided or guided tour, organised by many hotels and companies, such as Koli Active, in the area.

**Dogsled ride**
Whizz across the frozen Pielinen lake pulled by frisky huskies, bred by many local tour operators.

**Downhill skiing**
Koli has a downhill-skiing centre with four lifts and seven slopes of various difficulties.

### WHERE TO STAY AROUND KOLI NATIONAL PARK

**Kolin Ryynänen**
Rustic rooms in a barn, with shared kitchen and bathroom; sheets and breakfast cost extra. €

**Break Sokos Hotel Koli**
Atop Koli peak, with some rooms having views over Koli's slopes and the lake – the hotel spa has the same views. €€€

**Vanhan koulun majatalo**
Rooms with shared bathroom and kitchen, and two en-suite apartments with kitchenettes in an old school in the forest. €

# Beyond Koli

Koli surroundings offer some of Finland's best wilderness scenery. Grab the binoculars and go wildlife spotting.

Home to Finland's highest number of bears and wolves, remote Kuhmo has also been at the crossroads of many of the country's historic events, mainly due to its proximity to the Russian border, with Swedish and Russian monarchs fighting over their possessions. In 1809, when Finland became part of Russia as a Grand Duchy, Kuhmo's businesses started to thrive. In the winter of 1940, Kuhmo witnessed heavy fighting during the Winter War against Russia, and the Talvisotamuseo, dedicated to this war, is now one of the town's main sights. Kuhmo is home to less than 10,000 inhabitants, and instead of bustling city life, it's a place that's all about nature.

### TOP TIP

Combine wilderness and culture by visiting Kuhmo in July, when the city bursts into life for two weeks as it hosts an acclaimed chamber music festival, attended by thousands of visitors.

**Young wolves in Kuhmo**

LEFT: RISTO RAUNIO/SHUTTERSTOCK ©; TOP RIGHT: DOMINIK EHRHARDT/SHUTTERSTOCK ©

Wolverine in the forest

## Wildlife in Kuhmo

BEARS AND WOLVERINES

Around Kuhmo, the visitor experience is all about wildlife. It's an area dubbed as 'Wild Taiga', in reference to the landscape's untouched feel and the evergreen coniferous forest, which stretches all the way to Asia. Kuhmo's wilderness is a natural habitat for many of Finland's biggest carnivores, such as bears, wolves and wolverines. There are plenty of wildlife huts and tour operators in the area. Many visitors stay overnight in rented hides and cottages. With the sun barely setting around June and July in these latitudes, it makes an ideal setting for wildlife observation and photography. The season for bear spotting begins around April and lasts till September or October, when the animals start getting ready for hibernation. Wolverines and wolves move around the area throughout the year.

**Bear Centre** is a large viewing cottage with beds and bathrooms as well as small hides dotted around marshland that's roamed by bears and wolverines, while **Wild Taiga** has huts for wildlife watching in Kuhmo and nearby Suomussalmi. **Wildlife Safaris** offers versatile services and tours that range from wildlife watching in hides, to aurora borealis (Northern Lights) hunts, to snowshoeing, with the possibility of finishing with a sauna or smoke sauna.

### BEST EATS IN KUHMO

**Kaesan Kotileipomo** This bakery-cum-foodie souvenir shop makes for a refreshing coffee break, with local delicacies such as *rönttönen* (rye-crusted open pie with potato and lingonberry filling). €

**Neljä Kaesaa** Buffet lunch and bistro with baked goods from sister establishment Kaesan Kotileipomo. €

**Kahvila retro** A basic, Finnish-style cafe with sweet treats and savoury snacks as well as Italian ice cream. €

### GETTING AROUND

Kuhmo is pretty much surrounded by wilderness and you'll need a car to move around. Helsinki is 600km away, and the nearest airport is in Kajaani, 100km west of Kuhmo.

Kajaani also has railway and bus stations, with buses running to Kuhmo multiple times a day. Buses between Kuhmo and Nurmes, 80km to its south, run on Fridays and Sundays.

## THE MAIN AREAS

**RAUMA**
Charming old wooden town.
**p162**

**VAASA**
Buzzing university city and port. **p170**

# WEST COAST & NORTHERN OSTROBOTHNIA

## HARBOURS, BOATS, ISLANDS & CITIES

Explore historic and contemporary maritime towns, intriguing archipelagos and lake-strewn inland forests.

Finland's coast on the Gulf of Bothnia is a delightful sequence of small towns, fishing harbours, a few larger ports, rocky and sandy shorelines, and many thousands of low-lying islands. Quaint old wooden towns such as Rauma and Kristinestad contrast with the 21st-century buzz of the lively main cities, Oulu and Vaasa. Swedish influence from past centuries remains strong, with a number of towns still having majority Swedish-speaking populations. The islands are a magnet for anyone who likes boats and/or exploring. Assorted boat services carry people out to some of the islands, and Finland's longest bridge crosses to the Kvarken Archipelago near Vaasa. This is a coastline with a profile that has been continuously changing for millennia, thanks to the phenomenon of post-glacial uplift, which in some places has pushed the sea back as much as 100km since the last Ice Age.

The city of Oulu, near the northern end of the coast, is capital of the region of Northern Ostrobothnia (Pohjois-Pohjanmaa), which stretches across Finland to the Russian border. Its eastern forests and hills are home to some remote national parks, chief among them Oulanka, the rivers and canyons of which form some of the country's most dramatic scenery. They're a perfect canvas for anyone who likes walking, canoeing, rafting or simply being immersed in pristine nature.

LEFT: ESA RIUTTA/SHUTTERSTOCK ©; RIGHT: MAY_LANA/SHUTTERSTOCK ©

**OULU**
Growing cultural capital and tech hub. p175

**OULANKA NATIONAL PARK**
Dense forests and raging rivers. p179

# Find Your Way

The 600km of coast from Uusikaupunki to Oulu is home to many attractive towns and thousands of islands. Across Finland's central 'waist' lie remote forests, canyons, lakes and rivers. From four hubs you can explore this diverse slice of Finland.



## Oulu, p175

The likeable 'capital of the north', spread over several islands, with plenty of good food, drink, music, art and quirky humour.

## Oulanka National Park, p179

Forests, canyons, waterfalls, rapids, hanging bridges – Oulanka is one of Finland's top destinations for hikers, canoeists, rafters and all nature lovers.

LEFT: HIVAKA/SHUTTERSTOCK ©

**Vaasa, p170**
A bright, modern seaside city from which you can easily journey out to some remarkable islands and quaint historic towns.

**Rauma, p162**
This charming, World Heritage–listed old wooden town is very much alive with a multitude of good eateries, bars and shops.

## CAR & MOTORCYCLE

Your own wheels are by far the most convenient way of getting around the region. There are car rentals at all four airports (Pori, Vaasa, Oulu and Kuusamo) and in several town centres.

## TRAIN

Railways reach Pori, Vaasa, Seinäjoki, Jakobstad and Oulu, but for intra-regional travel they are only really useful on the northern section between Seinäjoki and Oulu, plus the Vaasa–Oulu route, which is better served by trains than buses.

## BUS

Buses are the only public transport between many towns – frequent on some routes, scarce on others. They also helpfully reach some very out-of-the-way places, such as Hailuoto Island near Oulu and the Karhunkierros trailheads around Oulanka National Park.

# Plan Your Time

As you travel this coast, enjoy the varied towns but be sure to get out to some of the islands. Check opening dates for anywhere you want to visit: some places have extremely short seasons.

IGOR GROCHEV/SHUTTERSTOCK ©

Rauma (p162)

## Just a Couple of Days

- Head to **Rauma** (p162), which arguably best preserves the coast's unique flavour. Start on the old wooden town's market square, **kauppatori** (p163), and have a wander, visiting landmarks such as the **old town hall** (p164), with a museum and crafts shop within, and the **Marela** (p164) house museum. Lunch at bistro **Sydvest** (p34), and visit **Pits-Priia** (p164) with its delightful lacework.

- On your second day, take a trip to **Kuuskajaskari** (p166) island, exploring its forests and old fortifications on the walking trail and enjoying lunch in the cafe in the old barracks.

## Seasonal Highlights

Almost throughout the region, the ideal months to visit are June to September. The weather is at its best, daylight is long and almost everything is open.

### JANUARY

A good month for winter sports at Ruka: New Year crowds have gone and the **Polar Night Light Festival** brightens everything.

### MARCH

Mainly classical and jazz concerts welcome the spring in the two-week **Oulu Music Festival**.

### JUNE

Schools break up and the summer season starts; the nights are bright, and the eastern lakes and trails have unfrozen.

FROM LEFT: BORISENKOFF, NATALIA FLEJSZAR, POPOVA VALERIYA/SHUTTERSTOCK ©

## A Few Days to Travel Around

- Spend a day and night in old **Rauma** (p162) then head out to the strange Stone Age mounds of **Sammallahdenmäki** (p168) and down to **Uusikaupunki** (p167) to check out the **Bonk-museo** (p167) and a couple of restaurants/bars.

- The following day, cycle the **Velhovesi Ring** (p167).

- Day four: travel up to Vaasa, breaking the journey at charming old **Kristinestad** (p174). Spend a day exploring **Vaasa** (p170) and its lively restaurants and bars, then venture out to the **Kvarken Archipelago** (p173) and see post-glacial uplift in action on the **Bodvattnet nature trail** (p173). Round things off with a tasty meal overlooking the waters at **Restaurant Arken** (p174).

## Exploring in Greater Depth

- Do everything in the previous itinerary then continue north to the interesting old-meets-modern town of **Jakobstad** (p174), the nearby **Nanoq (**p174**)** Arctic museum and pretty **Fäboda** (p174) beach.

- Head on to laid-back **Oulu** (p175) to enjoy a day of city life in northern Finland's biggest metropolis.

- Now cross the country to **Posio** (p185) and call in at the home base of leading Finnish interior style house Pentik. Continue to the forests of **Oulanka National Park** (p179) near the Russian border for a couple of days' hiking and maybe a day of gentle canoeing or thrilling white-water rafting.

**JULY**
Finland's peak holiday month: coastal towns fill, and festivals like **Pori Jazz** and **Rauma Lace Week** are celebrated.

**AUGUST**
Schools go back in the second week, so it's a more tranquil time to travel, still with decent weather.

**SEPTEMBER**
Best month for Oulanka and Hossa national parks: autumn colours, few insects, reasonable weather.

**NOVEMBER**
Oulu's **Lumo Light Festival** fends off the darkness; ski jumpers and cross-country skiers flock to **Ruka Nordic** weekend; you might see the aurora borealis.

FROM LEFT: TELIA, ANN-BRITT, ADAMIKARL, RAWPIXEL.COM/SHUTTERSTOCK ©

# RAUMA

Rauma preserves the imprint of the past like few other places in Finland. Its charming old quarter, Vanha Rauma, with some 600 old houses, has World Heritage listing as an outstanding example of an old Nordic wooden city.

Though Rauma got its charter in 1442, it burned down twice in the 17th century, so the old town mostly dates from the 18th and 19th centuries, when Rauma became one of Finland's biggest trading ports. It remains intimately linked with the sea. The making of fine lace also plays a big part in Rauma's story: in the early 19th century, when this cottage industry peaked, almost all Rauma women engaged in it.

Vanha Rauma remains the lively hub of town life, with over 100 shops, restaurants and cafes. The largest and most atmospheric of a few old wooden towns on Finland's west coast, it's also a base for some excellent mainland and island excursions.

## TOP TIP

Rauma's very professional tourist information service (visitrauma.fi) is normally based just outside the old town at Valtakatu 2, but from June to August it opens an office in the Vanha Raatihuone (old town hall) in the heart of old Rauma. Year-round, local guides offer a large variety of tourism-office-recommended experiences and tours: book at doerz .com/rauma.

JIKALZ/SHUTTERSTOCK ©

**Pyhän Ristin kirkko (p164)**

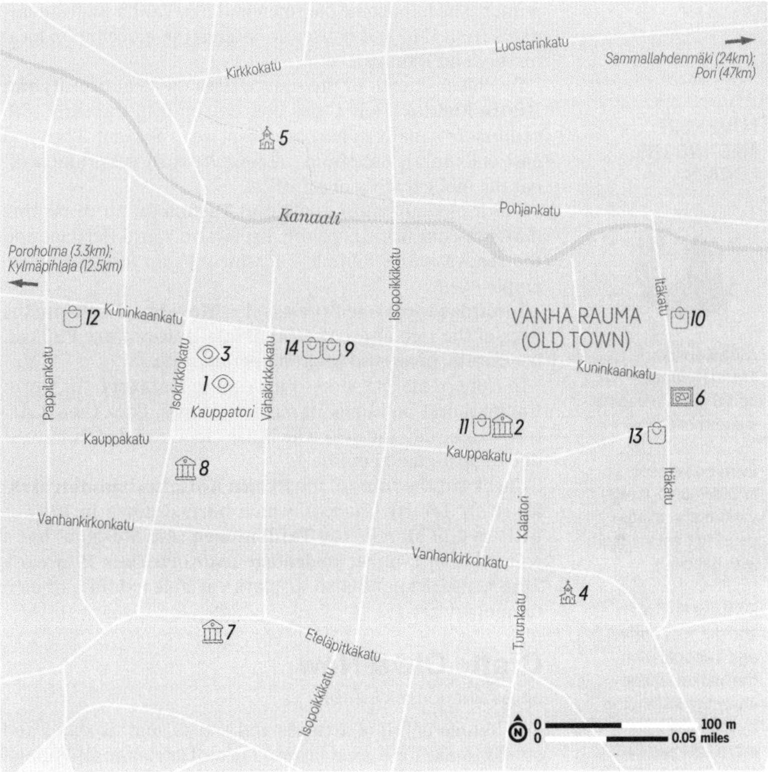

**SIGHTS**
1 Kauppatori
2 Marela
3 Old Rauma
4 Pyhän Kolminaisuuden kirkko
5 Pyhän Ristin Kirkko
6 Taidemuseo
7 Tammela
8 Vanha Raatihuone

**SHOPPING**
9 Ceramic Art Kirsi Backman
10 Heikklän Taidepiha
11 Kistupuad
12 Kultaseppä Laiho
13 Pits-Priia
14 TaruLiina

## Exploring Old Rauma

A LIVING PAST

It's a pleasure to pass a few hours wandering Vanha Rauma's cobbled streets lined with single-storey wooden houses, browsing the shops, dropping into cafes and visiting some of the main landmarks. The central market square, **Kauppatori**, is a lively scene with its produce and flower stalls, and the coffee stands that make it a gathering place even in

### WHERE TO STAY IN RAUMA

**Hotelli Vanha Rauma**
The only old town hotel, with comfortable, tasteful rooms and a top restaurant. €€€

**Hotelli Cityhovi**
Small, comfy hotel in greys, whites and silver, just outside the old town. €€

**Poroholman Lomakeskus**
Large RV/camping park on a picturesque bay with two-bedroom chalets and loads of facilities. €€

winter. The handsome old town hall, the Vanha Raatihuone, dates from 1776 and houses an interesting museum on local history and Rauma lace.

Two blocks north of the square rises the beautiful **Pyhän Ristin kirkko** (Holy Cross Church), built in the early 16th century, originally as part of a Franciscan convent. The vivid east-end murals date from the church's early years and present the biblical story of salvation.

South of Kauppatori you'll find **Tammela**, an intriguing museum-cum-workshop with displays on World Heritage and the renovation of Rauma – of which it's an fascinating example itself.

Towards the old town's east end is **Marela** – a look into the lives of the rich and powerful of late-19th-century Finland, beautifully preserved in grand period style.

In front of Marela spreads the square **Kalatori**, the site of Rauma's first buildings in medieval times. Back then Kalatori was beside the sea, which has since receded 2km west due to post-glacial uplift.

Check out the ruins of the **Pyhän Kolminaisuuden kirkko** (Holy Trinity Church), which burned down in 1640. A little east of Marela, the **Taidemuseo** (Art Museum) has a collection of Finnish golden age paintings (late 19th/early 20th centuries) and also displays variable exhibits of contemporary art.

### I LIVE HERE: MEETING THE LOCALS

**Aino Koivukari**, World Heritage coordinator in Rauma, shares her tips.

Everybody meets up in Old Rauma. It offers various charming cafes to treat yourself with delicious traditional pastries. Do it like the locals and get your coffee and a doughnut at the market square – enjoy them standing by the kiosk in the morning. *Pystökaffe* (standing-up coffee) is a traditional way to start the day.

The residents of Old Rauma are friendly: ask permission to have a peek into courtyards behind closed gates. The private courtyards are open for visitors also during the Lace Week festival in July. You'll get an authentic insight into people's daily lives!

## Crafts Old & New

BROWSING RAUMA'S SHOPS

Old Rauma is full of artisans and artists, and its shops and studios make for a great browse. As well as classic all-Finland design houses such as Pentik and Marimekko, you'll find numerous small-scale local enterprises.

**Kistupuad** in the old town hall has a good selection of local crafts, including lace items. The street Kuninkaankatu is a top hunting ground. At No 13, jeweller **Kultaseppä Laiho** makes some wonderfully intricate silver items based on Rauma lace designs. At No 21 is **Ceramic Art Kirsi Backman** – highly original works of pottery art. TaruLiina, two doors along (also No 21), has an eclectic collection, including some silver knives and key rings recycled from old spoons.

Off the east end of Kuninkaankatu, you'll find the **Heikklän taidepiha** (Heikklä art yard; Itäkatu 4) with the studios or galleries of four different artists, and Pits-Priia (Kauppakatu 29) with some exquisite lace pieces – and you can usually see a lacemaker at work here. For further ideas, check the Shopping and Art pages on visitrauma.fi.

### GETTING AROUND

Old Rauma is easily negotiated on foot. There's very limited parking in the old town, but plenty of spaces just outside it.

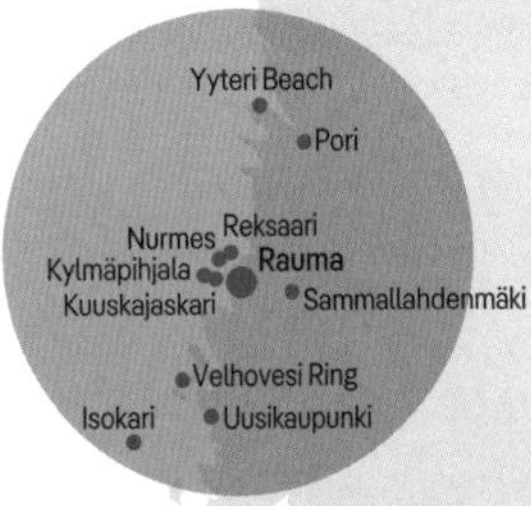

# Beyond Rauma

Yyteri Beach
Pori
Nurmes
Reksaari
Kylmäpihjala
Rauma
Kuuskajaskari
Sammallahdenmäki
Velhovesi Ring
Isokari
Uusikaupunki

## Islands, lighthouses, beaches, seafaring towns and dense forests wait to be discovered.

The labyrinthine archipelagos of Finland's southwest coast beg to be explored: hundreds of low-lying islands large and small, some little more than bare rocks, others with forests, beaches, lighthouses, accommodation and restaurants. You can reach them by summer water buses, on boat taxis, by paddling your own canoe or kayak or, in the Velhovesi Ring islands, by cycling or driving across small dams and bridges. The Bothnian Sea National Park groups dozens of separate tracts of sea and land strung along 160km of this coast. On land, the laid-back port of Uusikaupunki and the larger city of Pori, with the superb sweep of Yyteri beach nearby, are within an hour's drive of Rauma.

### TOP TIP

June to August is the choice period to visit this region. Outside those months, many tourism-related operations slash their opening times, or close completely.

**Yyteri beach (p168)**

O.KEMPPAINEN/SHUTTERSTOCK ©

**PORI JAZZ**

The city of Pori bursts into life in the first half of July for Pori Jazz, one of Finland's biggest festivals of any kind. Well over 300,000 people have attended some recent editions. The focus of the musical action is leafy Kirjurinluoto park, where dozens of free concerts happen during the first six days of the nine-day festival. The final three days see the big-name acts playing in a ticketed area also in Kirjurinluoto. Finnish jazz gets a big piece of the action, but the line-ups are broad. Megastars such as Elton John, Miles Davis and Björk have played Pori in the past, and recent editions have hosted the likes of Nick Cave, Brian Wilson, Toto and Emeli Sandé.

VVORONOV/SHUTTERSTOCK ©

Uusikaupunki harbour

## Discover Rauma's Archipelago

SAILING, ROWING, PADDLING AND WALKING

In summer it's a fun day out using the water buses from Rauma's Suvitien Merijakamo harbour to the islands of **Kuuskajaskari**, about 6km offshore, and **Kylmäpihjala** (10km).

The once fortified, largely forested Kuuskajaskari still houses four large guns, two watchtowers and several trenches; you can explore via a 3km walking circuit.

Smaller, barer Kylmäpihjala is home to a 36m-high lighthouse and is interesting for naturalists, with 28 nesting bird species. Each island has a restaurant and/or cafe, and assorted accommodation. From mid-June to around 20 August the water-bus timetables (raumansaaristokuljetus.fi) enable you to visit both islands in one day trip.

For a more back-to-nature experience, head to larger, thickly forested **Reksaari**, northwest of Rauma, which you can reach by a boat taxi service such as Eräheppu or a combination of bicycle/car, rowing boat (booked through Rauma tourist

### SLEEPING ON RAUMA'S ISLANDS

**Kylmäpihlaja**
There are 15 comfy, if compact, rooms in the island lighthouse itself. **€€**

**Kuuskajaskari**
Has 10 cottages for four to six people and army-style accommodation in old barracks. **€€**

**Reksaari**
A small, basic cottage at Rohela is rentable through Rauma tourist office (bring food, drinking water and bedding). **€**

office) and walking. Once on the island, there's 6km of walking trails to explore and a summer cafe at Karttu.

Or explore the inshore islands of the Rauma archipelago under your own steam in a canoe or kayak. It takes most people one to two hours to reach the large island of **Nurmes**, about 9km northwest of Rauma, for example. Firms such as Erähep-pu and Luontotaival rent equipment and do guided trips.

## Uusikaupunki: The Scent of the Sea

MARITIME FLAVOUR AND QUIRKY MUSEUMS

The town of Uusikaupunki, about an hour by car or bus south of Rauma, has almost as many old wooden houses as Rauma but the feel here is more maritime than olde-worlde. *Kaupunki* is Finnish for city and *uusi* means new, which Uki (as locals call it) was in 1617.

With a buzzing summer yachtie scene, a rich seafaring history, a line of inviting waterfront restaurant-bars on the Kaupunginlahti inlet, and some unusual museums, it's a fun place to wander for a few hours and maybe stay over.

Don't miss the **Bonk-museo**, a wonderful parody of an industrial museum that relates the glorious growth of Bonk Business Inc from a humble anchovy-fishing family to a mighty 'multiglobal enterprise' and world leader in 'fully defunctioned machinery'.

The **Wahlbergin museotalo** showcases the lifestyle of Uusikaupunki's richest family around 120 years ago and tells of the town's 19th-century shipbuilding and seafaring heyday. Admirers of beautiful cars should head out to the **Automuseo** on the east side of town, which lovingly displays more than 100 brilliantly gleaming 20th-century motors.

## Islands by Bike & Boat

TRIPS OUT FROM UUSIKAUPUNKI

Northwest of Uusikaupunki, an arc of islands around the Ruotsinvesi and Velhovesi bays is joined by short dams and bridges to create a circuit of country roads, the **Velhovesi Ring** (Velhoveden kierros in Finnish), that makes a great trip out for cyclists or drivers.

Pick up the map-brochure in town. The basic loop, from **Santtioranta Camping** on the edge of Uusikaupunki, is 55km. It runs through plenty of forest, with bays, inlets and a few beaches and scattered settlements opening up at regular intervals. The route is marked by little brown signs with an orange circle for the main circuit, and a green circle for detours.

### I LIVE HERE: HISTORY COMES ALIVE IN UUSIKAUPUNKI

**Irmeli Laiho-Andersson** is tourism designer at Uusikaupunki's tourist office.

The perfect place to start a visit to this seaside town is by the Kaupunginlahti inlet, where you can learn about our maritime history from info panels and ships' names set into the paving. The 19th-century storehouses along the south side of the inlet were originally used for storing salt, but now they house excellent restaurants.

According to the Finnish Heritage Agency, the large wooden-house district in Uusikaupunki is one of the best-preserved Empire-style wooden towns in Finland. Every second year, during the first weekend of September, dozens of idyllic wooden homes are opened to visitors in the Old Houses of Uusikaupunki event.

### WHERE TO STAY IN UUSIKAUPUNKI

**Hotelli Aittaranta**
Good, newish, medium-size hotel overlooking the inner harbour with classically Nordic clean-lined rooms. €€

**Hotelli Aquarius**
Large sea-facing holiday hotel with bowling, gym, nightclub and saunas. €€

**Gasthaus Pooki**
Four tastefully old-fashioned rooms upstairs from one of the town's best restaurants. Centrally located. €€

One particularly good detour is to the pretty village of **Pyhämaa**, with a cafe/restaurant, shop, guesthouse and two old churches side by side – the smaller, wooden one is the 17th-century **Uhri Kirkko** (Sacrifice Church), the entire interior of which is covered in colourful biblical-theme murals. From Pyhämaa a further scenic detour continues 8km to the remote fishing harbour of **Pitkäluoto**. You can rent bikes and e-bikes at Santtioranta Camping or Uusikaupunki's tourist office.

From late May to mid-September, **MS Kerttu** does day trips from Uusikaupunki to beautiful **Isokari island** (isokari.fi), 22km southwest of Uusikaupunki. Within the rocky shoreline of the 2.4km-long island are forests, meadows, a lake, a 19th-century lighthouse, a 2.2km nature trail and a restaurant.

The *Kerttu* also offers seal safaris, birdwatching trips and sightseeing cruises.

**BEST YYTERI ACTIVITIES**

**SUPing and Windsurfing**
Rent a board, or take a class, at Yyteri Surfcenter.

**Walking**
Prominent map boards display the trails: the Lietteiden Reiten, a 4.5km (one way) route from the south end of the main beach, traverses coastal wetlands, mainly on boardwalks, via several birdwatching platforms.

**Cycling**
Rent a fat bike or e-bike at Huikee Retkipiste.

**Adventure in the Trees**
Anyone over six (and 110cm in height) can clamber, swing, zip and jump along 2km of aerial obstacle courses at Huikee Seikkailupuisto adventure park.

## Glorious Beach, Top Museum

CONTRASTS OF PORI AND YYTERI

The city of **Pori** (Swedish: Björneborg), an hour north of Rauma by car or bus, is home to an excellent regional museum, **Satakunnan Museo** (check out the screen animation at the exhibits entrance showing how post-glacial uplift has pushed the sea back over eight millennia), and an expansive riverside park, **Kirjurinluoto**, with lots of diversions for kids.

Pori's grid-plan centre is uninspiring, but a short journey northwest brings you to one of Finland's finest stretches of sand: the broad, 3km sweep of **Yyteri beach**.

Very popular in summer, but with enough space for everyone, Yyteri is backed by dunes and pine forests strung with walking trails and is great for active summer pursuits, from standup paddleboarding (SUPing) to fat biking to trampolining.

Most facilities, and most of the eating options, cluster near the hotel Virkistyshotelli Yyteri, close to the north end of the beach.

## The Bronze Age Tombs of Sammallahdenmäki

ANCIENT MOUNDS IN PRISTINE FOREST

In the forests a half-hour drive east of Rauma stand the 36 mysterious stone burial cairns of Sammallahdenmäki, a remarkable World Heritage–listed group of rock mounds mostly constructed between 1500 and 500 BCE.

**WHERE TO STAY IN PORI & YYTERI**

**Lomakeskus Yyteri Beach**
High-quality wooden cabins and villas in the forest just behind Yyteri beach. **€€€**

**Hostel River**
Friendly and comfy hostel with private rooms and three-person dorms not far from central Pori. **€**

**Virkistyshotelli Yyteri**
Large spa-resort-type hotel with loads of facilities at the north end of Yyteri beach. **€€**

PECOLD/SHUTTERSTOCK ©

Sammallahdenmäki

Walking the paths through the beautiful forest, floored with reindeer lichen, you can almost feel yourself transported back to long-lost epochs.

Even stranger is that when the mounds were built, there was no forest here and they stood on rocky islets just above the sea. Since then the coastline has receded 20km west. The mounds – some impressively large and surprisingly shaped – are spread around an area about 700m long and 200m wide.

There are information panels with maps at the north and south ends of the site, both reachable by vehicle, but signage within is almost non-existent, so a trail map on your phone helps. Allow one to 1½ hours to explore.

## BEST RESTAURANTS IN & AROUND UUSIKAUPUNKI

**Gasthaus Pooki**
Nautically themed town-centre restaurant with very good dishes inventively prepared from local ingredients, and a lovely courtyard. €€

**Bistro Bay**
One of several restaurant-bars with waterfront decks along the inner harbour, with friendly service and straightforward but well-done fare (pizzas, burgers, beef, octopus...); sometimes has live music. €€

**Pyhämaan Pirtti**
Excellent little stop in Pyhämaa village on the Velhovesi Ring, doing buffet lunch with local fish and veggies. €€

**Kirsta**
Another in the town's waterside line-up, with good-value pizzas and burgers. €

## GETTING AROUND

Having your own vehicle certainly makes things easiest. Parking is straightforward everywhere. Otherwise, there are frequent buses between Rauma and Pori (where the bus station, the Matkakeskus, is 1.2km south of the city centre), and six each way (Monday to Friday only) between Rauma and Uusikaupunki. Pori city buses 34, 34M, 34R or 34W, which run about hourly, link the Matkakeskus with the central Kauppatori square and Yyteri (a 50-minute trip).

For Sammallahdenmäki, a taxi round trip should cost €60. In July and most of August, there are guided tours in English from Rauma for €10 per person, including transport: you can book at doerz.com/visitrauma.

# VAASA

The biggest city on the middle west coast, Vaasa (population 68,000) is a likeable and lively place that manages to be at once a port and an educational, summer-holiday and energy-industry hub. It has six universities or sections of universities, about 13,000 students and quite a youthful, cosmopolitan, cultural vibe.

There's plenty of eating, drinking and shopping action around the large market square, Kauppatori, and its nearby streets.

Vaasa was founded by order of Swedish king Karl IX in 1606 – 7km southeast of the current city centre, in a location that, at the time, had a sea harbour (since dried up). Old Vaasa burnt down in 1852 and was rebuilt in its current location.

The city's broad avenues and spacious feel owe a lot to its 19th-century planners' fire-prevention strategies. Around a quarter of Vaasa's population is Swedish-speaking, and there's a daily car-ferry link with Umeå, Sweden, 120km northwest.

### TOP TIP

It's only a little over 1km from Vaasa's picturesque old railway station to its inner-harbour seafront, passing through the bustling city-centre area as you go, so a pair of legs or a rented bicycle are the perfect ways to get around. City buses serve outlying areas. The town's tourism website, visitvaasa.fi, is helpful.

### BEST RESTAURANTS & BARS IN VAASA

**Sweet Vaasa**
City-centre cafe with big healthy salads, great quiches, wraps, cakes and pies. €

**Fröj**
Beautifully composed creations from Nordic ingredients in a bright space; book ahead and consider a tasting menu. €€€

**Strampen**
Wonderful 1860s pavilion with a large terrace overlooking the bay; go for an economical lunch or à la carte dinner. €€

**Faros**
Partly installed in an old sailing ship, Faros is a scenic spot for gourmet burgers, beetroot soup, and reindeer steaks. €€

## Waterfront Wanderings

CULTURE, FOOD AND ACTIVITY

Explore Vaasa's verdant inner-harbour area, with good museums, enticing restaurants and plenty of options for a little exercise.

The **Pohjanmaan museo** (Ostrobothnian Museum) is a great place to learn about the Vaasa area, the city's history and the region's nature and geology, especially the Kvarken Archipelago. The waterfront **Kuntsi Museum of Modern Art** exhibits top-rank modern Finnish and international art. A block inland from the monumental Court of Appeal, the **Tikanoja Art Museum** includes works by Gauguin and Matisse.

Across Vaasanpuistikko is a trio of waterfront restaurants: **Faros**, partly installed in an old sailing ship, and **Hejm** and

POPOVA VALERIYA/SHUTTERSTOCK ©

**Kuntsi Museum of Modern Art**

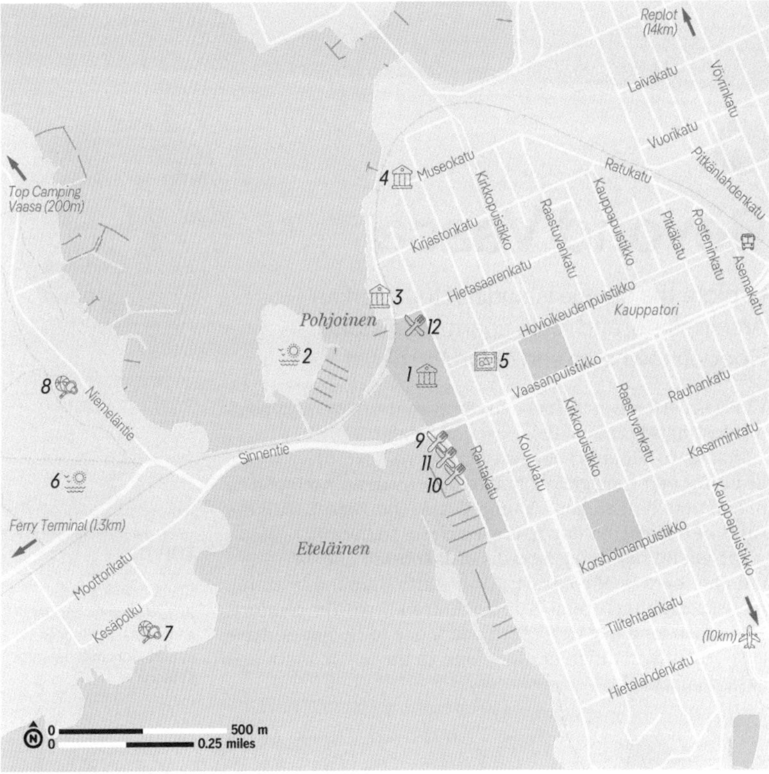

| SIGHTS | | ACTIVITIES, COURSES & TOURS | EATING |
|---|---|---|---|
| **1** Court of Appeal | **4** Pohjanmaan Museo | **7** Tropiclandia | **9** Faros |
| **2** Hietasaari | **5** Tikanoja Art Museum | **8** Zip Adventure Park | **10** Fiskdisken |
| **3** Kuntsi Museum of Modern Art | **6** Vaskiluoto | | **11** Hejm |
| | | | **12** Strampen |

**Fiskdisken** in a contemporary, wave-roofed wooden structure. From here, walkers can stroll along the delightful **Kaupunginselän Reitti**, winding through the shoreline trees for a full 10km (search 'City Bay Trail' on visitvaasa.fi). Alternatively, paddle on the inner harbour in a kayak from **Vaasankajakkivuokraus**, or cross the bridge to little **Hietasaari** island. The bridge continues to bigger **Vaskiluoto** island, where there's more fun at the large water-slide park and spa Tropiclandia and Zip Adventure Park.

## WHERE TO STAY IN VAASA

**Hotel Astor**
A touch of old-fashioned class: rooms are modestly sized but very cosy and the breakfast spread is superb. €€€

**GreenStar Hotel**
This medium-size hotel is carbon neutral and rooms are comfortable; location is a little off-centre. €€

**EC Hostel**
Student-like accommodation in plain but clean, comfy private rooms; shared kitchens. €

# Beyond Vaasa

Explore the unique islands of the Kvarken Archipelago, and roam charming historic wooden towns up and down the coast.



Vaasa is perfectly positioned for forays out to several appealing destinations along the coast and inland.

Thanks to Finland's longest bridge, you can drive to the beautiful and geologically remarkable Kvarken Archipelago in less than half an hour. Vanha-Vaasa (Old Vaasa), with the ruins of the original town, is even closer to the city.

The quaint old wooden towns of Jakobstad and Kristinestad and, by way of contrast, Alvar Aalto's ground-breaking modern architecture at Seinäjoki, are all within comfortable range for a day trip – each one is one to 1½ hours' drive away, though in different directions: to the north, south and east, respectively.

**TOP TIP**

Check opening dates for restaurants, cruises and sights. Some only operate for limited summer seasons.

**Kvarken**

ANN-BRITT/SHUTTERSTOCK ©

NBLX/SHUTTERSTOCK ©

Replot Bridge

## POST-GLACIAL UPLIFT

The land on the Kvarken islands is rebounding (slowly) upward after being squashed under 3km of ice during the last Ice Age, which ended around 10,000 years ago. The rate of uplift is currently nearly 1m per century, which can make a significant difference in a person's lifetime, as Björkö island's Bodvattnet nature trail, for example, bears witness. The whole of Finland's west coast is a case study in post-glacial uplift: islands such as Björkö, and Kylmäpihjala off Rauma, didn't even begin to emerge from the sea till about 1200 years ago, and Vaasa and Rauma themselves were founded just a few centuries ago on coastlines that have since retreated 2km or more. Ten thousand years ago, these towns' locations were 80km or more out to sea. For a fascinating animation, check out landupliftanimation. highcoastkvarken.org.

# A World Heritage Archipelago

THE STILL-RISING KVARKEN ISLANDS

The 5600 islands of the Kvarken Archipelago off Vaasa, together with Sweden's Höga Kusten (High Coast), comprise a Unesco World Heritage Site as the best place in the world to observe post-glacial uplift. The beautiful, low-lying islands, with countless inlets, bays and islets, forests, fields and scattered homesteads, make a lovely day's (or longer) outing from Vaasa.

The 1km-long **Replot Bridge**, 16km northwest of Vaasa, crosses to Replot island, with the **World Heritage Gateway** visitor centre at its far end. The main road continues to Björkö island by causeways. **Svedjehamn**, on Björkö's north coast, is a picturesque little harbour with rust-painted boathouses and a summer cafe over the water. The **Bodvattnet nature trail**, a 4km loop starting here, passes the **Bodback fishing harbour**, abandoned in the 1940s after land uplift rendered it useless, and the **Saltkaret observation tower** overlooking glacially formed ridges known as De Geer moraines, which almost seem to be rising out of the sea as you watch.

## WHERE TO STAY BEYOND VAASA

**Eleonora's Bed & Breakfast**
Charming, recently made-over B&B in an old Kristinestad house. **€€**

**Hotel Epoque**
Jakobstad's old customs house, elegantly modernised into a super-comfy hotel. **€€**

**Merenkurkun Camping**
Well-equipped seaside cabins on a tiny Kvarken island between Replot and Björkö. **€€**

**BEST RESTAURANTS & CAFES BEYOND VAASA**

**After Eight**
Chilled Jakobstad cafe/cultural centre, with a great courtyard-garden. Usually open daytime-only, with top-value lunch. Rents bicycles. €

**Eleonora's Bed & Breakfast**
Perfect cafe with salads, waffles, coffees, lemonade and William Morris wallpaper, in old Kristinestad. €

**Fäboda Kaffestuga**
Fresh fish, gourmet burgers, baked goods and fäb views to Fäboda's sands. €€

**Jungman**
Uplifting Kristinestad estuary panoramas and good lunch buffet, plus à la carte steaks, salmon and pizzas. €€

**Restaurant Arken**
Excellent soups, seafood, burgers and coastal views on the Kvarken island of Replot. €€

In summer you can rent bicycles at the World Heritage Gateway and Svedjehamn. If you'd prefer to see the archipelago by boat, **MS Tiira** (from Vaasa; jannensaluna.com) and **MS Corina** (from the World Heritage Gateway) do short cruises in the inner islands in July and early August; **Kvarkenturer** does charter trips (and, some summers, scheduled sailings) to the little-visited outer islands from Svedjehamn. For plenty more ideas on visiting Kvarken, see vaasa.fi/en/see-and-experience and nationalparks.fi/kvarken.

## Where Vaasa Began

A HANDFUL OF HAUNTING REMAINS

Seven kilometres southeast of central Vaasa, in the modern village of Vanha-Vaasa, it's a chastening experience to wander round the few evocative structures that survived the disastrous 1852 fire that destroyed Old Vaasa, the shell of **Pyhän Marian kirkko** (St Mary's Church), part of its **bell tower**, the **Vanhan Vaasan Museo**, the grand **Court of Appeal** (now a church) and the mound that was **Korsholm Castle**, from which Sweden controlled a large chunk of Finland for several centuries.

## A Tale of Three Towns

TWO OLD, ONE NEW

Of the three outings from Vaasa suggested here, **Kristinestad**, a 1¼-hour drive from Vaasa, is the most charming – an easygoing estuary-side town of just 2700 people, with around 300 mostly 19th-century wooden buildings; visitkristinestad.fi provides a helpful digital tour. Don't miss the beautiful leaning-towered church **Ulrika Eleonora kyrka**, built in 1700. **Jakobstad** (population 21,000) boasts another large old wooden-house quarter, **Skata**, but also an impressive cultural/educational complex, **Campus Allegro**, and the **Pedersöre kyrka** with a magnificently skyscraping spire. Nearby are sandy-bay beaches and forest trails at **Fäboda**, and the fascinating Arctic museum, **Nanoq**.

Larger **Seinäjoki** is of limited interest except for the **Aalto-keskus** (Aalto Centre), a complex designed in great detail in the 1950s and '60s by Finland's pioneering architect and designer, Alvar Aalto. It includes a city hall, theatre and library; its crowning glory is the wonderfully luminous **Lakeuden Risti kirkko** (Cross of the Plains Church). Take the lift up the adjacent tower for a good overview of the whole complex.

**GETTING AROUND**

Your own vehicle is easily easiest, especially on the islands, and essential for Fäboda and Nanoq. On school days there's a morning bus (wasabus.fi) into Vaasa from Björköby on Björkö island (1¼ hours), returning from Vaasa city hall at 2.45pm. Mostly rather slow buses run from Vaasa to Kristinestad, Jakobstad and Seinäjoki on weekdays, but few or none on weekends. For Seinäjoki the train is faster, more frequent and cheaper. City buses 1 and 4 link central Vaasa (Rewell Center, west side) with Vanha-Vaasa.

# OULU

There's something easily likeable about the 'capital of the north', which has a lot to do with its people's unhurried, humorous approach to life.

Much of Oulu's central area is spread over a number of islands in the mouth of the Oulujoki, linked by foot/bike and road bridges, which makes it an enjoyable city to stroll or cycle (a very popular mode of transport here).

With a very strong IT sector (Nokia is the biggest private employer, and there are many small start-ups), this is a fast-growing but clean city, now home to about 210,000 people. It has plenty of inviting restaurants, cafes and bars, and a creative vibe, with music and art year-round.

Oulu will be a European Capital of Culture in 2026. It considers itself the metal (music) capital of Finland, but one of its most renowned events is absolutely non-musical, and aptly sums up Ouluans' offbeat humour: the Air Guitar World Championships every August.

### TOP TIP

Oulu's train and bus stations are conveniently placed on the city centre's eastern edge, 1.5km from the waterfront market square, Kauppatori. The airport is 14km southwest, linked to the centre by buses 8 and 9. Bus 15 links Nallikari beach with the centre (Kaupungintalo stop).

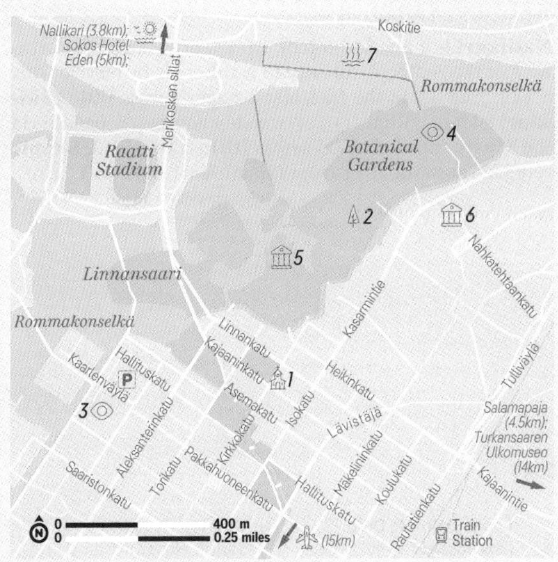


**SIGHTS**
1 Cathedral
2 Hupisaaret
3 Kauppatori
4 Merikosken Kalatie
5 Pohjois Pohjanmaan Museo
6 Tietomaa

**ACTIVITIES, COURSES & TOURS**
7 Kesän Sauna

**BEST RESTAURANTS & BARS IN OULU**

**Rooster**
Satisfying speciality burgers, plus pita breads and salads, and good-value lunch. Vegetarian/vegan leanings. €

**1881 Uleåborg**
Classy spot with creative French-influenced Finnish fare in an old wooden waterside warehouse off Kauppatori. €€€

**Sokeri-Jussin Kievari**
Wooden tavern overlooking the water on Pikisaari, good for traditional northern salmon or reindeer, or just a beer. €€€

**Kauppuri 5**
Casual spot with delicious handmade burgers and good craft beers. €

**Viinibaari Vox**
Cosy wine bar with numerous vintages by the glass; cheeses and tasty nibbles to accompany.

## Markets, Malls & Parks

TUNING INTO THE CITY

Start exploring Oulu at the large market square, Kauppatori, a lively summer scene with food stalls and pop-up restaurants. In one corner stands a famous city symbol: the **Toripolliisi statue** of a chubby policeman.

The downtown area inland from here is a grid of mainly concrete buildings, worth a short wander to take the city's pulse.

Then you might head north, passing by the impressive domed cathedral, and on to **Hupisaaret park** with its trees, waterways, bridges, summer cafe and the interesting if very large **Pohjois Pohjanmaan museo** (Northern Ostrobothnia Museum), focusing principally on the story of Oulu. Nearby is **Tietomaa**, an outstanding hands-on science museum with changing themed exhibits plus a giant-screen 3D cinema. Take the lift up the adjoining tower for city panoramas.

Back in the park, behind Hotel Lasaretti, find the curious **Merikosken kalatie** (Merikoski Fishway), a 750m channel for migrating fish to bypass the hydroelectric installations on the river.

Fancy some Finnish-style summer relaxation with a difference? Cross the dam here to find the **Kesän Sauna** floating off the river's north bank. This wood-burning sauna is (atypically) unisex, so bring your bathing suit. It operates from about mid-May to the end of September.

## To the Beach

PEDALLING OR PADDLING

**Nallikari** is a fine 500m-long stretch of broad sand northwest of the centre. A fun way to get there is by bicycle – it's a 4km ride using the foot/bike bridges across little **Pikisaari** island, with its quaint wooden houses. Or paddle via the **Mustasalmi** channel across Hietasaari island. **Lappis** rents kayaks and SUPs from Linnansaari near the centre.

**WHERE TO STAY IN OULU**

**Turusen Saha**
Great little guesthouse on Pikisaari island, with welcoming hosts and big home-cooked breakfasts. €€

**Lapland Hotels Oulu**
Luxurious hotel with antlers above the beds in mainly black-and-grey rooms; superb restaurant and pool. €€€

**Hotel Lasaretti**
Stylish 'Nordic art' hotel in peaceful Hupisaaret park; generous breakfast. €€

# Beyond Oulu

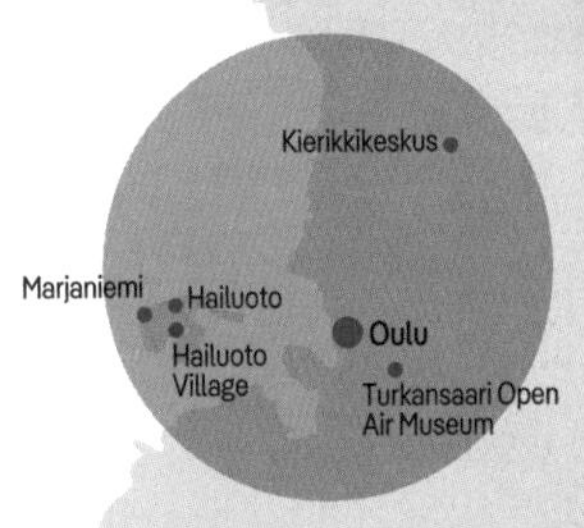


## Take a ferry out to one of Finland's biggest islands, or head inland to relive lifestyles of the past.

The top excursion from Oulu is to Hailuoto, the biggest island in the Bothnian Bay (the northern part of the sea between Finland and Sweden). At 200 sq km, and 30km from end to end, with a population of just 950 people, Hailuoto is like a microcosm of old Finnish rural life with its red-painted houses, wooden barns, occasional windmills, and open fields between dense pine forests. Also endowed with a picturesque coastline and some good sandy beaches, it's a favourite escape for Oulu city dwellers. Up the rivers inland from the city, you can try your hand in summer at Stone Age life at Kierikkikeskus, or walk among centuries-old wooden buildings on river islands at Turkansaari.

### TOP TIP

The official visithailuoto.fi website is in Finnish only, so the best online information source for Hailuoto in English is hailuoto.fi/en/tourism.

Marjaniemi beach (p178)

ABB PHOTO/SHUTTERSTOCK ©

**BEST ACCOMMODATION ON HAILUOTO**

**Arctic Lighthouse Hotel**
Most of the attractive, blond-wood rooms in this hotel in Marjaniemi's old lighthouse-pilot station provide wonderful sea views; the restaurant emphasises local fish. €€

**Hailuodon Majakkapiha**
Comfy old lighthouse-keeper's cottage and similar lodgings at Marjaniemi; also has budget rooms available. €€

**Pöllän Mökkimajoitus**
Well-equipped modern cabins at sandy Pöllänlahti beach in the island's south. €€

**Ailasto**
Restaurant/campground towards the east end of Hailuoto with two simple upstairs rooms and a four-person bunk cabin. Bikes for rent. €

## Island Escape

BEACHES, TRAILS, FERRY, FORESTS, BREWERY

Visiting Hailuoto, 1¼ hours by car from Oulu, is a chance to explore rural lanes by bicycle, walk forest and coastal trails (mostly starting from Marjaniemi), eat fresh local fish, sample excellent craft beers at **Hailuodon Panimo** brewery, enjoy sandy, dune-backed beaches, and watch birds from hides in the island's south.

Hailuoto has two main settlements: **Hailuoto village** in the centre, and the small fishing community of **Marjaniemi** with its landmark lighthouse at the western tip. Getting to Hailuoto by the free ferry from Oulunsalo (Riutunkari) is part of the fun. There are several accommodation options if you fancy a real island escape. Note that vehicle queues for the ferry can be many hours long at the busiest times, such as summer weekends.

## Going Back Centuries or Millennia

HISTORY IN THE OPEN AIR

Two mainly open-air museums in beautiful settings beckon for summer outings inland from Oulu. **Kierikkikeskus** (Kierikki Stone Age Centre), 55km northeast, is set on the site of a large Stone Age village occupied around 6000 years ago. In an impressively large modern log building, you can study finds from the site and watch films about it; outside, examine excavations and walk to a recreated Stone Age village beside the Iijoki to try your hand at archery or making stone tools.

**Turkansaari Open Air Museum** is an assembly of fine old wooden buildings, including a windmill and a still-functioning 17th-century church, on two islands in the Oulujoki, 15km southeast of Oulu. Staff demonstrate tar-making, once a major industry hereabouts.

**GETTING AROUND**

The ferry to Hailuoto (finferries.fi) takes 25 minutes and sails about hourly from Oulunsalo. Bus 59 from Oulu bus station runs to the island (as far as Marjaniemi, 1½ hours) up to three times daily. Buses and island residents have priority on the ferry.

You can rent bikes on Hailuoto at Marjaniemi, Ailosto and from the firm Luotorent.

There's no public transport to Kierikkikeskus; Saaga Travel runs day trips some summer Saturdays. Turkansaari is a nice bike ride from Oulu, or city bus 41 goes to within 1.6km of the museum.

# OULANKA NATIONAL PARK

On the east side of Finland's central 'waist', Oulanka is one of the country's most beloved national parks, in large measure for the rugged scenery of canyons, rapids, waterfalls, cliffs and lakes carved among the dense forests by its two main rivers, the Oulankajoki and Kitkajoki, which meet close to the Russian border.

It's a wonderful place for a walk – most famously along the 82km Karhunkierros (Bear's Ring) trail, which crosses the park from north to south, but also for many scenic shorter routes. But Oulanka is not just for hikers: the rivers are good for canoeing, kayaking and white-water rafting, and in winter there are snowshoe and cross-country skiing trails. Sleeping and eating options in and near the park are limited but there are plenty of both at Ruka, a ski and summer resort a short drive south.

### TOP TIP

A great deal of very good practical and background information on the park, the Karhunkierros and other activities, including route maps and descriptions, is published at nationalparks.fi. The national park's visitor centre, in Oulanka's heart, 13km along a sealed road from Käylä, is also an excellent source of info.

TEEMU TRETJAKOV/SHUTTERSTOCK ©

Oulanka National Park

## ACCOMMODATION IN & NEAR OULANKA NATIONAL PARK

**Basecamp Oulanka**
Well-run, cosy lodge near Juuma: good food, warm welcome, free sauna. €€

**Ajakka**
Guesthouse in a former school in large lakeside grounds 7km west of Juuma: characterful rooms, dynamic host, excellent local-produce meals. €€

**Oulangan Leirintäalue**
National-park summer campground near the visitor centre, with 10 simple four-person cabins, food-and-drink kiosk and plenty of tent and RV space. €

**Juuman Leirintäalue**
Juuma summer campground with sauna-equipped, year-round cottages, cafe, rowing boats and SUPs. €

**Retkietappi**
Three solidly comfy log cabins, plus camping space and a lakeside cafe, at Juuma. €€

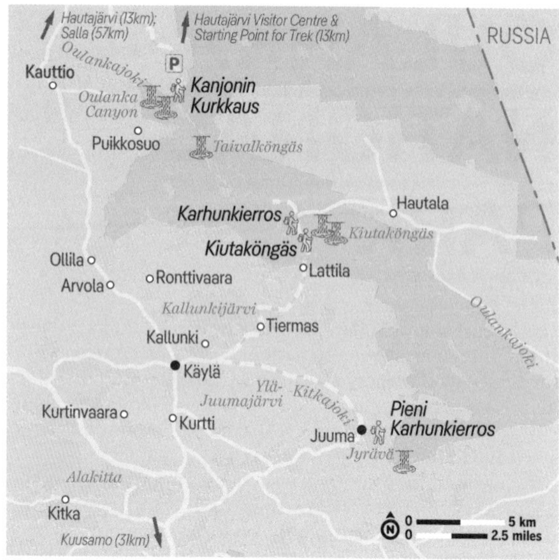


## Day Walks in the Park

OULANKA'S SHORTER GEMS

The highly popular **Pieni Karhunkierros** (Little Bear's Ring) incorporates some of Oulanka's most spectacular scenery in a 12km loop (3½ to four hours) from Juuma village. It's walkable almost year-round (in winter you might need snowshoes). Highlights include the Myllykoski and Aallokkokoski rapids, the thundering Jyrävä falls and two hanging bridges.

Another excellent, much less frequented circuit is the 6km **Kanjonin kurkkaus** (Canyon View) trail in the park's north, with views into the impressive Oulankajoki canyon.

Walkable June to October, it starts at the Savilampi parking area, 10km off Rd 950. A good extension (for a total of about four hours) is to continue 4km to Taivalköngäs rapids, and back.

The dramatic **Kiutaköngäs** falls, where the Oulankajoki funnels frantically between red cliffs, are an easy 1km walk from the park visitor centre. For a longer hike, continue round the Könkään keino forest circuit (8km).

## WHERE TO EAT IN & AROUND OULANKA NATIONAL PARK

**Basecamp Oulanka**
Hearty, well-prepared, local-produce meals in the lodge's bright, wood-beamed dining room. **€€**

**Ravintola Talonpöytä**
The restaurant at the park visitor centre serves up soup lunches, reindeer sausage and veggie burgers. **€**

**Kahvila Retkietappi**
Tempting baked goods at a lakeside cafe at the start of the Pieni Karhunkierros. **€**

## Running the Rivers

RAFTING AND KAYAKING OULANKA'S WATERWAYS

When they're unfrozen (approximately June to some time in October), Oulanka's rivers make for excellent paddling. The main paddle is a 25km canoe and kayak route down the **Oulankajoki** from Mataraniemi (reachable by car, near the park visitor centre) to Jäkälämutka. This usually takes five to seven hours and is fine for beginners, including families with children. Firms such as Ruka-based Kuusamo Safaris will provide all the gear and bring you back to Mataraniemi at the end (€35 to €40 per person).

The rafting river is the **Kitkajoki**, with three sections. The 14km 'family route' extends from Rd 950 near Käylä to Juuma, with seven rapids (class I to III). Then there's the 'wild route' from Juuma to just before Jyrävä falls, with three rapids, including the thrilling class IV Myllykkoski and Aallokkokoski (minimum age: 18). Easiest is the 13km 'scenery route' from just below Jyrävä to Huotinniemi. Firms offering these routes include Basecamp Oulanka and Retkietappi at Juuma, and Ruka-based Stella Polaris and Ruka Safaris. Typical prices (children pay less) are €50 to €75 per route.

## Karhunkierros: The Bear's Ring

FINLAND'S MOST POPULAR TRAIL

Despite its name, the Karhunkierros is a linear route: 82km for the full hike from Hautajärvi, just north of Oulanka National Park, to Ruka, south of the park. It takes most people four to six days. There's plenty of up and down along the way, but it's not mountainous terrain. Dense, silent forests are interspersed with rivers, lakes, waterfalls, rapids, canyons, cliffs and hanging bridges. The trail is normally snow-free from about the beginning of June to mid-October. July is peak mosquito season. September, with autumn colours, is an ideal month.

There are six wilderness huts for sleeping on the main trail, plus a campground near the park visitor centre and accommodation options at Juuma. You'll find cafes or restaurants at the park visitor centre and Juuma.

### WHY I LOVE OULANKA NATIONAL PARK

**John Noble,** writer

I love Finnish nature – the deep, quiet forests, broad mirror-like lakes, swift rivers, clean air, the sense of space. Oulanka abounds in all these and has an extra dimension in the drama of its deep canyons and thundering rapids and waterfalls. So many great hikes here. You can get deep into the forest quickly from the trailheads. The icing on the cake is Basecamp Oulanka, a perfect forest lodge from which to launch explorations.

### WHERE THE WILD THINGS ARE

The **Kuhmo area** (p155), aka Finland's Wild Taiga, is another excellent zone for sighting bears – and, maybe, wolves and wolverines.

### GETTING AROUND

The airport at Kuusamo, 26km south of Ruka, is many people's entry point to the area. It has car-hire desks. An airport bus (pohjolanmatka.fi) runs to and from Ruka (30 minutes) for all arriving and departing flights, with some services extending to/from Hautajärvi (1¼ hours). A taxi from the airport to Ruka/Hautajärvi costs around €65/140.

Sealed or good unsealed roads reach all the national park and Karhunkierros access points. There's a daily morning bus from Ruka to Hautajärvi, and a service also calling at Juuma and the national park visitor centre Monday to Saturday from early June to early August. Check ruka.fi for schedules. A taxi from Ruka costs around €55/90 to Juuma/Hautajärvi.

# Beyond Oulanka National Park

Oulanka National Park
Ruka
Karhu-Kuusamo
Posio
Kujalan Porotila
Lammintupa Winter Village
Erä-Susi
Hossa National Park

A top ski and summer resort and a less visited national park are within reach, plus there's summer bear spotting.

About 20km southwest of Oulanka National Park lies Ruka, one of Finland's most popular ski resorts and a base for other winter activities such as snowmobiling and ice fishing. It's also an active place in summer and a good jumping-off point for Oulanka as well as for cycling, bear spotting and trips to reindeer and husky farms. Around 100km south of Ruka is Hossa National Park, considerably less visited than Oulanka and with an expanse of forest, lakes and rivers with famous rock paintings and good hiking, cycling and canoeing. For something different, why not take a trip to Posio, 65km west of Ruka, the home of one of Finland's leading design houses, Pentik?

**TOP TIP**

The website ruka.fi has comprehensive, detailed information on the Ruka area – a big help in planning, and making bookings, for your visit.

**Hossa National Park (p185)**

HIVAKA/SHUTTERSTOCK ©

TORSTENGRIEGER/SHUTTERSTOCK ©

Ruka ski slopes

## Winter Sport in Ruka

SKI SLOPES AND PLENTY MORE

With over 200 days of skiing a year on 39 varied slopes, and a lively après-ski scene, carbon-neutral Ruka, 20 minutes' drive from Oulanka, is among Finland's top ski destinations.

The resort divides into Ruka Village (Rukan Kylä) and Ruka Valley (Rukan Laakso), with the slopes on Rukatunturi hill between the two. Only six slopes are black-rated but the 600m **FIS** is a worthy challenge for advanced skiers.

Also at Ruka are an outstanding snow park (**Ruka Park**), the **Rosa & Rudolf Family Park** for beginners, and 88km of cross-country trails. **PisteVuokraamo**, in Ruka Village and Ruka Valley, is a one-stop shop for ski passes, equipment rental and ski school bookings; you can also book everything at ruka.fi.

There's plenty more winter diversion beyond the ski slopes. Ride a snowmobile through the forests (if you have experience you can rent one; otherwise join a guided trip). Visit a husky farm such as the experienced **Erä-Susi** (8km southeast of Ruka) to drive a husky team across snowy landscapes; or

### I LIVE HERE: A PERFECT DAY ON RUKA'S SLOPES

**Tuomas Lipasti** is a keen snowboarder based in Ruka.

In midwinter the days are short, so I suggest starting early by getting the first lift up to ride some fresh groomers (or, if you are lucky, some powder snow). My favourite runs for carving are the **front slopes** and **Kelo**, which are wide, steep and usually in a great condition. I would also recommend checking out the **Ruka Park** – there's something for everyone there. To watch the sunset, take a little hike over to **Juhannuskallio** for a beautiful view. For après-ski, I recommend trying **Hanki Baari**, a cosy little restaurant in the heart of Ruka.

### WHERE TO STAY IN RUKA

**Iisakki Village**
Charming recreation of an old Karelian village with cosy rooms on a lakeside 7km southeast of Ruka Village. €€

**Arctic Zone Hotel**
Well-kept, reasonably priced, sparsely decorated rooms in the heart of Ruka Village. €€

**Ski-Inn RukaValley**
Good contemporary-styled rooms and apartments near the lifts in Ruka Valley; has sister premises in Ruka Village. €€€

## RUKA ACTIVITY OPERATORS

**Tailored Adventures Rukapalvelu**
A host of summer and winter activities, from snowmobiling and snowshoeing to fishing and river floating; convenient office in Ruka Village.

**Kuusamo Safaris**
Specialist in snowmobile trips and summer canoeing.

**Ruka Bikes**
Friendly outfit renting high-quality electric mountain bikes.

**Ruka Safaris**
Has a full programme, including SUPing on a local lake and winter husky and reindeer activities.

**Stella Polaris**
Snowmobile rentals in winter, white-water rafting in summer.

a reindeer farm such as **Kujalan Porotila** (13km south on the Kuusamo road), a generations-old operation well set up for tourism, from one-hour farm visits to sleigh rides, full-day experiences and even reindeer yoga!

**Lammintupa Winter Village**, 9km east of Ruka, is popular for both reindeer and husky sledding, plus snowmobiling for kids. Or go snowshoeing or fat biking (several trails are open in winter), or join a night-time safari to view the aurora borealis (Northern Lights). Several well-established operators offer these experiences. You can combine more than one of them on one trip by, for example, snowmobiling to a husky farm or snowshoeing in search of the aurora.

## Ruka Summer Fun

MOUNTAIN BIKING, TOBOGGANING, REINDEER

In the summer season (roughly mid-June to mid-September), **Ruka Bike Park** is in full swing with its mix of downhill tracks from the top of ski lifts and up-and-down cross-country trails.

There's a further 70km of mountain-bike routes winding over the hills and surrounding country.

Several bike rental outlets are in town. Or speed down the 1km-long **summer toboggan track**, or glide over Rukatunturi in the **Village2Valley gondola**.

Reindeer and husky farms often have summer programmes, too: you'll be walking with the animals instead of being pulled over the snow.

## There's a Bear in There

SIGHTING FINLAND'S NATIONAL ANIMAL

In summer you have a very good chance of seeing wild brown bears at the comfortable hide of **Karhu-Kuusamo** (karhujenkatselu.fi), about 40km east of Ruka.

Often several bears can be seen visiting the pond here in one evening, enticed by fish bones. You may also see ospreys. Four-hour sessions (€120 per person) start at 6pm, May to September; you make your own way to its hut.

Similar experiences at a hide 75km from Ruka are offered by **Lammintupa**.

### WHERE TO EAT IN RUKA

**Pizzeria Ruka**
Pleasant ambience and very tasty pizzas, 600m south of central Ruka Village. **€€**

**Restaurant KaltioKivi**
Nicely done fish, reindeer, burgers, pasta and soups in the middle of Ruka Village. **€€**

**Riipinen Riistaravintola**
This log-cabin-style restaurant is the place to come for northern game classics – elk, reindeer and, yes, bear. **€€€**

## Hossa National Park

HIKING, CYCLING, CANOEING AND ANCIENT ART

A labyrinth of forest lakes and rivers makes this 110-sq-km national park a summer treat for walkers, mountain bikers and canoeists.

It's an 80-minute drive south from Ruka to the visitor centre (Hossan Luontokeskus), situated 700m off Rd 843. The centre dispenses information on the park (also available online at nationalparks.fi and hossa.fi), has a restaurant, and rents canoes, kayaks and fat bikes.

The **Karhunkainalon** campground, with modern cabins and apartments, is next door. There are further lodgings in Hossa village, 4km south of the visitor centre. On a short visit, a good place to head is **Julma-Ölkky canyon lake** in the north of the park. Julma-Ölkky is 3km long, 50m deep, lined by cliffs rising to 50m, and is just 10m wide at its narrowest point.

A summer boat service does half-hour trips on the lake, or you can rent a canoe or walk around the lake on the 10km **Ölökyn ähkäsy** trail (about five hours) – or cut that in half by crossing the lake on a hanging bridge halfway along, an option called **Ölökyn ylitys**. Either way, it's a good leg-stretch, with a lot of up and down and rocky terrain.

In the other direction (south) from the Julma-Ölkky trailhead, you can walk 4.4km to Finland's largest group of prehistoric rock paintings at **Värikallio**. The ochre-toned paintings, on a cliff face directly above the waters of Somerjärvi, date back at least 3500 years and mainly depict animals and human-like, possibly shamanic, figures.

### A FINNISH DESIGN EPICENTRE

Fans of Finnish style should make a beeline 65km west from Ruka to the small town of **Posio**, home base of the outstanding interior-design house **Pentik**, founded here in 1971 by ceramic artist Anu Pentik and her husband Topi Pentikäinen. Pentik's readily appealing, never overcomplicated homeware ranges, with designs often inspired by northern Finnish nature, are now sold in the company's nearly 50 shops (and many others) around Finland. Pentik's ceramics (some still designed by Anu) and candles are still made here in Posio. The **Kulttuurikeskus Pentik-mäki** (Pentik Hill Culture Centre) embraces the Anu Pentik Galleria with its stunning 20m-wide mosaic facade, the Pentik kotimuseo (Pentik Home Museum) in the family's old log house, a cafe and, of course, shops (outlet and vintage).

### GETTING AROUND

Winter Skibus services link the centre of Ruka Village with Ruka Valley and other outlying areas of Ruka. To head further afield, your own vehicle is by far easiest. Kuusamo airport, 26km south of Ruka, has car-hire desks. From early June to early August (except Sundays), Hossa Bussi runs from Ruka to Hossa National Park in the morning and back in the evening. A taxi from Ruka to Posio and back will cost around €90, plus about €50 an hour for waiting.

# LAPLAND

## THE ARCTIC NORTH

A vast land of vast extremes, where in summer there's no night, and in winter no real day.

Lapland is the land of the midnight sun, the polar night and the magical aurora borealis ('Northern Lights'). It occupies more than a quarter of Finland, mostly north of the Arctic Circle, with just 3% of the country's people. It's a region of extremes where snow covers the ground for half the year, but the sun doesn't set for weeks in summer.

Northern Lapland is the Homeland of the indigenous Sámi, long accustomed to Arctic life. The Sámi still herd reindeer (which roam Lapland's countryside freely much of the year), though many of them now follow other livelihoods and/or live outside the Homeland. Lapland is also the location of the 'official hometown of Santa Claus' – the regional capital Rovaniemi, to which Santa helps attract hundreds of thousands of visitors annually. Lapland's extensive tourism sector makes it easy for visitors to ride in reindeer sleighs, drive husky sleds, scoot around on snowmobiles or search the backwoods for elk (moose). For those who like to explore independently, the forests, fells, lakes, and rivers of this beautiful land offer infinite scope and space. The superb network of national parks and other protected areas is equipped with excellent infrastructure, including numerous information centres and hundreds of marked trails and wilderness huts. Lapland is a world far removed from the everyday experience of the great majority of its visitors. It's just waiting to be discovered.

IGOR VICTOR MASCHEK/SHUTTERSTOCK ©; RIGHT: MOSHE EINHORN/SHUTTERSTOCK ©

### THE MAIN AREAS

**ROVANIEMI**
Regional capital and busy tourism hub. p192

**INARI**
Centre of Sámi culture. p200

**KILPISJÄRVI**
Remote outpost with great hiking. p213

# Find Your Way

Easily Finland's biggest region, Lapland stretches 500km from north to south. The few larger towns are all in the south: beyond the Arctic Circle it's villages (and a few ski resorts) only.

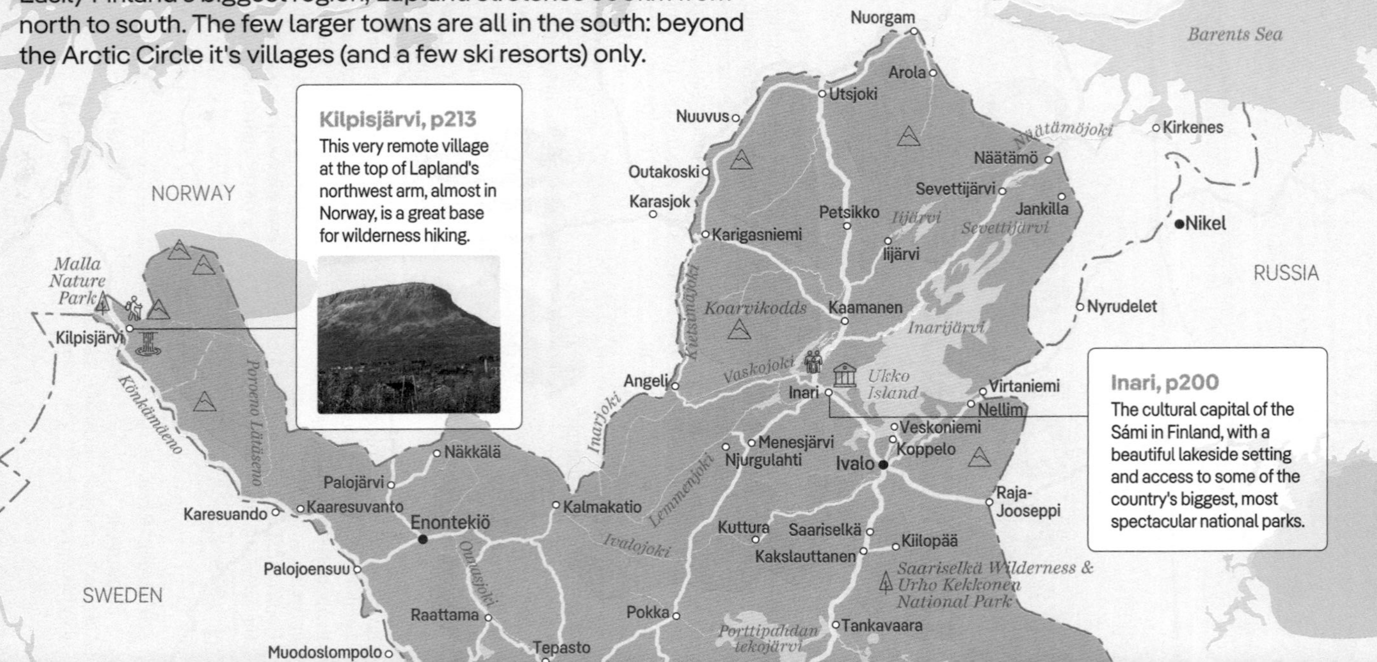


**Kilpisjärvi, p213**
This very remote village at the top of Lapland's northwest arm, almost in Norway, is a great base for wilderness hiking.

**Inari, p200**
The cultural capital of the Sámi in Finland, with a beautiful lakeside setting and access to some of the country's biggest, most spectacular national parks.

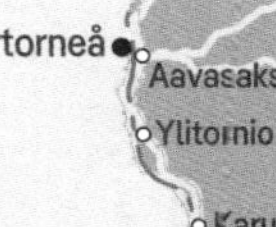

## CAR & MOTORCYCLE

Unless you're just visiting one place, with limited excursions, having your own vehicle is the easiest way to go. Just watch out for reindeer on the roads, know where the next filling station is, and in winter use snow tyres and check the weather.

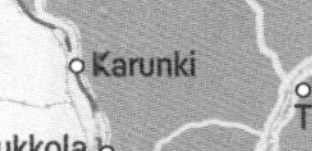

## BUS

Buses fan out to the main towns and villages from Rovaniemi, but most services are not too frequent. Just two or three buses a day head up to Inari (one goes on into Norway) and Kilpisjärvi.

## CAR RENTAL

All Lapland's four airports – Rovaniemi, Kemi-Tornio, Ivalo and Kittilä – have car rental desks. You can also pick up cars at Rovaniemi railway station.

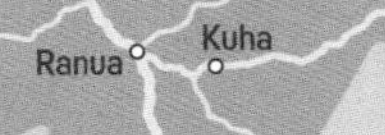

**Rovaniemi, p192**

Springboard for Santa Claus experiences and other classic Lapland tourist activities, but also a lively city with good cultural life, restaurants and bars.

LEFT: TSUGULIEV/SHUTTERSTOCK ©, RIGHT: ROMAN BABAKIN/SHUTTERSTOCK ©

# Plan Your Time

Visiting Lapland is all about getting out into the countryside and visiting reindeer farms, hiking or skiing the forests and fells, husky-sledding or gaping at the aurora borealis.

STEFANO ZACCARIA/SHUTTERSTOCK ©

Inari (p200)

## If you only visit one place

- Basing yourself at **Inari** (p200) will give you a taste of the north, which some consider the 'real' Lapland. If you have just two days, spend one visiting the brilliant Sámi museum **Siida** (p201) and **Sajos** (the Sámi cultural centre and Parliament; p201), and then either taking a boat trip on **Inarijärvi lake** (p203) or walking out to the **Pielpajärvi Wilderness Church** (p203) and back.
- On the second day get yourself out early to **Lemmenjoki National Park** (p208) and, if it's summer, ride the river boat along the Lemmenjoki and take a hike among the hilly forests.

## Seasonal Highlights

There's no night in summer and little light in winter. It gets more pronounced heading north: Rovaniemi has 30 days of midnight sun, Utsjoki has 70.

**MARCH**

Usually a good month for snow-based activities, as there's plenty of snow but also daylight, and temperatures are climbing.

**MAY**

The snowmelt make streams overflow and the wetlands wetter, curtailing activities in the countryside.

**JUNE**

The midnight-sun season starts in most of Lapland; it's party time, as Finns soak up the blessed rays.

FROM LEFT: TANHU, JUHANI VILPO, POPOVA VALERIYA/SHUTTERSTOCK ©

## A few more days

- Start at **Rovaniemi** (p192), the regional capital and 'official hometown of Santa Claus'. In two days you can visit the excellent **Arktikum** (p194) and **Pilke Tiedekeskus museums** (p192), enjoy a spot of shopping, a riverside walk and some of the town's excellent restaurants and bars, and take a trip out to meet the man himself at **Santa Claus Village** (p197).

- Days three and four: head up to **Saariselkä** (p210) for some hiking in the endless hilly expanses of **Urho Kekkonen National Park** (p000) or (if it's winter) some skiing.

- Days five and six: Continue to **Inari** (p200) and follow the 'one place' itinerary (left) before heading out on day seven.

## Two weeks

- Now we're talking. Do everything in and around **Rovaniemi** and **Saariselkä** in the previous itinerary (left), and give yourself an extra day based in Inari to visit **Reindeer Farm Petri Mattus** (p207) or the Sámi home of **Tuula Airamo** (p207).

- Add in a one- or two-day driving trip to Finland's northernmost extremities along the beautiful **Tenojoki** (p204), and stay overnight at **Lemmenjoki National Park** (p208) to allow for lengthier explorations.

- Then head to remote **Kilpisjarvi** (p213) at the northwest tip of the country for some superb wilderness hiking, including another extremity of mainland Finland, the **triple border point** (p214) where Finland, Norway and Sweden all converge.

**JULY**

Still high summer, the main Finnish holiday month, but also peak mosquito season, so not a great time for hiking.

**SEPTEMBER**

Magnificent autumn colours, moderate temperatures, no mosquitoes: ideal for hiking and other countryside pursuits.

**OCTOBER**

First snows normally arrive over northern Lapland in the second half of the month (early November in the south).

**DECEMBER**

Peak season (continuing into January) at winter tourism destinations Rovaniemi and Saariselkä: prices go up, crowds thicken. Little daylight.



FROM LEFT: IURII BURIAK, IMRELE, BLUEORANGE STUDIO, PETER GUDELLA/SHUTTERSTOCK ©

# ROVANIEMI

Capital of Finnish Lapland, Rovaniemi (population: 55,000) styles itself as the 'official hometown of Santa Claus'. He resides year-round on the Arctic Circle, 8km northeast of town, and has contributed mightily to Rovaniemi's booming tourism sector. From here you can easily visit Santa Claus Village and not just take reindeer/husky/snowmobile/aurora borealis safaris (the four most popular activities) but also go berry foraging, elk (moose) spotting or fatbiking under midnight sun. Old Rovaniemi was almost razed by fire in the 1944 Wehrmacht retreat. It was rebuilt to a plan by Alvar Aalto, with its main streets in the form of a reindeer head (the stadium near the bus station is the eye. Modern Rovaniemi has a great setting at the confluence of the Kemijoki and the Ounasjoki, and its Arktikum museum is one of Finland's best.

**TOP TIP**

There's usually snow from about mid-November to late April. In December and the first half of January the sun is up less than four hours a day. Despite that, and temperatures well below zero, peak season is December and January. Book ahead for accommodation and activities at that time.

**BEST BARS IN ROVANIEMI**

**Cafe & Bar 21**
Chilled spot for an early-evening wine or cocktail.

**Paha Kurki**
Dark but friendly rock bar, with autographed guitars. Try a Lapland Red Ale or two.

**Bar Hemingway's**
For a straightforward pub with good beer, and maybe TV sport, head for wood-panelled Hemingway's.

**Gustav Kitchen & Bar**
Ideal bar for a cocktail, wine or beer and maybe some light snacks.

**Mökkiterrassi**
Soak in the late-night sun at Hostel Koti's popular summer roof bar.

## Rovaniemi's Action Playground

OUNASVAARA FOR SUMMER & WINTER

Ounasvaara, the forest-clad fell across the river just east of Rovaniemi, is where the city lets off steam. On its northern side, the **Ounasvaara Ski Resort** has 10 varied downhill slopes (including freeride), a snow park and an area for beginners. There are also 200km of cross-country ski tracks on Ounasvaara and around Rovaniemi. In summer (late June to mid-August) the ski station operates a summer bobsleigh run and a bike park with downhill runs. There are also plenty of unmarked bike tracks on the hill. The main walking trail is the **Talvikävelyreitti** ('Winter Trail', but walkable year-round), which starts near the east end of Jätkänkynttilä-silta and climbs to the Sky Ounasvaara hotel via a lookout tower, does a circuit from there then heads back down; about 8km in all. There's a shorter **'nature trail'** loop from the hotel .

## Cultural Triangle

THREE TOP MUSEUMS

Rovaniemi is home to three excellent museums, all worth a piece of your time. A combined ticket for all three, the Culture Pass, saves you a few euros.

**Arktikum** is a very well-presented introduction to Lapland's history, culture and nature and an eye-opener on the whole Arctic world – all in a stunning building that extends beneath a road to emerge in a long glass-roofed atrium. The Arctic sections range from peoples and wildlife to icebergs and climate change. Lie back and watch a simulation of the aurora borealis. The Lapland halls cover topics such as the indigenous

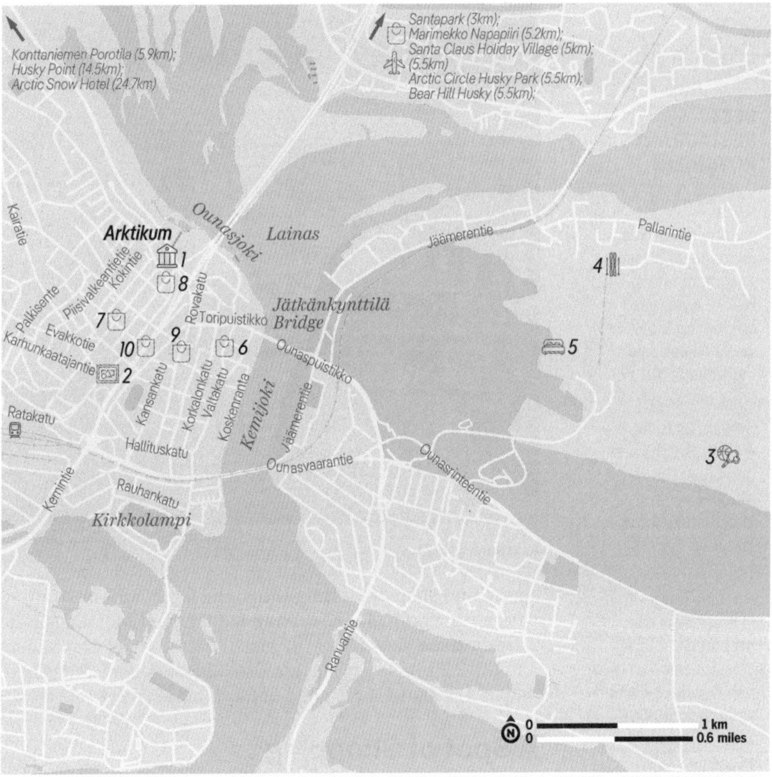

Konttaniemen Porotila (5.9km); Husky Point (14.5km); Arctic Snow Hotel (24.7km)

Santapark (3km); Marimekko Napapiiri (5.2km); Santa Claus Holiday Village (5km); (5.5km) Arctic Circle Husky Park (5.5km); Bear Hill Husky (5.5km);

**HIGHLIGHTS**
1 Arktikum

**SIGHTS**
**see 1** Pilke Tiedekeskus
**2** Rovaniemen Taidemuseo

**ACTIVITIES, COURSES & TOURS**
**3** Ounasvaara
**4** Ounasvaara Ski Resort

**SLEEPING**
**5** Sky Ounasvaara

**EATING**
**see 1** Arktikum Cafe

**SHOPPING**
**6** Arctic Design
**7** Lauri Tuotteet
**8** Marttiini
**9** Pentik
**10** Rinteenkulma

**see 9** Sampokeskus

**INFORMATION**
see 1 Metsähallitus

Sámi and reindeer herding, wildlife and Lapland during WWII, with models showing the devastation wrought on Rovaniemi.

**Pilke tiedekeskus** (Pilke Science Centre), adjacent to Arktikum, is an entertaining exhibition on Finnish forestry with a sustainable focus. Kids of all ages can climb up into a giant logging vehicle or a birdhouse. There is an information

## WHERE TO STAY IN ROVANIEMI

**Arctic Light Hotel**
Inspired conversion of former city hall with individually designed, Arctic-themed rooms; superb breakfast. **€€€**

**Hostel Cafe Koti**
Centrally located, popular hostel with 24 rooms and two dorms in neat, clean Nordic style. **€€**

**Arctic City Hotel**
Rooms are compact but plush fabrics give them an intimate feel; location is super-central. **€€**

### BEST RESTAURANTS IN ROVANIEMI

**Roka**
Communal tables, exposed-brick walls and imaginative bistro-style fare combining local and international ingredients. €€

**Cafe & Bar 21**
Stylish haunt for waffles, salads and bao buns, sharing premises with excellent Mexican Taquería Yuca. €

**Nili**
Hunting-lodge-style interior; very well-prepared Lapland classics, such as lake fish, reindeer, elk and salmon soup. €€€

**Sky Kitchen & View**
Sky Ounasvaara hotel's atmospheric restaurant has specialities including wild-mushroom risotto and reindeer of the day. €€€

**Monterosa Restaurant**
Wooden booths and candles enhance the experience at this long-established steak specialist. €€€

KETKAR/SHUTTERSTOCK ©

**Arktikum (p192)**

centre and shop of Metsähallitus, the forest administration, where you can pick up walking leaflets and buy maps. The **Taidemuseo** showcases the visual creativity of Laplanders and other Finnish artists. It's also a music venue. Cafes here and at Arktikum serve good buffet lunches.

## A Spot of Shopping

CRAFTS & DESIGN

Lauri is a unique shop with Sámi and Finnish handicrafts – rings, plates, spoons, earrings, *kuksa* birchwood cups – in one of Rovaniemi's few wooden houses. Many items are finely crafted on the spot, from reindeer antler or wood. The **Arktikum**, **Pilke** and **Taidemuseo** museums all have interesting shops – forest-themed products at Pilke, ranges of quality artisanship at the other two. **Arctic Design** sells a big variety of Lapland-made items, from soaps and sauna scents to wallets, bags, hats, even some remarkable earrings, made from reindeer hide. **Sampokeskus** has branches of Finnish design houses **Pentik** and **Marimekko**; in **Rinteenkulma** you'll find a shop of Marttiini, the famous, formerly Rovaniemi-based, knife maker.

### GETTING AROUND

Rovaniemi airport is 8km northeast of the city centre. City bus 11 runs to/from the city centre (Ruokasenkatu) every 40 minutes daily from December to February (departures from the airport: 8.40am to 8pm). Airport Express minibuses (www.airportbus.fi) run into the centre but don't always operate outside the winter season (about November to April). A taxi from airport to city costs €20 to €30. The city is walkable: the train and bus stations are within a 20-minute walk of the central square Lordinaukio. City bus 9 serves the Ounasvaara ski station and Santasport, and bus 10 serves Santasport. No buses go to the top of the hill.

## AN OFF-CENTRE STROLL

Rovaniemi's rivers are its great scenic blessings. Starting from the **1 Arktikum museum** you can enjoy a 2km riverside stroll beside first the Ounasjoki then the Kemijoki, then turn inland to check out some of the city's most interesting architecture.

From the car park on the northwest side of Arktikum find the underpass that leads below the busy Kantatie into the **2 Arktinen puutarha** (Arctic Garden) riverside park. Walk east through another underpass and you're at the confluence of the Ounasjoki and Kemijoki.

Continue south beneath the **3 Jätkänkynttilä-silta**(Lumberjack's Candle Bridge), an impressive city symbol erected in 1989, then 1km along the straight riverside path, with the wooded hill Ounasvaara rising on the opposite bank of the Kemijoki.

Pass under the **4 Ounaskosken rautatiesilta** rail-and-road bridge. Turn right up the next street to find the **5 Rovaniemen Kirkko**, a high-spired 1950 church designed by Bertel Liljequist. Its wooden predecessor (along with much of Rovaniemi) was destroyed in the German army's scorched-earth retreat across Lapland in 1944. The large, impressive fresco behind the altar, by Lennart Segerstråle, depicts the battle between good and bad in the human heart, with a Christ figure emerging from Lappish scenery between a group of the faithful on one side and brawling drunkards and ravening wolves on the other.

In the **6 cemetery** behind the church you'll find the neat rows of graves of over 600 people who died during WWII. Continue 300m west and cross the railway footbridge to see buildings designed by Alvar Aalto in the 1960s and 70s: the city hall, the city library and the beautiful, wave-roofed **7 Lappia-talo** arts and conference centre.

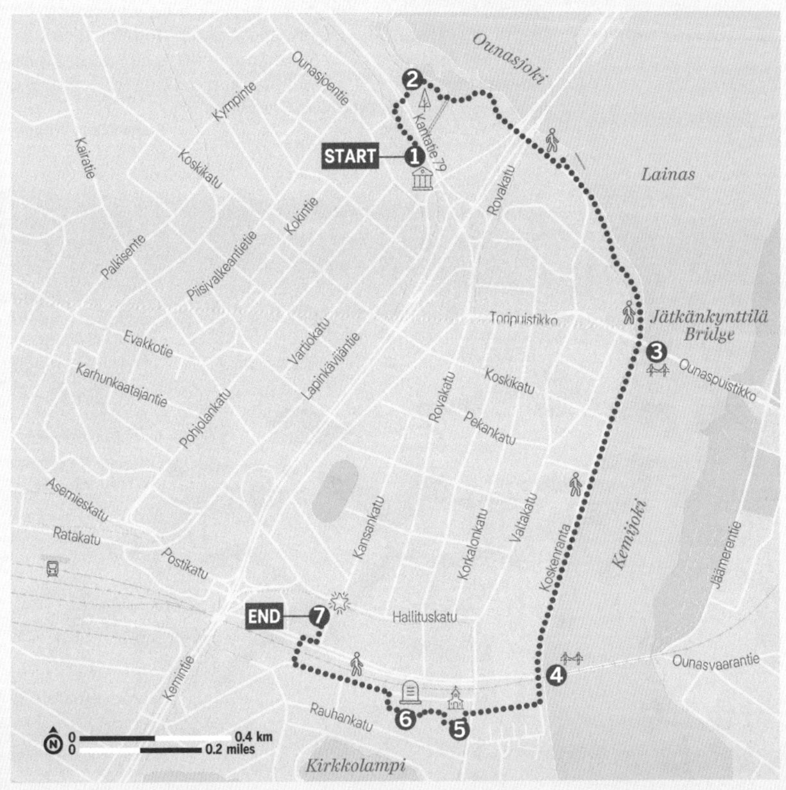

# Beyond Rovaniemi

Almost everyone goes to Santa's village, then there's a world of diverse experiences to enjoy year-round in the countryside beyond.

### TOP TIP

Making arrangements directly with establishments you want to visit can often result in a lower price and/or more personal experience.

Just 8km outside Rovaniemi, right on the Arctic Circle (Napapiiri in Finnish), lies Santa Claus Village, where Santa is in residence year-round, and an array of Santa- and Arctic-related attractions keeps visitors rolling in. There are many other good reasons to venture into the Lapland countryside, from reindeer and husky farms tucked away on lakesides to berries and mushrooms to forage in the forests, wildlife such as elk (moose) to search for, and clear skies ideal for witnessing the aurora borealis. A host of providers awaits to offer these experiences. And for direct communion with Arctic nature, just head out along some of the well-marked walking trails that get right away from the roads and crowds.

**Santa Claus Village**

MARCELO SOUZA DE ARAUJO/SHUTTERSTOCK ©

KRISKIT/SHUTTERSTOCK ©

A bright aurora borealis

## Santa's Village

CHRISTMAS SPIRIT ALL YEAR ROUND

Santa Claus himself welcomes visitors of all ages every day of the year, free of charge, at his 'office' in **Santa Claus Village**, a 20-minute bus ride northeast of Rovaniemi. The Village, spread over a forest-fringe site scattered with Santa-related attractions and several hotels, restaurants, cafes and shops, is a fun place to visit any time of year, though it really comes into its own with snow.

**Santa's office** is inside a curious, pointy-towered, wood-and-stone building. You may or may not have to queue up to see him, depending on the time of year and day. He's a friendly fellow and quite a linguist. Taking photos inside isn't permitted, but your three-minute chat will be photographed and videoed by elves and you can download the results for €45 (or pay €35 for an A4 print).

Any mail you send from the **Santa Claus Main Post Office** will be stamped with a special Arctic Circle/Santa/Reindeer postmark. Post it in special boxes for it to arrive just before

### BEST HOTELS IN SANTA CLAUS VILLAGE

There are no budget options here, and in the winter high season (roughly December to March) prices can be stratospheric.

**Santa Claus Holiday Village**
Least-expensive option. In high season well-kept standard cottages, with large rooms, cost €250 a double. €€€

**Glass Resort**
Luxurious 2-floor 'glass apartments': glass bedroom ceilings and full-wall glass windows for comfortable aurora viewing. €€€

**Nova Skyland**
Comfy Nordic-style apartments and suites for up to eight guests, among the trees. €€€

### ROVANIEMI ACTIVITY OPERATORS

**Safartica**
Quality local outfit offering huge range, from berry foraging to gasoline-free electric-snowmobile safaris.

**Lapland Welcome**
Has a strong nature focus on trips, including elk (moose) spotting and wilderness wildlife photography.

**Beyond Arctic Adventures**
Experts in aurora borealis photography tours; carefully chosen locations up to 100km out of town.

**I LIVE HERE: TIPS FOR WITNESSING THE AURORA BOREALIS**

**Juho Uutela**, CEO of Rovaniemi's Beyond Arctic Adventures, specialists in Northern Lights photography tours, shares some tips.

**Location**
You need to be away from light pollution and have a good view to the northern sky. Go at least 20 to 30km from the city.

**Weather**
Should be clear or partly clear for you to see the night sky. For the best chances, select the location according to local weather.

**Solar activity**
Solar wind colliding with the earth is why we see the Northern Lights in Lapland. For the lights to appear, we need enough solar activity. A KP (geomagnetic activity) index of 2 to 3 (or more) suggests Rovaniemi may get some kind of light show; check www.gi.alaska.edu/monitors/aurora-forecast.

Christmas. The office receives around 500,000 letters a year to Santa from around the world.

Elsewhere in the Village, try a sleigh ride with **Santa's Reindeer** (or in summer just visit or walk with them), or pet huskies and take a short ride in a husky-pulled sled (or wheeled carriage in summer) at **Husky Park**. **Elf's Farmyard**, with a selection of domestic animals and more reindeer, is an agreeably inexpensive option. For winter only, there's children's snowmobiling at **Arctic Circle Snowmobile Park**, and **Snowman World** with ice skating, ice and snow slides, ice restaurant and ice bar. A historical curiosity is the **Roosevelt Cottage**, a log cabin built for a visit by Eleanor Roosevelt in 1950. It's now a reindeer-horn souvenir workshop.

## Reindeer, Huskies & a Zoo

TALK TO THE ANIMALS

Winter husky-sledding safaris with sustainability-conscious **Bearhill Husky**, a half-hour drive northwest of Rovaniemi, range from short outings suitable for families to three-hour, 25–30km adventures.

The guides are excellent and the dogs well cared for. Also good for husky sledding is **Huskypoint** at Käpälämäki, a 15-minute drive northwest of Rovaniemi, belonging to champion husky racer Aki Holck. Both places provide transport; book in advance.

You can feed and learn about reindeer, and take 1km or 3km winter sleigh rides, at **Konttaniemen Porotila** (Napapiirin Porofarmi), a reindeer farm among pine woods, 10 minutes' drive northwest of Rovaniemi. Book by 3pm the day before.

Popular **Ranua Wildlife Park**, a one-hour drive or bus ride southeast of Rovaniemi, focuses chiefly on Finnish wildlife, including the brown bear, elk, lynx, wolverine, otter, Arctic fox, owls and eagles. A 2.8km trail runs round the various enclosures – plus there's horse-sleigh rides and mini-snowmobiles for kids.

## Out into Nature

RIVERS, RAPIDS & WATERFALLS

The **Arctic Circle Hiking Area** (Napapiirin retkeilyalue), northeast of Rovaniemi, comprises marked trails of varied lengths crossing forests, rocky hilltops and wetlands. The 4km **Vaattunkivaara Nature Trail** circuit from Vikaköngäs parking area (just off the Sodankylä road, a 25-minute drive

**ROVANIEMI ACTIVITY OPERATORS**

**Nordic Unique Travels**
Wide-ranging operator with offerings from a midnight-sun sauna boat to ice fishing and cross-country skiing.

**Roll Outdoors**
Mountain bike, fatbike and e-fatbike rentals, route ideas and guided rides.

**Lapland Safaris**
The largest of Rovaniemi's tour operators, a very professional operation with a vast activities range.

from Rovaniemi) crosses rapids of the Raudanjoki on a hanging bridge then ascends 85m to a lookout tower atop Vaattunkivaara hill.

You can extend the walk by heading 3.5km south from Vaattunkivaara on the Könkäiden polku trail as far as **Vaattunkilampi** pond, then returning via the **Kivalonaapa Mire trail**, for a total of about 11.5km (four to five hours plus stops). Spring floods sometimes make the path impassable near Vaattunkilampi.

The 16m **Auttiköngäs** falls are about one minute's walk from a parking area off the Kuusamo road (about 1¼ hours' drive southeast of Rovaniemi), but you can stretch your legs round a 3.6km nature trail that crosses the Auttijoki on a hanging bridge. There's a summer cafe at the car park.

In winter you'll need snowshoes for these trails.

## A Hotel Made of Snow

BEDS OF ICE

The **Arctic Snow Hotel**, a half-hour drive northwest of Rovaniemi on the shore of beautiful Lehtojärvi, is your chance to sleep on a bed of ice and eat on ice chairs and ice tables. Room temperatures never exceed 0°C but reindeer furs and sleeping bags keep you warm.

The 30-room building is constructed anew each winter and opens from mid-December to March. Also here, lines of glass-igloo rooms, available from late September, are designed for aurora-watching in comfort. Day tickets, enabling you to look at snow rooms, cost €24/12 per adult/child.

### CHASING THE AURORA BOREALIS

The aurora borealis is one of the earth's most ethereally beautiful phenomena. What exactly is it? Why does it appear when and where it does? Turn to p232 for some answers.

### LAPLAND'S FAVOURITE FOODS

**Reindeer** The most common meat here – in fillets, sausages, soup, sautéed or as a great hunk of shoulder roasted over an open fire.

**Elk** Also known as moose, hunted in Lapland's forests; tastes like venison.

**Salmon** Especially good from the Tenojoki in the far north.

**Whitefish** A tender treat from Inarijärvi.

**Berries** Cranberries, lingonberries, blueberries, and the beloved cloudberries. Laplanders love late-summer foraging then turning berries into jams, juices and desserts. Ranua is Lapland's unofficial cloudberry capital and holds a cloudberry festival in August.

**Wild mushrooms** Another foragers' favourite.

**Leipäjuusto** 'Bread cheese', also known as squeaky cheese.

### GETTING AROUND

As ever, having your own transport is most convenient, though you can get out to Santa Claus Village from Rovaniemi by city bus 8 and the privately operated Santa Claus Bus, and many activity operators offer transport to their locations. There are several buses daily to/from Ranua zoo, and several Kemijärvi- or Sodankylä-bound buses from Rovaniemi will stop at the Köngästie stop, a 500m walk from the start of the Vaattunkivaara walking trail. Some tour firms offer trips to Auttiköngäs.

# INARI

Inari
Helsinki

The small, spread-out village of Inari (population: about 650) occupies a big and important place in the Lapland picture as the seat of the Sámi Parliament in Finland and effectively the Sámi people's cultural capital in Finland.

You can learn about Sámi life and culture not just at the excellent Siida museum and Sajos cultural centre but also by visiting Sámi reindeer farms and homes. The village is strung along the shore of Inarijärvi, Lapland's very beautiful, island-studded biggest lake (1084 sq km). The Inari Sámi have been fishing and hunting around the lake since time immemorial.

Today Inari is a hub of tourism in northern Lapland, a good base for local walks and lake trips, winter husky sledding and aurora borealis viewing, and for access to the outstanding Lemmenjoki and Urho Kekkonen national parks. But it remains an agreeably low-key place, far from overwhelmed by its visitors.

**TOP TIP**

The centre of the village is effectively the K-Market supermarket, with a large parking area around it, some shops nearby and Hotel Inari across the main road. Sajos and Siida are to the northwest; a few places to stay are dotted along the lakeshore for 2km or 3km to the southeast.

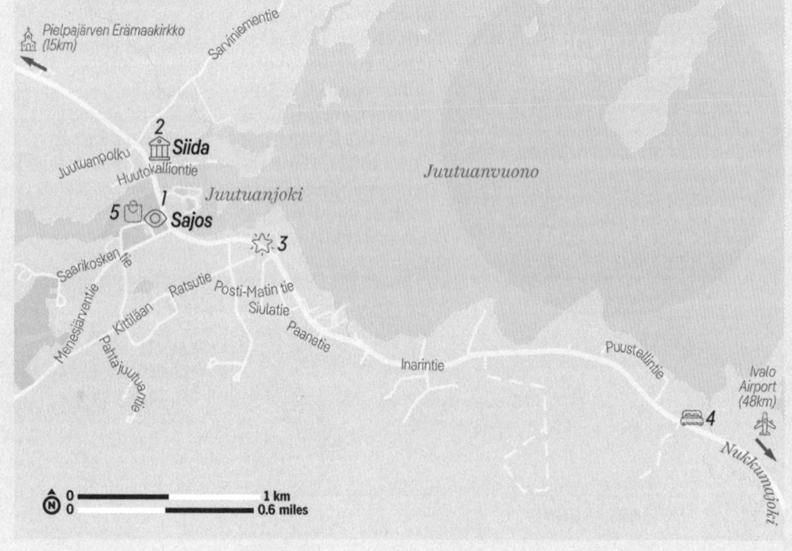


**HIGHLIGHTS**
**1** Sajos
**2** Siida

**ACTIVITIES, COURSES & TOURS**
**3** Visit Inari

**SLEEPING**
**4** Wilderness Hotel Inari

**SHOPPING**
**5** Sámi Duodji Ry

PRIMI2/SHUTTERSTOCK ©

Siida

### BEST CRAFTS SHOPPING IN INARI

**Duodji Shop**
Sámi handicrafts association's shop, inside Sajos: clothing, jewellery, bags, knives, *kuksa* birchwood cups, books, CDs.

**Siida**
Museum shop has good range of Sámi-made crafts, including Samekki silver jewellery, Ságat decorated bags.

**Inarin Hopea**
Matti Qvick crafts superb silver and gold jewellery in his workshop across from Siida.

**Samekki**
Sámi artisan Sami Laiti produces finely worked silver jewellery and traditional Sámi crafts, including knives.

## Discover Sámi Culture

OUTSTANDING MUSEUM & A PARLIAMENT

You can't get a better introduction to Sámi culture than by visiting Inari's outstanding Siida museum and Sajos, the Sámi Cultural Centre.

The recently renovated **Siida** (the Sámi Museum and Northern Lapland Nature Centre) gives a detailed, superbly displayed presentation of Sámi history and culture and northern Lapland nature. In the larger of its two permanent-exhibition rooms, huge, beautiful photo panels illustrate the region's different ecosystems and the cycle of the seasons, while displays of artefacts, info panels and photos demonstrate the holistic connection between livelihoods, nature, language, costume, handicrafts and other elements in Sámi life.

**SÁMI LIFE TODAY**

Turn to p244 for background on the Sámi – where they live, their reindeer herding and other traditions, their modern lifestyles and their situation in Finland today, with an article by Tuomas Aslak Juuso, their president (2020–23).

### WHERE TO STAY IN & NEAR INARI

**Hotel Inari**
Well-run, comfortable, medium-sized lakeside hotel in the middle of town; great views from the restaurant. €€

**Wilderness Hotels**
Inari's classiest rooms, at the lakeside Wilderness Hotel Inari and the riverside Wilderness Hotel Juutua. €€€

**Villa Lanca**
Friendly, relatively economical, centrally located place; the Sámi owner has a husky farm outside Inari. €€

Outside, there's an open-air museum of historical Sámi buildings along an 800m walking trail. Also here are a shop, a cafe, and a helpful desk offering both local tourist information and maps and info on national parks.

**Sajos**, in a spectacular wood-and-glass-faced building opened in 2012, houses the Sámi Parliament in Finland (with its oval meeting chamber), a Sámi library and archives, a crafts shop, a good cafe and several Sámi organisations.

One-hour guided tours, including a 15-minute film on Sámi life, are normally available at noon, but you can visit without taking a tour.

The Sámi Duodji shop here is the official shop of the Sámi handicrafts association; its Sámi Duodji trademark guarantees that an item is an authentic Sámi handicraft made by Sámi.

### WHY I LOVE INARI

**John Noble**, writer

I love Inari for the views over Inarijärvi with its changing moods and, if you're lucky, the aurora borealis reflected in its waters. For the brilliant insights into Sámi culture, and its intimate connection with northern nature, provided by Siida and Sajos. For the walks through forests, alongside rivers and lakes and to the tops of fells. And because from here the wonderful Lemmenjoki and Urho Kekkonen national parks and the Teno valley villages at the very top of Finland are within easy reach. And yes, because this really is the far north, with little except unspoiled Arctic nature stretching for hundreds of kilometres all around.

## Walks in the Woods

LAKES, RIVERS, A HISTORIC CHURCH

Several well-marked trails invite you to explore the Inari countryside. One delightful walk, through mossy, boulder-strewn forests and past several lakes, leads to the handsome wooden Pielpajärven erämaakirkko (Pielpajärvi Wilderness Church), pictured, built in the 1750s in a now-vanished Sámi winter village.

DANIELE ALOISI/SHUTTERSTOCK ©

The route starts along Sarviniementie running northeast from Siida: it's 2.5km along roads to a parking area (you can drive this far if you have a vehicle), then about 5km by forest paths to the church (total if walking the whole way: about 4½ hours there and back, plus stops).

The church is always open, and you can open its shutters (just close everything behind you when leaving). Nowadays services are held there at Easter and midsummer; it's also a popular wedding venue. Retrace your steps to return to Inari. This walk can be done in winter with snowshoes.

A shorter, year-round walk is the **Juutuanpolku** (Juutua Path), a 6km loop starting along the riverbank behind

### WHERE TO STAY IN & NEAR INARI

**Guesthouse Husky**
Good-sized rooms in a traditional-style wooden house on husky farm near Ivalo; great husky activities. **€€**

**Uruniemi Camping**
Lakeside summer campground 2.5km from centre; a few cabins; cafe; bikes, kayaks, canoes for rent. **€**

**Holiday Village Inari**
Modern wooden two-to-four-person cabins. Various models, some right by lakeshore, 1km from the village centre. **€€€**

Sajos. It follows the Juutuanjoki upstream to a hanging bridge over the fierce Jäniskoski rapids, then returns along the north side of the valley.

For a longer outing, take the 'Otsamo' path from the shelter on the north side of the hanging bridge. This leads in about 6.5km to the top of Otsamo hill (419m), with a steepish bit towards the end rewarded by panoramas as far as Inarijärvi. Retrace your steps to return.

There are also cross-country ski trails to the Wilderness Church and Otsamo, open from about mid-February to late April.

## A Cruise on the Lake

SAIL TO A SACRED ISLAND

A great way to experience Inarijärvi is to take a summer cruise from the dock at the Siida car park in the 120-seat catamaran operated by Visit Inari.

The boat sails to (but does not land on) **Ukko** (Ukonsaari) Island, an old Sámi sacred site. Departures are at 1pm from mid-June to mid-September, and 5pm in July. On request the 1pm cruise will drop you at Pielpavuono, from where you can walk back to Inari via Pielpajärvi Wilderness Church.

**Visit Inari**, with an office next to Hotel Inari, offers a range of other summer, autumn and winter activities, such as reindeer- and husky-farm visits, snowmobiling and aurora borealis outings, with transport from Inari included. It also rents gear, such as snowshoes, skis, fatbikes, SUP boards and rowing boats.

If you're interested in a paddling trip on Inarijärvi, bear in mind that it's a very large lake and its waters can get very rough. A sea kayak is the best craft. LuontoLoma in Saariselkä is one outfit renting them. There's a lot of excellent information at www.nationalparks.fi/inarijarvi.

## Meet a Reindeer Family

LEARN ABOUT THE HERDING LIFE

**Renniina Reindeer Family** is a convenient option for close-up reindeer contact from November to March, when this Sámi family brings a few of their herd into an enclosure by their house on the edge of Inari village. You can feed the animals and have a chat about reindeer husbandry and Sámi culture.

### BEST CAFES & RESTAURANTS IN INARI

**Café Čaiju**
The cafe in Sajos does great organic coffee, cinnamon rolls and good-value set lunches. €

**Aanaar**
Seasonal local produce in deliciously original preparations at the restaurant in Wilderness Hotel Juutua. €€€

**Restaurant Aurora**
Hotel Inari's panoramic restaurant; shortish, satisfying menu, including white fish from the lake, roast reindeer. €€€

**PaPaNa**
Pine-panelled PaPaNa, with an outdoor terrace, serves thin-crust pizzas – also serves as village pub. €

### GETTING AROUND

Inari is a small place and easy to walk around. Most lodgings can rent or lend you a bicycle if you wish. Many people get here by flying to Ivalo Airport, 49km south of Inari. The airport has car-hire desks. Ilmari Slant (www.kuljetusliikeilmarislant.fi) runs buses to Inari (€30), departing the airport 20 minutes after flight arrivals. It will drop and pick up at hotels. To go to the airport, call or email them no later than 3pm the day before.

ROAD TRIP

# To the Far North

The great feature of this drive is the Tenojoki (Deatnu in the North Sámi language), a majestic river, famous for salmon fishing, that forms the Finland–Norway border for over 140km. The drive can be done in one long day but it's enjoyable to stay a night or two. Much of the route is within Utsjoki municipality, the only one in Finland with a majority Sámi population. Outside summer, check road conditions before setting out.

### 1 Inari

Start at **Inari**, the lakeside village that is the effective Sámi cultural capital in Finland.

**The Drive:** Head 32km north on Rd 4, then 65km west to Karigasniemi on Rd 95 (about 1½ hours total).

### 2 Karigasniemi

A bridge crosses the Inarijoki to Norway but we turn north through the village on Rd 970. The last petrol station before Utsjoki is here, and you could stop for a break at the Guossi cafe. After 5km the Inarijoki combines with the Karasjohka entering from Norway, to become the Tenojoki (unfortunately trees block the view of the confluence).

**The Drive:** Just enjoy the scenery as the road winds 1½ hours along the Teno Valley to Utsjoki, paralleling the broad river as it flows powerfully between the enclosing fells.

WJAREK/SHUTTERSTOCK ©

Tenojoki, on the border of Finland and Norway

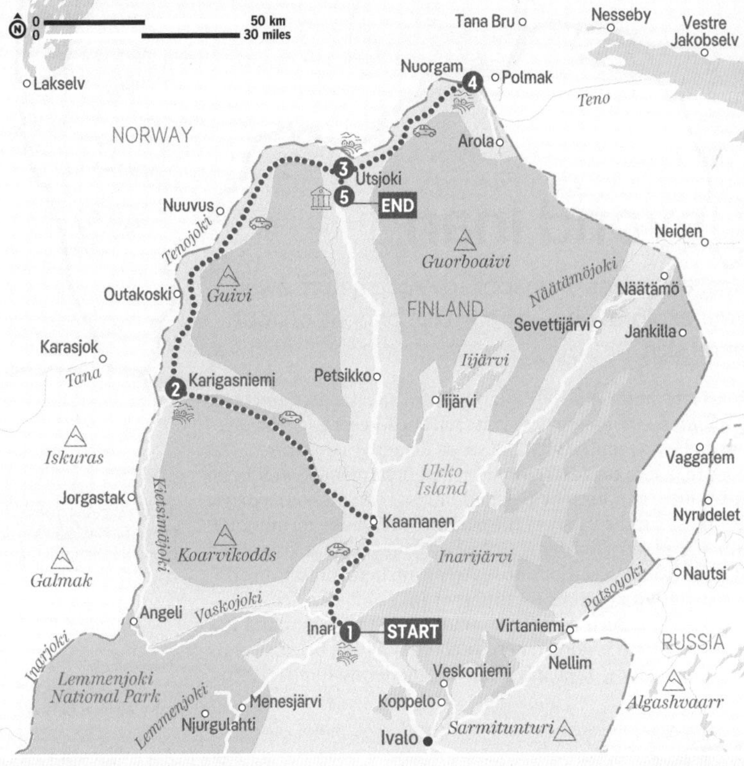


## 3 Utsjoki

You reach Lomakylä Valle (Holiday Village Valle), the route's classiest accommodation, with a restaurant right over the riverbank, 99km from Karigasniemi. Two kilometres further is Utsjoki, where the impressive Sámi Bridge spans the Tenojoki. Utsjoki (population: 340) has a craft shop, tourist information and cafe in its village hall (Kylätalo Giisá), decent rooms, restaurant and bar at the midrange Hotel Utsjoki, and a handful of mostly short (2km to 6km) walking trails.

**The Drive:** Keep right on to the end of the road (well, the end of Finland), about 45 minutes further along the Teno valley at Nuorgam.

## 4 Nuorgam

This is Finland's northernmost village. At its far end you reach the Norwegian border and a roadside rock labelled 'The Northernmost Point in EU and Finland'. Maps indicate the real northernmost point is in the river, about 400m north of here, but let's not quibble. The busiest place in town, when open, is Nuorgamin Lomakeskus, with good cabins, apartments and cafe/restaurant.

**The Drive:** Return to Utsjoki and turn south towards Inari. In 5km you reach the Utsjoen kirkkotuvat (Utsjoki church huts) beside Mantojärvi.

## 5 Utsjoki church huts

The wooden huts (13 today, though there were once more than 20) date back in some cases to the 18th century and were used until the 1940s by Sámi families attending the church here. The existing church, uphill, was built in 1853 to replace an earlier wooden one that had crumbled into disrepair. A trail leads south from the huts to the area of the old church. From here, head about two hours south along Rd 4 back to Inari.

# Beyond Inari

Tulvalahti
Inari
Lemmenjoki National Park
Njurgulahti
Joenkielinen
Ravadasköngäs
Saariselkä
Kiilopää
Urho Kekkonen National Park

**Vast expanses of unspoiled Arctic nature await your explorations – by car, bike or boat, on foot or on skis.**

Inari sits amid some of Finland's most spectacular and least populated territory, where lakes, rivers, forests and fells present endless scenic beauty and scope for active adventures. The country's two biggest national parks, Lemmenjoki and Urho Kekkonen, can both be reached in less than an hour's drive. To the north the valley of the beautiful Tenojoki, forming 140 km of Finland's border with Norway, makes for a great road trip. Seasonal variations are extreme up here, presenting different activity options for different times of year. September is an ideal month for hiking, with autumn colours and few insects. March is good for cross-country skiing because of its reasonably long days and relatively moderate temperatures.

### TOP TIP

It is practicable to visit the major national parks in day trips from Inari, but they will amply reward longer stays.

**Urho Kekkonen National Park** (p211)

VICTOR MASCHEK/SHUTTERSTOCK ©

DELBO ANDREA/SHUTTERSTOCK ©

Reindeer rides

## BEST INARI AREA FESTIVALS

**Poro-Kuninkuusajot**
Inari's 'Royal Reindeer Race' (late March/early April): animals and skiing 'jockeys' on frozen Inarijärvi.

**Ijahis Idja**
Two-day 'Nightless Night' indigenous music festival (August) focuses on the multiple genres of Sámi music.

**Inari Viikot**
'Inari Weeks' (late July): concerts, markets, parties and more in Inari, Saariselkä, Lemmenjoki and elsewhere.

**Skábmagovat**
Indigenous peoples' film festival (late January) includes films in English, with some open-air screenings.

**Kaamosjazz**
'World's darkest jazz festival' brightens up Saariselkä winter nights with a January weekend of gigs.

## Visit to a Sámi Home

CRAFTS, REINDEER & COFFEE

Learn about Sámi life first hand on a visit to the friendly lakeside home of Tuula Airamo, at Tulvalahti, a 20-minute drive northwest of Inari (off the Angeli road).

In a three-hour visit you get to feed Tuula's reindeer, see how reindeer-hide shoes are made and wool dyed from natural plants, and learn about local folklore and history over coffee and home-baked goodies. Shorter options are also possible; booking ahead is essential (www.tuulasreindeer.weebly.com).

## Reindeer & Huskies

ANIMAL FARMS

Several reindeer and husky farms in the Inari area open for visits. **Reindeer Farm** Petri Mattus, a half-hour drive southwest of Inari and belonging to a friendly Sámi family, gives visitors a taste of authentic reindeer husbandry on their daily visit to tend their herd (December to April).

### WHERE TO FIND CRAFTS BEYOND INARI

**Ateljee Huopapirtti**
Paltto Elämysretket, Lemmenjoki, has superb works of felt art, many incorporating old shamanic symbols.

**Kammigalleria**
Sámi artisan Kikka Laakso at Lemmenjoki creates detailed jewellery and other items from reindeer antler and leather.

**Kaunispään Huippu**
Amazing artisanship, including beautiful jewellery with local gemstones, at the top of Saariselkä's Kaunispää ski lift.

### I LIVE HERE: FAMILY HISTORY

Sámi **Margetta Jompan-Tiainen** is hostess of Ahkun Tupa guesthouse, Njurgulahti.

My grandfather and his two brothers, Sámi reindeer herders from Norway, founded this village when they settled here in the late 19th century. My father Juhani Jomppanen started tourism here in 1946 by transporting travellers on his Nuoli boats on Inarijärvi and the Lemmenjoki river. He was also a goldminer and our family still has the same claim. Our boats continue to operate from Njurgulahti to the gold-panning areas through Lemmenjoki National Park, driven by my husband Juha Tiainen. During winter, I still have reindeer in the yard. This is my birthplace and I enjoy working in this peaceful, beautiful nature.

You'll see hundreds of reindeer and learn about the reindeer-herding life over coffee and snacks. It's essential to make contact at least a day ahead. In May there's the chance to head out to the calving area to see newborns.

Over 140 huskies live at family-run Guesthouse Husky, off the Ivalo road about 45 minutes' drive south of Inari, and they'll pull you on a range of sled rides – from a quick one-hour spin to three-day expeditions with nights in a cabin on an Inarijärvi island.

Each winter there are several guaranteed-departure small-group two- or three-day safaris.

In summer, wheeled-cart husky rides are available if the temperatures aren't too high for the dogs (maximum 10°C). Owner Juha-Pekka was one of the first people in Lapland to offer husky tours and is a champion long-distance husky racer.

**Ride North Inari**, a Sámi-owned lakeside husky farm about 10 minutes' drive north of Inari, offers mostly shorter experiences, including simple farm visits on which you can hug the amiable dogs, and a two-hour 'husky experience', where you can join in preparing the dogs as well as go mushing for 7km or so. It also has wheeled-cart rides on cooler summer days, and snowshoeing and aurora borealis outings in winter.

EMKA74/SHUTTERSTOCK ©

## Lemmenjoki: Finland's Biggest National Park

RIVERS, FORESTS, FELLS & GOLD

Finland's biggest national park, Lemmenjoki, stretches over 2860 sq km of virtually uninhabited forests, fells, river valleys and wetlands southwest of Inari.

It's an excellent summer hiking area, with a helpful scheduled summer boat service along the river. Most of the marked walking trails are within the park's 'recreation zone', a strip about 40km long and up to 12km wide embracing the Lemmenjoki valley and the old-growth forests and fells either side of it.

Accommodation and services are concentrated around the small, scattered Sámi village of **Njurgulahti**, on the national

### WHERE TO EAT IN SAARISELKÄ

**Kaunispään Huippu**
Panoramic lunch restaurant on Kaunispää hill with reindeer soup, salad buffet and wonderful fish pies. **€€**

**Laanilan Kievari**
Restaurant 2.5km south of Saariselkä with well-prepared game, fish and veggie options; reservations advised. **€€**

**Petronella**
Artfully presented northern favourites – elk, snow grouse, lake fish – in an attractive dining room. **€€€**

GUIM/SHUTTERSTOCK ©

Ravadasköngäs

park's eastern fringe, a 45-minute drive from Inari.

The most popular route is along the river from Njurgulahti to **Ravadasköngäs**, where the Ravadasjoki tumbles into the Lemmenjoki in 10m-high falls (17km from Njurgulahti by boat, slightly less on foot), and a further 6km to **Kultahamina**. The boat service run by **Ahkun Tupa** from Njurgulahti operates from early June to mid-September. From mid-June to mid-August there's a morning and an evening service in each direction; otherwise it's evening only. Journey time to Ravadasköngäs (€25 one way) is about an hour, to Kultahamina (€30) 1½ hours. The forest-lined river sometimes broadens to around 300m wide in stretches that the locals call lakes; at other times it passes through cliff-lined narrows.

A good day-trip plan is to walk up to Ravadasköngäs then take the boat back. When there are two sailings each day, you could boat up and walk back, or boat up to Kultahamina then walk to Ravadasköngäs and catch the evening boat back from there.

The **marked walking trails** start from a parking area about 1.5km south of the middle of Njurgulahti. From here it's about 14.5km along the river valley to a wilderness hut at Ravadasjärvi, then a further 700m to Ravadasköngäs. The trail spends a lot of its time on ridges above the river, but you have to descend to cross the river on a cable boat at either Searitniva or Härkäkoski. Another good trail from the

## BEST LEMMENJOKI NATIONAL PARK ACCOMMODATION

**Hotel Korpikartano**
Hotel on Menesjärvi lake, 15km from Njurgulahti; Pine-panelled rooms, local-produce restaurant, many activities almost year-round. Sámi-owned. €€

**Ahkun Tupa**
Sámi-owned Njurgulahti accommodation, from shared-bathroom rooms to log cottages with private sauna. Runs Lemmenjoki boat service. €

**Paltto Elämysretket**
Four well-equipped, comfy cottages for up to six people at Njurgulahti. Organises its own river trips. Sámi-owned. €€

**Lomakylä Valkeaporo**
Sámi-owned campground with good-quality cabins beside Menesjärvi on Njurgulahti approach road. Does river trips, rents canoes. €

**Lemmenjoen Lumo**
HI-affiliated summer campground at Njurgulahti with basic rooms and cabins and a cafe. €

## WHERE TO EAT IN SAARISELKÄ

**Restaurant Kaltio**
Lapland specialities, from salmon soup to grilled reindeer, in stylish surroundings at Santa's Hotel Tunturi. €€€

**Pirkon Pirtti**
Try the bouillabaisse and fish dishes in this bright, well-spaced dining room. €€€

**Rakka Restaurant**
Reliable hotel restaurant with burgers and a children's menu, as well as reindeer and snails. €€

### WILDERNESS HUTS

Metsähallitus, the forest administration, operates a marvellous network of several hundred hikers'/skiers'/canoeists' huts in Finland's national parks and other protected areas.

**Open wilderness huts** Unlocked huts with bunks or boards for sleeping, wood stove, cooking equipment, dry toilet and firewood. Often sociable places, in peak seasons some can fill up. Last arrivals have priority.

**Day-trip huts** Like open wilderness huts, without sleeping space.

**Campfire huts** Day huts with benches round a fireplace.

**Reservable huts** Like open wilderness huts but locked; you pay to reserve an overnight place and get a key.

**Rental huts** Pay to rent the whole thing.

For further information see Metsähallitus info centres and http://nationalparks.fi.

ERKKI MAKKONEN/SHUTTERSTOCK ©

Saariselkä

parking area is the 16km circuit via the top of **Joenkielinen** fell (535m), with great panoramas rewarding a 300m ascent (and descent).

Kultahamina (meaning 'Gold Harbour') is the gateway to an area where much of the prospecting and panning happened during the 1940s and '50s Lemmenjoki gold rush. It's a 1.6km walk to the site of the first gold find, next to the Morgamoja stream. If you're up for an overnight trip with some steepish parts, the **Kultareitti** (Gold Trail) is a 25km loop from Kultahamina up through the pine and birch forests on to the open fells then back down to Ravadasjärvi. There are wilderness huts for sleeping at both ends of the route and at Morgamoja (after 4.5km). You can also camp.

## Europe's Most Northerly Ski Resort

SAARISELKÄ IN WINTER

Saariselkä, an hour's drive south of Inari along Rd 4, is a pleasant, scattered settlement, far bigger than its permanent population of around 300 might suggest – because so many of its buildings are holiday cottages and hotels. It is busiest (and looks prettiest) in winter. **Ski Saariselkä**, as the ski resort calls itself, comprises 20 slopes on two hills, Kaunispää and Isisakkipää, rising either side of the same valley.

### WHERE TO STAY IN & AROUND SAARISELKÄ

**Log House Kuukkeli Teerenpesä**
Delightfully cosy, up-to-date rooms in a long log building in Saariselkä; free sauna. €€

**Suomen Latu Kiilopää**
Excellent establishment at the Kiilopää trailheads, with hotel rooms, hostel, cabins, apartments and equipment rentals. €€

**Star Arctic Hotel**
Classy, panoramic, Scandi-style hotel with suites and aurora-view glass-roofed cabins up on Kaunispää hill. €€€

The season here can last from mid-November to the beginning of May. The longest run is 2km with a vertical drop of 180m. You can also career down Finland's longest toboggan run (1.3km).

Over 150km of maintained cross-country skiing tracks roam the fells and valleys around Saariselkä. Bikers, hikers and snowshoers aren't allowed to use these – but never fear, plenty of bike and walking trails are maintained in winter too. Drop into the helpful **Kieninen information centre** for trail maps and answers to any questions.

The full panoply of husky, reindeer, snowmobile and aurora borealis safaris is on offer from local operators, such as **LuontoLoma** and **Husky & Co**, as well as the Saariselkä branch of **Lapland Safaris**.

When the day is done you won't find a better watering hole in northern Lapland than **Local Pub Panimo**, with its long wooden tables, roaring fire, plenty of beers and other drinks, and sometimes live music.

## Saariselkä Summer

FUN UNDER THE MIDNIGHT SUN

The winter resort Saariselkä, an hour's drive south of Inari, buzzes in summer too. You have l-o-n-g days to enjoy being out and about, with the sun never setting from late May to late July.

Several marked Urho Kekkonen National Park walking and bike trails start at a trailhead on Lutontie in the village. A good day's walk is the **Rumakuru trail**, a 14km circuit with views into gorges along the way.

A number of places in Saariselkä rent fatbikes, mountain bikes, e-fatbikes and e-mountain bikes. **LuontoLoma** will take you rafting or canoeing on rivers in the area, or rent you a canoe to go it alone.

## Rambles & Treks

URHO KEKKONEN NATIONAL PARK

A 2550 sq km expanse of forests, open fells, ridges and valleys, **Urho Kekkonen National Park** rolls more than 40km east from Saariselkä to the Russian border and even further to the south.

It's a perfect canvas for anyone who likes vast expanses of pristine nature. The panoramas from the tops of its hills are awe-inspiring. You can walk into the park's northwest corner at the edge of Saariselkä village, or reach deeper into the

### I LIVE HERE: HOW TO TRAVEL RESPONSIBLY IN SÁMI HOMELAND

**Kirsi Suomi** coordinates the Responsible Sámi Tourism project of the Sámi Parliament in Finland.

**Sámi people's home**
Visitors may see Sámiland as an untouched wilderness, but it's been a home for indigenous Sámi people since time immemorial. The land provides a livelihood and subsistence economy for local Sámi, who herd their reindeer and hunt, gather and fish here. Be considerate of their cultural practices.

**Don't objectify the Sámi**
If you're visiting indigenous Sámi communities, let local people go about their everyday lives undisturbed. Don't objectify the Sámi by photographing them without permission. They value privacy.

**Before your visit**
Read our guidance: samediggi.fi/saamelaismat kailu/en/.

### WHERE TO STAY IN & AROUND SAARISELKÄ

**Saariselkä Kuukkeli Inn**
Relatively economical option in the village; seven plain, well-kept rooms sharing bathrooms, kitchen/dining and sauna. €€

**Wilderness Hotel Muotka**
Attractive wood-panelled rooms, log cabins, glass-roofed aurora cabins in the forest 2km off Kiilopää road. €€€

**Saariselkä Keskusvaraamo**
Central reservation service for cottages, cabins and apartments, which can be convenient. €€

## EIGHT SEASONS

It's often said that northern Lapland has not just four seasons, but eight. Siida in Inari characterises them as follows (we've added approximate Gregorian-month equivalents):

**Spring–winter** (March–April) Migratory birds start arriving; sunlight combined with low nighttime temperatures forms a walkable crust on the snow.

**Spring** (May) Snow and ice melt, reindeer calves are born.

**Spring–summer** (June) Nightless night starts.

**Summer** (late June and July) The insect season, good for birds, bad for reindeer and humans.

**Autumn–summer** (August) Berry- and mushroom-collecting time.

**Autumn** (September–October) Glorious autumn colours *(ruska)*, then first snowfalls.

**Autumn–winter** (November–December) Lakes freeze, snow settles, polar night starts.

**Winter** (January–February) Very low temperatures; once the sun reappears, daylight hours increase rapidly.

park from **Kiilopää**, about 1½ hours' drive from Inari at the end of a 6km road from Kakslauttanen, which is 11km south of Saariselkä on Rd 4. Kiilopää consists almost solely of the buildings of **Suomen Latu Kiilopää**, an excellent base with accommodation at various prices, a cafe, two restaurants and rental of bikes, skis and camping gear.

Numerous trails start at Kiilopää. The 6km **Kiirunapolku** loop takes you to the top of **Kiilopää fell** (546m) with superb panoramas.

The hill is home to the poor Kiilopää birch, a type of tree which instead of growing upwards like normal trees creeps along the ground to survive the ferocious winter winds and temperatures up here. You can extend this walk by switching to the Luulampi trail on the way down for a total circuit of about 10km.

A classic, more demanding, route is the 22km **Rautulampi circuit**, over superb fell scenery. It's only partly marked so requires navigation skills.

Serious fit trekkers can head out for days on end, using the park's numerous wilderness huts for overnighting. One of the most popular unmarked routes is the four-to-six-day loop (70 to 80km) from Kiilopää to **Luirojärvi** via Suomuruoktu and Tuiskukuru and back via Lankojärvi (70–80km). From Luirojärvi you can spend an extra day climbing up and down the park's highest peak, Sokosti (718m).

Some good mountain bike trails for summer or winter, and cross-country skiing tracks, also start from, or pass through, Kiilopää.

There's comprehensive information on the national park at www.nationalparks.fi/urhokekkonennp. The **Kiehinen** information centre in Saariselkä is very helpful and sells maps (and national park t-shirts) and takes bookings for the reservable and rental huts in the park.

## GETTING AROUND

As ever, your own wheels are most convenient. Eskelisen Lapin Linjat buses depart Ivalo airport for Saariselkä and Kiilopää 20 minutes after flight arrivals. Returning, they leave Kiilopää 2½ hours before flight departures, stopping in Saariselkä about half an hour later. Eskelisen also runs a daily bus from Karasjok (Norway) to Rovaniemi that stops at Inari, Saariselkä and Kiilopää, plus a daily bus from Inari to Rovaniemi stopping at Saariselkä. Heading north, buses depart Kiilopää and Saariselka in the afternoons. A ski bus shuttles around Saariselkä hotels and the ski lifts during the season. There's no public transport to Lemmenjoki National Park. If you don't have your own wheels you have to take a tour or a taxi.

Kilpisjärvi
Helsinki

# KILPISJÄRVI

If you like remote places, come to the village of Kilpisjärvi, right up at the top of Finland's northwest arm. There's only one settlement of any size (the small village of Karesuvanto) along the entire 200km road leading up here from Muonio.

Kilpisjärvi sits under the stern gaze of Saana fell, on the east side of beautiful Kilpisjärvi (lake), looking across to northern Swedish hills on the far shore.

The Norwegian border is just a few kilometres north, and Skibotn on Norway's Lyngen fjord is just 50km away. Kilpisjärvi is also the highest village in Finland, at 490m above sea level, situated as it is on the fringe of the northern end of the Scandinavian Mountains.

It's a great spot for some wilderness hiking in the snow-free season (typically early June to early/mid October), and that, along with transit to/from Norway, is why most visitors come here.

## TOP TIP

The main section of the village includes most accommodation and restaurants, the useful visitor centre of Metsähallitus (the forestry administration, which manages protected natural areas), a small shopping centre and a petrol station. Five kilometres up the road towards Norway is the Kilpisjärven Retkeilykeskus accommodation, and 2km beyond that is the main hiking trailhead.

OLIVER BIALLAWONS/SHUTTERSTOCK ©

**Kolmen valtakunnan rajapyykki (Three-Country Cairn; p214)**

### A REINDEER YEAR

Almost all reindeer in Finland are semi-domesticated and are husbanded mainly for their meat. A typical reindeer year goes something like this:
**April/May** Move to calving areas.
**May** Calves are born. Females drop their antlers about two weeks later.
**Late June/early July** Roundup for earmarking of calves.
**October** The mating season (rut). Afterwards, male reindeer drop their antlers (antlers of both sexes grow back each summer).
**End October/ November/ December** Roundup, and slaughter of selected animals.
**24 December** A very lucky few fly off with Santa Claus to circumnavigate the globe.
**December-March/ April** Reindeer stay on winter pastures, often close to their owner's homestead.
To learn much more about reindeer visit http://paliskunnat.fi (Finland's Reindeer Herders' Association).

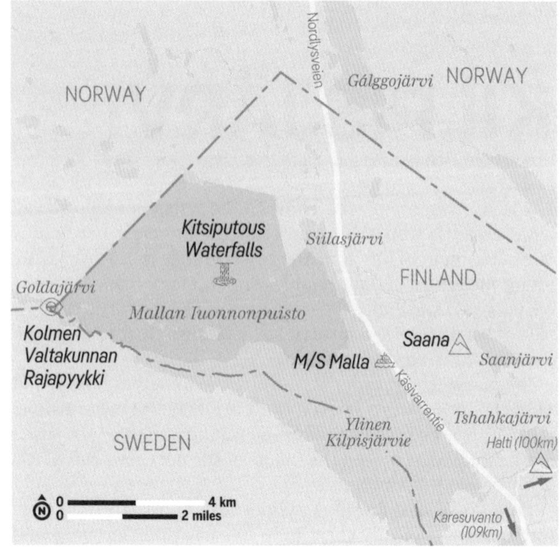


## Where Three Countries Meet

TRIP TO THE TRIPLE BORDER

Finland, Norway and Sweden all converge not far west of Kilpisjärvi, and their meeting point at the **Kolmen valtakunnan rajapyykki** (Three-Country Cairn) is a fabulous outing.

From about mid-June to the end of September, MS Malla sails at 10am and 3pm from the Kilpisjärvi lakeshore (opposite Kilpisjärven Retkeilykeskus) to **Koltaluokta** on the Swedish shore (30 minutes; one-way/return €35/50). The boat waits two hours before returning – time to walk the easy 3km to the border point and back.

The Three-Country Cairn stands just off the shore of Goldajávri (a metal walkway leads to it). Nearby, on the Finnish side, are the Kuohkimajärvi open and reservable wilderness huts for those who want to sleep here.

It's a great idea to return to Kilpisjärvi on foot. The path back (11km, about three hours) parallels a reindeer fence northeast

### WHERE TO EAT IN KILPISJÄRVI

**Tundrea**
Hotel restaurant good for northern favourites (salmon soup, reindeer steak) and also pizza and pasta. €€

**Cahkal Hotel**
Panoramic hotel restaurant with creative preparations (pike ceviche and reindeer sausages). €€€

**Kilpisjärven Retkeilykeskus**
Good-value, no-frills restaurant doing a decent buffet lunch plus waffles, salads, pizzas and burgers. €

for some 2km, then veers eastward up through birch forest, then traverses open moorland with fabulous views over Kilpisjärvi and other smaller lakes.

Approaching **Kitsiputous Waterfalls** (100m high, in several stages) it becomes rockier. Crossing the stream below the falls might be tricky when there's a lot of water. You climb to a small pass with a **reconstructed German WWII bunker**, then it's a gradually descending 4.5km to the roadside trailhead 2km north of the Retkeilykeskus.

Walking to the border and returning by boat, or walking both ways, are also quite feasible.

## Up the Hills

SAANA & FINLAND'S HIGHEST POINT

Cliff-girt **Saana**, looming above Kilpisjärvi, looks distinctly forbidding when it's wreathed in cloud. But in decent weather this 1029m fell rewards a climb with spectacular panoramas.

The main trail to its summit starts 2km along the main road past the Kilpisjärven Retkeilykeskus. After 1.5km the trail crosses a path coming from the Retkeilykeskus, which continues eastward round to Saanajärvi (5km).

Head straight on over this up the treeless hillside. A flight of 200 steps surmounts the steepest part, then the often rocky path continues upward, with the gradient easing near the summit (4.3km from the start). Head down the way you came up.

To make a full day of it, turn east towards Saanajärvi along the path you crossed earlier. This makes an 11km circuit right round the base of Saana, via Saanajärvi (with campfire huts) and the Retkeilykeskus. Some streams en route may have strong currents when they're running high.

Finland's highest point (1324m), on **Halti** fell on the Norwegian border, is a 55km trek of about four days (one way) from Kilpisjärvi, practicable July to mid-September.

For a quicker expedition, some Kilpisjärvi hotels and tour firms offer day-trips including transport to/from **Guolasjávri** in Norway and a quite strenuous hike up and down the hill from there (7km each way).

The hill's actual summit, Ráisduattarháldi (1361m), is in Norway, 2km north of Finland's highest point.

### BEST ACCOMMODATION IN KILPISJÄRVI

**Tundrea**
Range of attractive apartments, chalets and cottages, some with private sauna; a good seasonal restaurant. €€

**Kilpisjärven Retkeilykeskus**
Well-kept, no-frills rooms and campground close to MS *Malla* and hiking trailheads. €€

**Cahkal Hotel**
Classy, contemporary-styled, 23-room boutique hotel in a panoramic position, opened in 2022. €€€

**Arctic Polar Holiday Village**
Fairly simple wood-lined apartments in the main village, with a restaurant. €€

### GETTING AROUND

If you don't have your own transport you can get here by two daily buses from Rovaniemi via Muonio. In this case, staying at the Kilpisjärven Retkeilykeskus is the convenient option for MS Malla and hiking trails. If you stay in the main part of the village you've got a long walk up to the north end unless you can rent or borrow a bicycle. It is, however, possible to access the Saanajärvi circuit path at its south end by a 2.3km trail from the main part of the village.

# TOOLKIT

The chapters in this section cover the most important topics you'll need to know about in Finland. They're full of nuts-and-bolts information and valuable insights to help you understand and navigate Finland and get the most out of your trip.



Oulanka National Park (p179)

MAZUR TRAVEL/SHUTTERSTOCK ©

# Arriving

Helsinki-Vantaa Airport is the primary point of entry for most visitors arriving in Finland. The airport, with a railway station underneath, is located 28km from Helsinki city centre. Renovated in 2021, it now has one terminal for both arrivals and and departures, a lot of cafes, restaurants and shops. A new baggage claim area will open in the summer of 2023.

**Visas**

EU and Nordic nationals don't need a visa to enter Finland. Those from the UK, Canada, Australia, New Zealand, the US and South America can stay for up to 90 days.

**SIM cards**

Prepaid SIM cards can be purchased at the airport R-kiosks; one is located in the arrivals terminal and the other by gate 50 in the non-Schengen area. The WHSmith stores also sell SIM cards.

**Border crossing**

If entering Finland by ferry, there are normal passport and visa requirements. Foreign nationals arriving from outside Schengen countries by land must enter via official border crossings, with valid documents.

**Wi-fi**

Free 100 Mbps wi-fi is available in the airport without requiring a password. The wi-fi in Finland is typically fast and access is widespread.

### Public transport from Airport to city centre

| | Helsinki | Tampere | Rovaniemi |
|---|---|---|---|
| TRAIN | 30 mins €4.10 | N/A | N/A |
| BUS | 45 mins €2.80 | 30 mins €4.50 | 10 mins €8 |
| TAXI | 30 mins €35 | 20 mins €35 | 10 mins €25 |

## AIRPORTS IN FINLAND

Finland's busiest airport is Helsinki-Vantaa Airport, but international flights from European countries also use smaller airports, especially the Rovaniemi airport in Lapland. From Helsinki, it takes approximately 1.5 hours to fly to Rovaniemi. But at half the price, you'll get there also by using the train in about 8 to 9 hours, or the 11–12-hour night train.

Apart from Rovaniemi, Lapland's airports are in Kemi-Tornio, Kittilä and Ivalo and are mainly used for domestic flights. After Helsinki, Tampere-Pirkkala Airport has the biggest number of international flights, planes landing mainly from the UK, the Netherlands, Denmark and Germany.



GEORGE MDIVANIAN/EYEEM/GETTY IMAGES © BRESTER IRINA/ SHUTTERSTOCK ©, FUSE/GETTY IMAGES ©

# Getting Around

Trains are an easy and comfortable option when exploring the bigger cities, but for more remote destinations buses are necessary, and some will require a car.

### TRAVEL COSTS

Rental
**From €70/day**

Petrol
**Approx €2.04/litre**

EV charging
**from €0.2/KWh**

Train ticket from Helsinki to Tampere
**from €8.90**

### Hiring a car

It is best to rent cars in the bigger cities or airports for cheaper prices and availability. Some smaller cities don't offer car rentals. Both manual and automatic options are available. You can rent hybrid or electric cars – the charging network is constantly expanding.

### Road conditions

Bigger highways are in good shape but the remoter the road, the bumpier it gets. Take notice of warning signs for moose/deer. Roads are well-maintained but can get slippery in winter, so speed limits are lowered. Rental cars will have winter tyres.

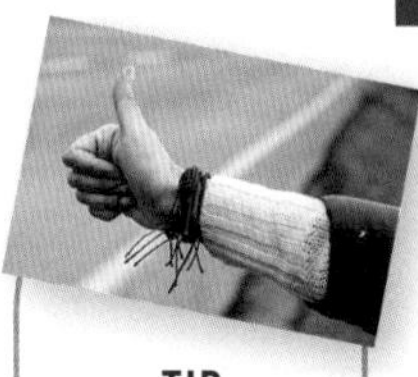

### TIP

Hitchhiking is safe but relatively uncommon, especially in Finland's remoter areas – ensure you have time and patience if attempting it.

### FERRY ROUTES

Finland is connected to several other European countries by ferry. Ferries from Tallinn arrive at Länsisatama terminal. Some boats from Tallinn also used the city centre Katajanokan terminaali. Ferries from Sweden arrive at Helsinki, Turku, Naantali and Vaasa, whereas the long-distance ferry from Germany arrives at Helsinki's Vuosaari. The quickest – and most budget-friendly – ferries shuttle between Helsinki and Tallinn in two hours (starting from 17€). The overnight ferries from Finland to Tallinn and Sweden are popular for parties and can get rowdy.

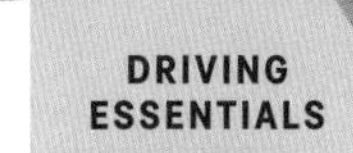

### DRIVING ESSENTIALS

Drive on the right.

Speed limit is 50km/h in urban areas, 80km/h in secondary roads and 120km/h in motorways, 100km/h during winter.

**.05**

Blood alcohol limit is 0.5‰

### Bus & train

Bigger cities, especially below Lapland, are well-connected by rail and long-distance bus networks. In Lapland, Tornio, Rovaniemi, Kemijärvi and Kajaani can be reached by train, with few stops in between. Buses and trains are reliable and comfortable, although snow might cause delays occasionally in winter.

### Train tickets

Train tickets are cheaper if you purchase online at least a month before the journey. Finland's train provider is the government-owned VR. Long-distance tickets have to be bought before boarding the train, commuter tickets can be purchased on the train. Stations will have ticket machines and service desks.

### Plane

Finnair operates in over a dozen airports around Finland, for example Helsinki–Turku (40 minutes) and Helsinki–Ivalo in Lapland (1 hour, 45 minutes). Unless you are in a hurry, opt for the more carbon-friendly trains, which also gives you time to see more of the country in one trip.

# Money

CURRENCY: **EURO (€)**

### Credit cards

Hotels, cafes, restaurants and shops accept credit cards, as do most stalls in the market squares, especially in bigger cities. In more remote spots it is convenient to have some cash at hand in case credit card machines are down.

### Digital payments

Digital payments are growing in popularity but credit cards and cash are still widely used. MobilePay is the most popular app for mobile payments in Finland but other apps, such as ApplePay, work as well.

### Taxes & refunds

Prices in Finland include 24% VAT in consumer goods and 14% in food products. People with permanent residence outside the EU can claim tax back for unused purchases that cost over €40. You can process the taxes in some stores, at the airport or electronically.

### Tipping

Tipping is not customary in Finland, although some restaurants have started providing the option for tipping, especially when paying with card. Staff will always appreciate extra income.

### HOW MUCH FOR A...

Night in a Lapland igloo
**approx €300**

Reindeer farm & sleigh ride
**from €100**

Public saunas
**€8-15**

Ferry ticket to Tallinn
**€20**

### HOW TO... Save some euros

Student-card holders, pensioners and people over 65 years old get a reduction to many main sights and for train and bus tickets. If you are keen on a sightseeing spree in Helsinki, buy a Helsinki Card from the tourist office and get free admission to many main sights, museums and the sightseeing bus.
In the rising foodie hub Turku, the Turku Food Walk Card will showcase the flavours of the city.

### LOCAL TIP

When travelling by car, keep a few coins handy, as cities outside Helsinki might still have one or two parking metres operating with coins – although payment with an app/card is more common.

### BEST THINGS IN LIFE ARE FREE

With the price of pizza easily reaching over €20 in Helsinki, Finland can feel like a pricey country to visit. Today, more and more Finns are also starting to feel the pinch, as living costs are rising due to the recent changes in the economic situation. Train and bus tickets can also feel expensive at times, but remember: the distances are long. On the other hand, some of the most valuable things here are free: that is, education and healthcare, so in the end, Finns in general are happy to pay their heavy taxes

# Accommodation

## Rental cottages

Finland is a nation of cottages and there is a good supply in the rental markets, too. Lomarengas (lomarengas.fi) has the biggest selection. Many cottages are located by lakes or the seaside and come with a sauna. Traditionally, Finnish cottages have been very modest places (with outdoor toilets) but recently, more luxurious cottages have been built.

## Camp out

Freedom to roam guarantees that camping is allowed almost everywhere, especially if you pitch your tent for a day or two, and not on cultivated land. In nature reserves and national parks camping is allowed in designated areas. Some beaches have restricted camping possibilities. A landowner's permission is always needed before you make a fire.

## Glass igloos & the ice hotel

Glass igloos are a fabulous way to see the aurora borealis (Northern Lights), especially in Lapland where you can find many options, from Rovaniemi to all the way to the northernmost parts of Saariselkä. In southern parts of Finland, glass igloos are normally located by lakes and seashores and provide calm vistas and starry night skies. Or sleep in temperatures below zero (0 to -5°C) in Rovaniemi's Arctic SnowHotel made of snow and ice.

### HOW MUCH FOR A NIGHT IN...

a rustic lakeside cottage
**€200**

a hostel dorm
**€30**

a manor house
**€150**

### Budget sleeps

Hostel dorms start from around €30 in high season, although (especially in Helsinki) a bed in a dorm can be as expensive as €70. Hostellit.fi is a good resource for finding a budget spot around Finland. You can also find budget hotels for around €50 to €70. Some guesthouses can be more budget-friendly, too, offering private rooms with shared bathrooms.

## Manor houses

Finland doesn't have a big B&B culture but in more remote areas there are some charming guesthouses transformed from old manor and farm houses. The manor houses normally offer a feast of local produce. The range of manor houses vary from swish stays with spas to more modest, yet equally, enchanting settings.

## SUSTAINABLE STAYS

Nolla ('zero' in Finnish) cabins are modest huts with a design twist, located at Helsinki's seaside and the Archipelago Sea near Turku. The A-shaped cabins are based on a zero-waste ethos and part of the profits go to The Finnish Association for Nature Conservation. Ollero has sustainable glass igloos in Lapland, and Rovaniemi's Arctic TreeHouse has won sustainability awards, as well as the Solo Sokos Hotel Seurahuone in Lahti. Look for the Green Key and the Sustainable Travel Finland labels when booking a sustainable stay; there are plenty of options around Finland.

PANDO HALL/GETTY IMAGES ©; RYAN MCVAY/GETTY IMAGES ©; POM BAKERY/SHUTTERSTOCK ©

# Family Travel

Finland is incredibly child friendly, and a terrific place to holiday with kids. A trip with kids to this outdoorsy destination could include splashing about in lakes and rivers, hikes in national parks, cycling and open-air theme parks. In winter, the reliable snow opens up a world of outdoor possibilities, and there's a year-round seat on Santa's knee.

## Getting Around

In Helsinki, children age seven and under travel free on all public transport and ferries. If a child is in a stroller, the adult with them travels free as well. Most other transport tickets for children tend to be around 60% of the adult charge. At car-hire firms, child safety seats must be booked in advance and cost about €45 a day; consider bringing one as plane carry-on luggage.

## Sights

Finnish children are on school holidays from mid-June to early August, and many child-oriented activities are closed outside this period. This is when campgrounds are buzzing with Finnish families, and temperatures are usually warm. If your kids are older and you want to get active in the snow, go in March or April: there's plenty of daylight, better snow and the cold isn't so extreme.

## Accommodation

Finland's rental cabins, apartments and cottages make excellent family bases. Campgrounds are also good, often have a lake beach and playground, and rent out boats and bikes. Most hotels will provide an extra bed for little added cost. Kids under 12 often sleep free.

## Going Out

Most museums in Helsinki have free admission for kids. High chairs and cots (cribs) are standard in many restaurants, but numbers may be limited. Most resort hotels always have family-friendly restaurants with a kids' menu, or deals where children eat free if accompanied by adults.

## KID-FRIENDLY PICKS

**Muumimaailma (Moominworld) (p84)**

Moomin theme-park extravaganza.

**Santa Claus Village (p197)**

Visit the big man in red and his post office.

**Snowman World (p197)**

Skate, slide and dine at an ice restaurant.

**Särkänniemi (p123)**

Amusement park with roller coasters and a rotating restaurant.

**Children's Town (p52)**

Helsinki's history experienced through imaginative playtime.

**Jukupark (p83)**

Finland's biggest water park, with wild slides.

**Ranua Wildlife Park (p198)**

Nature spotting plus horse-sleigh rides and mini-snowmobiles.

## PARENTING IN FINLAND

Finland's parenting culture typically places a high importance on independent, outdoor play. Children are encouraged to explore nature freely. In the forests of regions such as Lapland, they may learn to build fires and use certain tools from a young age. Children's programming and activities are sometimes less structured than in many other countries, and leave space for wandering, yet this approach also lends to a high focus on interactive, educational and fun museums. It's typical for such attractions to have many summer demonstrations and activities, making visits interesting for grown-ups and kids alike.



CANBEDONE/SHUTTERSTOCK ©; ONDREJ PROSICKY/SHUTTERSTOCK ©; ROAD SIGNS SOURCE: WIKIPEDIA

# Health & Safe Travel

## BEAR ENCOUNTERS

Bear encounters are extremely unlikely as bears generally want to avoid human contact. Should you see one, back away quietly without eye contact: running won't help as they will win. Bears are good climbers and swimmers. If a bear chases you, lie on the ground covering your head and neck with your hands and pretend to be dead.

### Mosquitos

Around June and July, mosquitos are everywhere in Finland, but especially in rural areas and Lapland. In cities you will barely see them; they are at their worst in forests when there's no breeze. Wear clothing that covers you from head to toe, including a mosquito head net, and use repellents. Apart from the itching bites, Finland's mosquitos are harmless.

### Winter

In winter, Finland is a true wonderland, but it comes with a price: the cold. Dress in layers, as the air between the clothing works as insulation. When the temperature drops below -15°C, cover your face with a scarf or a commando hat and avoid using products with water on your face. These can include foundation and certain moisturisers.

**SOLO TRAVEL**

Finland is a relatively safe country for women travelling alone. Taking the same precautions, as when travelling everywhere, is advised.

## SAFETY TIPS

Danger of moose on the road

Danger of reindeer on the road

Danger of deer on the road

Railroad crossing without a safety barrier

Forest fire warning: lighting a fire in nature forbidden

### Scams

Finland is pretty safe regarding pickpocketing, but some incidences occur, especially in crowded city spots, such as in shops and on public transport. If you drop your phone, wallet or other valuables, contact Löytötavaratoimisto (lost and found, phone +358600 41006, available 24/7) or the local police – chances are you will get it back.

**NIGHTLIFE**

In general, Finns are a bit reserved but polite. Open aggression is most typically encountered during nighttime in bars, clubs and city streets when alcohol has been consumed, but the nightlife scene is still safe. For visitors, Finns' alcohol consumption might seem excessive, although in recent years more and more people are opting for mocktails instead of cocktails.

# Food, Drink & Nightli

### When to Eat

**Aamiainen** (breakfast, 7am to 10am) is a simple affair, with filter coffee or tea and bread, yogurt or porridge.

**Lounas** (lunch, 11am to 1pm) is served often as a buffet.

**Illallinen** (dinner, 5pm to 6pm) normally consists of slightly pricier dishes and can be eaten later, especially when celebrating or meeting with friends.

### Where to Eat

**Ravintola (restaurant):** Can vary from a lunch buffet or corner shop bar to fine dining.

**Leipomo or leipomo-kahvila (bakery or coffee shop and bakery):** Normally artisanal or traditional Finnish bakeries with a small eating area.

**Panimoravintola (brewery restaurant):** Typically you will find one or two in the biggest cities. Food can vary from street food and gastropub dishes to German-influenced plates.

**Baari (a bar):** Includes swish spots with classy cocktails as well as more relaxed neighbourhood joints.

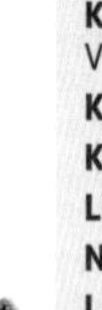

### MENU DECODER

**Ruokalista:** menu
**Alkuruoka:** Starters
**Pääruoka:** Mains
**Jälkiruoka:** Dessert
**Brunssi:** Brunch
**Lasten lista:** Kids menu
**Sesongin menu:** Seasonal menu
**Maistelumenu:** Tasting menu
**Kasvismenu:** Vegetarian menu
**Kasvisvaihtoehto:** Vegetarian option
**Kala:** Fish
**Kana:** Chicken
**Liha:** Meat
**Naudanliha:** Beef
**Lammas:** Lamb
**Possu:** Pork
**Pihvi:** Steak
**Keitto:** Soup
**Salaatti:** Salad
**Ranskanperunat**: French fries
**Voileipä:** Sandwhich
**Juomat:** Drinks
**Tuoppi:** A pint
**Pullo:** A bottle
**Lasi:** A glass
**Limonadi:** Soft drink
**Mehu:** Juice
**Viini:** Wine
**Punaviini:** Red wine
**Valkoviini:** White wine
**Rosé-viini:** Rosé wine
**Kuiva:** Dry
**Makea:** Sweet
**Siideri:** Cider
**Olut:** Beer
**Kuohuviini:** Sparkling wine
**Kahvi:** Coffee
**Päivän erikoinen:** The day's special
**Keittiö suosittelee:** Kitchen recommends

HOW TO...

### Order (& clear your table)

Normally coffee shops have counter service where you order and pay by the till. Some cafes will bring your orders to the table, in others you are supposed to carry them yourself. Often, you are expected to clear your own table; check if there is a trolley to place your dishes. If not, the staff will clear after you are finished.

Lunch restaurants, especially the budget-friendly ones, are often buffets where you pay first and then collect your food and drinks. Normally there are salads, soups, and meat and vegetarian options, as well as gluten-and lactose-free products. Buffets include coffee/tea and dessert.

Dinner and à la carte lunch restaurants have table service. Sit down, and the staff will take care of you.



ALENA MATROSOVA/SHUTTERSTOCK ©; MAREKULIASZ/SHUTTERSTOCK ©

**HOW MUCH FOR A...**

Cinnamon bun
**€2-4 (varies according to size and place)**

Filter coffee (third-wave coffee houses are the priciest)
**€2.50-5**

Lunch at a buffet
**€9-13**

Pizza
**€13-16**

Dinner at a Michelin-star restaurant
**€200**

Beer
**€7-10**

Wine
**€8-15**

## HOW TO... Drink your coffee

Finns drink the most coffee in the world per capita (12kg per person to be exact, according to the International Coffee Association) so you might find it odd that much of the coffee here is light roasted filter coffee instead of the strong espressos or creamy cappuccinos, as in many other coffee-obsessed countries.

Typically, Finns start their mornings with a big mug (or three) of coffee. In the work environment there are scheduled coffee breaks in place based on employment contracts, and sometimes people even have a special cup of coffee after their evening saunas.

In coffee shops, people normally order filter coffee – as sometimes *santsikuppi* (a second cup/refill) is included in the price – or cappuccinos.

For more than a decade Finland has also enjoyed the rise of third-wave cafes, with beans roasted in artisan roasteries and smooth flat whites available.

Purists still have their coffees black, the daring ones with a dash of milk – and the modern radicals even with oat milk.

If you want to befriend a Finn, invite them for coffee – they'll find it hard to refuse.

Enjoying a cup of coffee and a chat is also oddly reassuring to the Finns, as many have fond memories associated with the ritual, so apart from having a sauna with them, a shared coffee moment might turn out to be a true icebreaker.

### No small talk, no offence taken

Remember that the Finnish language doesn't have a specific word for 'please' when ordering and there is no culture of small talk. Short sentences may not be a sign of rudeness, but just the way of the Finns.

## GOING OUT

For a long time, Finns have been known for their heavy use of alcohol, but in recent years, the tendency has been easing up, especially among the younger generations: friends can meet up for a dinner and a few cocktails or mocktails, and be home by midnight.

But still, as alcohol is expensive in restaurants and bars, many Finns also prefer gathering at home parties before heading out, typically around midnight.

In the summertime, gatherings take place also in parks and on beaches. In winter, it is common to go to fancier clubs in winter-ready shoes but change into heels by the cloakroom.

Pubs normally close at 2am on weekdays and 3am or 4am on Fridays and Saturdays, whereas clubs and bars stay open until 4am. After closing time, there are snack trucks or pizzerias open to cater to the party people in bigger cities and towns.

Karaoke is popular throughout the country and it is easy to partake in the fun; the crowds, normally a bit tipsy, are welcoming and there's much good cheer.

When ordering a pint of beer, don't expect the glass to be full: Finland has strict alcohol laws and measurements apply to all drinks, from wines to cocktails.

A glass of wine is sold in three sizes, 12cL, 16cL and 24cL.

In food stores, you will find alcohol products that are less than 5.5% alcohol – for heavier drinks, such as wine and spirits, head to Alko, Finland's national alcoholic beverage retailing monopoly.

# Responsible Travel

## Climate Change & Travel

It's impossible to ignore the impact we have when travelling, and the importance of making changes where we can. Lonely Planet urges all travellers to engage with their travel carbon footprint. There are many carbon calculators online that allow travellers to estimate the carbon emissions generated by their journey; try resurgence.org/resources/carbon-calculator.html. Many airlines and booking sites off er travellers the option of off setting the impact of greenhouse gas emissions by contributing to climate-friendly initiatives around the world. We continue to off set the carbon footprint of all Lonely Planet staff travel, while recognising this is a mitigation more than a solution.

## Everyman's Right

Jokamiehenoikeus ('everyman's right') is an ancient Finnish code that allows people to walk, ski or cycle anywhere in wilderness – even on private lands – so long as they act responsibly.

## Trekking

Enjoy a multiday adventure, hiking the nature trails of Koli National Park (p152). The longest hike, winding around Herajärvi lake, is 60km long and takes four days (although a shorter, 35km version is also possible).

## Cycling Tour

Indulge in emissions-free island hopping on the Archipelago Trail (p87). The 230km circular cycling route starts and ends in Turku, winding through lush southern countryside and over bridges connecting tiny islands and their unique maritime communities.

## Sámi Handicrafts

Look for products with the colourful Sámi Duodji (Sámi handicrafts association) logo, guaranteeing authentic Sámi craftsmanship and proceeds for indigenous northern communities. The association also runs a shop (p201) in Inari.

Finland's forest administration operates well-maintained wilderness huts across national parks and protected areas. Be sure to leave the hut as you found it – replenish the firewood and take away your rubbish.

Take home a Lappish souvenir made from recycled natural materials such as dropped reindeer antlers and fish leather. At shops like Lauri (p194) and Kangasniemi Hornwork (p29), you can see the artisans at work.

Consider donating to conservation efforts for the endangered Saimaa ringed seal (p132). Over recent years, campaigns from **WWF Suomi** (wwf.fi) and others have helped numbers rise from only dozens to 400.



TOP: RAUNO KOIVUNEN / SÁMI CULTURAL CENTRE SAJOS ©, RIGHT: THOMACA/SHUTTERSTOCK ©, LEFT: BORIS15/SHUTTERSTOCK ©

In Turku, shop at stores supporting a circular economy. Discover local boutiques and designers using natural fabrics, upcycling and selling vintage. Many antique shops give furniture and decorations a new chance at life.

### Wildlife Spotting

The rugged, untouched forests of Kuhmo are home to thriving numbers of bears, wolves and wolverines. Grab some binoculars and observe them ethically from a wilderness hut in June and July, when the sun never sets.

### Northern Lights Chasing

In Lapland, skip the tour buses and go looking for the aurora borealis yourself on a pair of snowshoes. Resources such as the 'My Aurora Forecast & Alerts' app can help.

Visit Finland's first zero-waste pizzeria: the slices at YLP! (p107) are made entirely with local produce.

Finland's favourite forest fruit is the cloudberry. Pick them yourself in Ranua (p109), Lapland's unofficial cloudberry capital.

3

Finland is an excellent responsible-travel destination. The 2022 Environmental Performance Index (EPI) ranked Finland in third place worldwide for overall sustainability, and first for sustainability in marine areas. The country has also been recognised for ethical wildlife tourism

### Lake Bathing

Skip a shower and join locals at Hanko's tiny bathing house (p101) for a cold, refreshing dip to start the day. The cost of key rental (€5 a day) goes towards the hut's maintenance.

## RESOURCES

**ymparisto.fi**
Understand everyman's rights via Finland's environmental administration

**eceat.fi**
Organic, sustainable farm stays

**metsa.fi**
Well-maintained huts in national parks and protected wilderness area

# LGBTIQ+ Travellers

In 2021, Spartacus Gay Travel index ranked Finland the world's 22nd most LGBTIQ+ friendly place, leaving the country far behind its more progressive Nordic neighbours, Denmark and Sweden. Same-sex marriage was legalised in 2017, and same-sex adoption a year earlier. Generally speaking, Finns are friendly to all, though underlying prejudice still lingers, as well as in some laws concerning sex reassignment therapy.

## Biggest Parties

The home of Tom of Finland (see below), Helsinki throws Finland's biggest LGBTIQ+ party in June, when the Helsinki Pride (pride.fi) celebrations last for a week. There has been an annual Helsinki Pride since 2006, but its history dates back to the 1970s, when organised activities to improve the status of sexual minorities in Finland began. Another event is the cinema festival Vinokino (vinokino.fi) held in five cities – including Helsinki, Turku and Tampere – in October and November. The festival showcases international queer cinema, from documentaries to films.

### …OR SEXUAL MINORITIES

Seta ry (seta.fi; from Finnish for 'sexual equality') is Finland's main LGBTIQ+ rights organisation, established in 1974 to advance equality in Finland, and successful with many legal battles, such as equal marriage and adoption laws. Seta's most notable chairperson is Tarja Halonen, Finland's first female president (2000–2012).

### MINDSETS

In general, Finns won't show their approval or disapproval of other people's comings and goings, especially in bigger cities, but some negative attitudes can still be picked up. This can manifest especially when alcohol is consumed, as some might get rowdier and more outspoken about their personal views. Some conservative priests may also refuse to hold a ceremony for a same-sex marriage.

## Gay-Friendly Districts & Bars

Kallio is Helsinki's bohemian gay-friendly district, with bars such as the classic Fairytale, and Kvääristö, which offers a dedicated safe space for queer women and gender minorities, but also to anyone who shares Kvääristö's values. Near Kallio in Vallila, is Finland's only gay sauna Vogue. The more upscale/bohemian Punavuori district is also favoured by Helsinki's gay population. Tampere's only gay bar is Mixei. In Turku, check out Bar Suxes.

### Tourism

Gay Travel Finland (gaytravelfinland.com) is a member of IGLTA, the International LGBTQ+ Travel Association, and a great resource for gay travels in Finland. The international Gaily Tour (gailytour.com) organises LGTBIQ-themed tours.

### TOM OF FINLAND

Tom of Finland is the country's most celebrated gay icon and artist. His art can adorn T-shirts as well as sheets, and you can also taste his namesake vodka. In 2023, Helsinki's Kiasma Modern Art Museum hosts an exhibition of his artwork.

 ALEXANDER SPATARI/GETTY IMAGES ©

# Accessible Travel

Finland's public infrastructure, from offices to transport, takes into account accessibility, and work is being done to make nature and sights more accessible to all, too.

### Accessible nature

The National Parks website (nationalparks.fi) features a searchable map for accessible destinations. These include 56 different types of accessible locations (for example, boardwalks and accessible toilets), from Helsinki to the top of Lapland.

### Airport

Helsinki airport was renovated in 2021 and offers wheelchairs and other assistance for people with reduced mobility. There are helpdesks at the airport, but calling prior to arrival is advised to guarantee assistance.

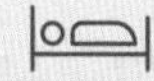

### Accommodation

Chain hotels in particular have worked to improve accessibility in their facilities, but there are more smaller and family owned hotels getting on board, too. To check your accommodation's accessibility, it's best to call in advance.

## RESOURCES

**Respecta** (*respecta.fi)* provides the largest variety of assistive devices and related services in Finland. Contact them to reserve equipment.

**The Finnish Association of People with Physical Disabilities** ((*invalidiliitto.fi*) is dedicated to advocacy and service provision for people with physical disabilities or functional impairment.

**The Finnish Federation of the Visually Impaired** (*Näkövammaisten liitto; nkl.fi*) has hotel rooms and a museum of visual impairment in its Iiris Centre in Helsinki's Itäkeskus.

## TRANSPORT

Helsinki's public transport is free for people with vision impairment and for people using wheelchairs or mobility scooters (only allowed on metros). The EU Disability Card is a valid method to prove various types of disabilities.

### Accessibility award

Helsinki came second in ENAT's (European Network for Accessible Tourism) Accessible Cities Awards in 2022 in recognition of the city's long-term efforts, the newest additions being more light trails, new trams, and accessible nature areas.

### Helsinki's beaches

Helsinki's Aurinkolahti and Hietaranta beaches have a floating bathing chair and a Mobi-mat® carpet to make travelling easier on the sand. These services are handled by the lifeguard on duty.

## HELSINKI'S STREETS

Helsinki's Senate Sq and Market Sq areas have cobblestoned streets. Traffic lights have little assistance for people with vision impairments, especially around the Market Sq and Mannerheimintie St. Winter makes the streets snowy.

Ekeventjohku.com organises accessible tours in and around Lohja, 60km from Helsinki.

S Adventureapes.fi provides nature-driven accessible expeditions and is a leader in accessible travel for the visually impaired.

Palmuasema.fi has tips for accessible hotels, spas and nature spots.

Santa Claus Village (p197)

# HOW TO... Find Santa

You want to take the family for a treat to see Father Christmas, in the Arctic, where he lives. You've heard that Rovaniemi in Finnish Lapland is his 'official hometown'. But you've found that a three-night package for a family of four from the UK (for example) can cost £3500 or more – with no guarantee that you'll visit the actual Santa Claus Village.

Well, it's not hard to set it all up independently and, if you book far enough ahead, probably save a chunk of money. For starters, several airlines fly direct scheduled flights to Rovaniemi from around Europe, especially in winter, among them Easyjet, Ryanair, Air France, KLM and Eurowings.

## Where to stay

Rovaniemi town has plenty of accommodation, from hostels and self-catering apartments to luxury hotels.

At the budget end, a family room in winter high season can cost in the region of €200 a night. The hotels at Santa Claus Village itself tend to be luxurious, and expensive, but the well-kept standard cottages at Santa Claus Holiday Village are more moderately priced.

## What to do

Santa Claus Village, a sort of Christmas theme park scattered around the forest edge, is 8km from Rovaniemi town, easily reached by bus. There, you can visit a genial Santa in his 'office' any day of the year for free (you might have to queue a bit at busy times) and, for mostly reasonable prices, take a sleigh ride with his reindeer and have a go at snowmobiling or husky sledding.

The Village can be magical in deep winter. With another day, try some skiing at Ounasvaara, visit the Arktikum or Pilke museums, look for the aurora borealis, or head out for a longer sled/sleigh ride at Bearhill Husky or Konttaniemen Porotila reindeer farm (book these in advance).

## When to go

If you're not dead set on Christmas, consider March. There's still plenty of snow, plus more daylight and not-quite-so-low temperatures, and accommodation can be cheaper.

In summer? Well, there's no snow, but there is midnight sun, lower room rates, and Santa is still there!

### HOW MANY SANTAS?

Santa Claus is magical of course, so it's perfectly reasonable that he can be in two, or four, or six places at once. But his tendency to pop up at unexpected times and places can cause puzzlement for people of any age. He even has a second manifestation in Santa Claus Village itself – in 'Christmas House', which is near the Santa Claus Holiday Village reception building. He has another office in central Rovaniemi as well. And he makes special appearances at other locations for some tour groups. Some parents try to avoid too many Santa appearances to avert overdose and confusion!

# Nuts & Bolts

## OPENING HOURS

Opening hours vary between weekdays and weekends. Rural areas offer fewer services. Here are the typical opening hours in bigger cities.

**Banks** 10am–4.30pm weekdays

**Bars** 3pm–2am weekdays

**Cafes** 8am–7pm weekdays

**Clubs** 8pm–5am Friday and Saturday

**Restaurants** 11am–9.30pm

**Shopping malls** 10am–8pm

**Shops** 10am–6pm Monday to Friday, 11am–5pm weekends

### Smoking

Smoking is not allowed inside public buildings. Most restaurants and cafes don't have smoking sections. Cigarette packets are sold by cashiers in shops.

## GOOD TO KNOW

**Time Zone**
GMT/UTC plus two hours

**Country Code**
358

**Emergency number**
112

**Population**
5.5 million

## PUBLIC HOLIDAYS

There are 13 public holidays in Finland. Some businesses and nonessential services are closed or operate with restricted opening hours.

**New Year's Day** 1 January

**Epiphany** 6 January

**Good Friday** The Friday preceding Easter

**Easter** March/April

**Easter Monday** The Monday following Easter Sunday

**Labour Day** 1 May

**Feast of the Ascension** The 40th day after Easter, Thursday

**Pentecost** Seventh Sunday after Easter

**Midsummer** Saturday between 20 and 26 June

**All Saints' Day** Saturday between 31 October and 6 November

**Independence Day** 6 December

**Christmas Day** 25 December

**St Stephen's Day** 26 December

### Weights & measures

Finland uses the metric system. Decimals are indicated with commas. Thousands are marked with commas, for example: 2,000.

### Tap water

Tap water is safe to drink and is of a high quality throughout Finland.

**Electricity** 220V/50Hz; 230V/50Hz

Type C
220V/50Hz

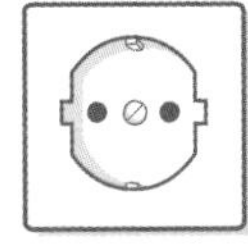

Type F
230V/50Hz

KUZNETSOVA JULIA/SHUTTERSTOCK ©

Aurora borealis (Northern Lights)

**APPS TO ASSIST**

There are many apps and websites that can assist when on a hunt for the aurora borealis. For example, My Aurora Forecast sends phone alerts if there's a chance of seeing the lights in your area. It also helps you to predict when and where are the best chances to see them. There's no point looking for the lights when the sky is covered with clouds, so it's also worth checking the Finnish Meteorological Institute's cloud map (ilmatieteenlaitos.fi/pilvet-pohjoismaat). Other good sources include the USA-based NOAA (National Oceanic and Atmospheric Administration; swpc.noaa.gov) with 30-minute and three-day forecasts, and gi.alaska.edu/monitors/aurora-forecast.

# HOW TO... Chase the Northern Lights

Imagine a firefox running across a snowy landscape under a dark winter sky. As it goes, its furry tail keeps hitting the snow, creating sparkles that illuminate the sky. These are *revontulet* (fires of the fox), or the aurora borealis (Northern Lights). In reality, the phenomenon is less poetic, and more scientific, caused by particles coming from the sun and slamming against Earth's protective, upper atmosphere at speeds of up to 72 million km/h, causing them to emit light of varying colours. Still, when you see the Northern Lights in Finland, you might just start believing in the firefox.

## When to Spot

The best time to see the aurora borealis is March, when the skies are at their clearest. In winter, the snowy landscapes will also make the experience even more magical. September is another good time to chase the lights, as nights are dark enough by then for the phenomenon to be visible.The best time of night to see the aurora is from 11pm to 1am.

## Where to Spot

With its vast open areas and darkness, Lapland is the best place to see the aurora borealis . In its most northernmost parts you can see them up to three nights out of four. In the middle of Lapland, it comes down to 60% of nights. It's possible to see the lights as south as Helsinki, where in dark months they light up the sky approximately once a month. Bear in mind that they're harder to see around light pollution.

## Hotels for Spotting

Many hotels around Finland offer glass igloos and glass-walled hotel rooms to see the aurora comfortably from your bed. For example, the Arctic Snow Hotel (p199), northwest of Rovaniemi, has lines of glass-walled rooms designed specifically for aurora viewing. There are also glass igloos in and around many of Lapland's skiing centres.

## Gear for Spotting

Layers, layers, layers! That's the mantra if heading outdoors on cold winter nights, especially in Lapland, where the temperatures can drop as low as -30°C or -40°C . Remember gloves or mittens, hat and warm shoes with enough space in them for thick woollen socks.

MR. TEMPTER/SHUTTERSTOCK ©

Finnish sauna

# HOW TO... Navigate Finnish Sauna Etiquette

Sisu, Sibelius and sauna: this is the holy trinity Finns learn from an early age as representative of the nation. Sisu (perseverance): just enough to survive the long and dark winter months. The composer Sibelius is renowned all over the world. And sauna, well, maybe the institution has given the nation a less complicated attitude towards nudity. But it is the one thing Finns miss the most when living abroad.

## How common is a sauna?

There are over three million saunas in Finland, which makes saunas more common than cars in the country. Most private homes and apartments have their own saunas, and if not, there is a sauna in the block of flats for the residents to use. Summer cottages also have saunas, normally close to the water. Note the Finnish pronunciation of sauna, which sounds something like 'sour-na'.

## Where to have a sauna

Almost all hotels have saunas for their guests. There are also historic and public neighbourhood saunas in bigger cities, such as Tampere and Helsinki. Then there are the leisure centres you can visit for a couple of euros, and have a swim and a sauna. Some cities also have modern sauna complexes lining the lakes and seashores, such as in Jyväskylä.

## How to have a sauna

A sauna should be a simple affair, so don't stress about it. First, in public saunas, the locker and shower rooms are separate for men and women. Second, always have a shower before the sauna. When you go into a common sauna, you should wear a swimsuit – unless it is specifically pointed out that it is optional. If so, you can still wear your bathing suit. Some Finns go naked, others don't, and both ways are fine. Lastly, remember to drink water.

## What not to do

Avoid engaging in too-loud behaviour. It is totally fine to exchange words with others in the sauna – in fact, this might be the one environment where Finns are at their most chatty – but in general, sauna is for quiet enjoyment.

### HOW TO MAKE AND TAKE THE HEAT?

In public saunas, the closest person to the stove normally throws water on the stones. The heat should be tolerable for all, so if you are in charge of the 'sauna ladle', don't go crazy with throwing the water and ask if people want more heat. For some Finns, it is a matter of pride to be able to take the heat no matter what, but should the sauna be too hot, it is normal to go and sit down on the lower benches – the heat is the hottest on the top bench. The steam is known as *löyly*. If you enjoy your sauna, you can say that the *löyly* was good.

# Language

## Basics

**Hello.** Hei/Terve (pol) Moi (inf). *hay/tehrr-veh/moy*

**Goodbye.** Näkemiin (pol)/Moi (inf). *na-keh-meen/moy*

**Yes.** Kyllä (pol)/Joo (inf). *kül-lah/yoo*

**No.** Ei. *ay*

**Please.** There's no frequently used word for 'please' in Finnish. Often kiitos (thank you) is used.

**Thank you.** Kiitos/Kiitti (inf). *kee-toss/keet-ti*

**Excuse me.** Anteeksi. *uhn-teehk-si*

**Sorry.** Olen pahoillani/Sori (inf). *o-lehn puh-hoyl-luh-ni/ so-rri*

**What's your name?** Mikä teidän nimenne on?/Mikä sun nimi on? (inf). *mi-ka tay-dan ni-mehn-neh on?/ mi-ka sun ni-mi on?*

**My name is ...** Minun nimeni on .../ Mun nimi on ... (inf). *mi-nun ni-mehn-ni on .../mun ni-mi on...*

**Do you speak English?** Puhutko englantia? *pu-hut-ko ehng-luhn-ti-uh?*

**I don't understand.** En ymmärrä. *ehn üm-marr-rra*

## Directions

**Where's ...(train station)?** Missä on ...? *mis-sa on ...?* (juna-asema (inf)/rautatie-asema *yu-nuh-uh-se-muh/ row-tuh-ti-eh-uh-se-muh)*

**I'm looking for...?** Etsin....? *et sin...?*

**Can you show me (on the map)?** Voitko näyttää minulle (kartasta)? *voyt-ko na-üt-taa mi-nul-leh (kuhrr-tuhs-tuh)?*

## Time

**What time is it?** Paljonko kello on? *puhl-yon-ko kehl-lo on?*

**It's (one) o'clock.** Kello on (yksi). *kehl-lo on (ük-si)*

**morning** aamu. *ah-mu*

**afternoon** iltapäivä. *il-tuh-pa-i-va*

**evening/night** ilta. *il-tuh*

**today** tänään. *ta-naan*

**tomorrow** huomenna. *hu-o-mehn-nuh*

## Emergencies

**Help!** Apua! *uh-pu-uh!*

**Go away!** Mene pois!/Häivy! (inf). *meh-neh poys!/ha-i-vü!*

**I'm ill.** Minä olen sairas. *mi-na o-lehn sai-rruhs*

**Call the police** Soittakaa poliisi! *soyt-tuh-kah po-lee-si!*

## Eating & drinking

**What would you recommend?** Mitä suosittelisit? *mi-ta su-o-sit-teh-li-sit?*

**Can I see the menu please?** Saisinko ruokalistan? *sai-sin-ko-ru-o-kuh-lis-tuhn?*

### NUMBERS

1 **yksi** *ük-si*

2 **kaksi** *kuhk-si*

3 **kolme** *kol-meh*

4 **neljä** *nehl-ya*

5 **viisi** *vee-si*

6 **kuusi** *koo-si*

7 **seitsemän** *sayt-seh-man*

8 **kahdeksan** *kuhkh-dehk-suhn*

9 **yhdeksän** *ükh-dehk-san*

10 **kymmenen** *küm-meh-nehn*

**DONATIONS TO ENGLISH**

The most commonly used Finnish word in English is **sauna**.

## UNIQUE LANGUAGE

Finnish is not closely related to any language other than Estonian and Karelian and a handful of other rare languages. There is also a notable Swedish-speaking minority in Finland, and all Finns learn Swedish in school, so you may need your Swedish vocabulary in Finland from time to time.

### Must-Know Grammar

The main difficulties with Finnish are the endings added to noun and verb roots, which often alter in this process, and the habit of building long words by putting several small words together.

### Sounds Familiar

Finnish isn't related to any Indo-European languages. There are, however, many loan words from Baltic, Slavonic and Germanic languages, and many words deriving from French and, especially, English.

### Sámi Languages

There are nine different Sámi languages, of which three are spoken in Finland. It's estimated about one-third of Sámi people in Finland today speak a Sámi language.

**bures** - *pu res* - u is a long vowel - is how you say 'how are you, hello' when shaking hands in Northern Sámi.

**oaidnaleapmái** *oa y-dna-leap-may* means 'see you'.

**giitu** *ki y-htu* is how you say 'thank you'.

boazu *po a-tsu* is 'reindeer' in Northern Sámi; it's **poro** *po ro* in Finnish.

**guovssahasat** *ku ovs sa ha-saht* is 'Northern Lights' in Northern Sámi; it's *revontulet re von tu let* in Finnish.

**Juovlastállu** *juo v-la-stal-lu* is Santa Claus in Northern Sámi and **Joulupukki** *yo loo pu ki* in Finnish.

## WHO SPEAKS FINNISH?

There are around six million Finnish speakers in Finland, Sweden, Norway and Russian Karelia. In Finnish, Finland is known as Suomi and the language itself as suomi.

# STORYBOOK

Our writers delve deep into different aspects of Finnish life



JAMO IMAGES/SHUTTERSTOCK ©

# A HISTORY OF FINLAND IN 15 PLACES

For centuries, Finland's destiny was decided by its two neighbours Sweden and Russia, battling over lands and possessions. Both countries left their mark in architecture, foods, language and the people. But yet, the Finns have also always been characteristically their own people.

**AS A REMOTE** country tucked away in the northern corner of Europe, Finland's history doesn't often appear in schoolbooks around the world. Yet the small nation of some five million people has pushed through harsh environments and even harsher times during conquests from the East and West.

Finland's earliest written history, which started around the 12th century, is a tale of a nation stuck between two rivals, Sweden and Russia. As battles were fought and borders were drawn and redrawn, the people continued with their own lives as much as they could.

Finland's borders were last defined in 1940 and 1945, as the country lost some of its eastern territories to the Soviet Union. The nation also had to pay hefty reparations in money and equipment to the Soviet Union, boosting further the already developed metal industries. In fact, Finland became a modern welfare state quite swiftly after coming out of WWII.

In politics, the nation got used to balancing between East and West, but in ideology the West prevailed: in 1995 Finland became part of the EU and replaced its markka with the euro in 2002.

Following Russia's invasion of Ukraine, Finland applied to join NATO in May 2022.

## 1. Astuvansalmi rock paintings

PREHISTORIC ART

Located in Mikkeli, Astuvansalmi's prehistoric rock paintings, the oldest ones dating from 3000 to 2500 BCE, are among northern Europe's biggest. The 65 paintings depict human and animal figures, most notably moose, an animal the ancient Finns believed to be the centre of the universe.

The images were painted with a mixture of red ochre and oil or blood, and it is thought that they were done from a boat or standing on the frozen lake when Saimaa's waters were 4–9m higher than they are now. The site is still today best approached by boat.

*For more on Mikkeli, see page 119*

## 2. Sammallahdenmäki

BRONZE AGE BURIAL MOUNDS

These 36 mysterious stone burial cairns from 1500 to 500 BCE stand near the coastal city of Rauma (Raumo), forming a remarkable Unesco World Heritage Site.

The walk to the group of rock mounds feels like a step back in time, as the path winds through the forest, floored with the ethereal-looking reindeer lichen. Originally the mounds stood on rocky islets just above the sea, as there was no forest in the area.

The coastline has since receded 20km west, leaving the site on dry ground, revealing snippets on how the Finns lived and died in the Bronze and Iron ages.

*For more on Sammallahdenmäki, see page 168*

## 3. Siida & Sajos

INTRODUCTION TO LAPLAND'S SÁMI CULTURE

Around 1600 BCE, the Sámi people used to live all around central Finland, before reaching and settling down in Lapland around the beginning of the Common Era.

Siida (the Sámi Museum and Northern Lapland Nature Centre), with its permanent exhibition showcasing how nature and culture are closely linked in the Sámi concept of cultural environment, and Sajos (Sámi Parliament in Finland) are good spots to get to know the Sámi people's past and present.

Both Siida and Sajos are easily visited in one day, and are very worthwhile to see while in Inari, as they are about 500m apart.

*For more on Siida and Sajos, see page 201*

## 4. Häme Castle

HIGHS AND LOWS

One of Finland's medieval castles, Häme Castle dates from the late 13th century when it was built to solidify the Swedish rule in the area. During its centuries-old history, the castle has witnessed highs and lows. The former, for example, in the hands of the mighty Lady Ingeborg, the de facto queen consort of Sweden and the fief holder of Häme Castle. The latter were the many fires and conquests the castle experienced during its heyday.

From 1881 to 1972, a women's prison was located here, and now you can visit both castle and prison museums as well as the neighbouring military museum.

*For more on Häme Castle, see page 147*

**Astuvansalmi rock paintings**

JUKKA PALM/SHUTTERSTOCK ©

## 5. Turku Castle

MEDIEVAL SPLENDOUR IN STONE

Turku Castle showcases Turku's importance as Finland's medieval capital. The castle dates from the 13th century, when southern parts of Finland became part of Sweden.

In the 1560s Catherine Jagiellon, a Polish princess who married John III of Sweden, lived in the castle, upgrading its interiors – and introducing Finland to forks.

Later the castle suffered damages and was used mainly as barracks – first for Swedish troops, and from 1809 onward for Russian troops.

The final blow came from Russian bombings during WWII, but after the war, long-awaited restoration work began.

Now visitors can sense the castle's medieval history in its whitewashed vaulted rooms and cobblestoned courtyard.

*For more on Turku Castle, see page 80*

## 6. Suomenlinna sea fortress

FORTRESS TURNED IDYLL

A 15-minute ferry ride from Helsinki's city centre, Suomenlinna (Sveaborg in Swedish) has a long history. From the 1740s it was under Swedish rule, then under Russian rule from 1808, until finally it belonged to Finland, following the country's independence in 1917. This is also when the fortress, formerly known as Viaborg, got its present Finnish name 'Suomenlinna', Castle of Finland.

The fortress island is Helsinki's only Unesco Heritage Site and hosts 800 inhabitants as well as 6km of walls, 100 cannons, tunnels, museums, beautiful parks and seaside coves, which make it a thrilling day trip.

*For more on Suomenlinna, see page 51*

### 7. Vanha Rauma

WOODEN HOUSES & COBBLESTONE STREETS

Walk the streets of Old Rauma, one of Finland's seven Unesco Heritage Sites and home to the Nordic countries' largest and most well-preserved wooden house quarters, dating from medieval times.

You can also find small boutiques, cafes and restaurants here, which makes the historic site even more pleasant to visit.

The oldest building is the Church of the Holy Cross, dating from the 16th century, whereas the wooden private homes are from the beginning of the 18th century.

Strolling the streets, you can really get the feel of how the bourgeois of the city might have lived a few hundred years ago.

*For more on Vanha Rauma, see page 240*

### 8. Koli National Park

PAINTINGS & PEAKS

When the mainly upper-class Finnish and Swedish-Finnish populace started to talk about the 'Finnish identity' in the 19th century, some with Swedish origins even changed their names into Finnish ones, and dozens of artists set across Finland to document – and invent – the country's ethos. One was Eero Järnefelt who climbed Koli's peaks, took out his easel and brushes and started to paint.

Today, Järnefelt's Koli paintings are renowned in Finland, making Koli's bare quartzite peaks and twisted tree trunks, pine-covered slopes and views over Lake Pielinen Finland's most familiar national landscape.

*For more on Koli, see page 153*

### 9. Uspenski Cathedral

RUSSIAN INFLUENCES

The Eastern Orthodox Uspenski Cathedral, rising on top of a little cliff near Helsinki Market Sq in Katajanokka district, is one of the city's most photographed sights.

The cathedral is the biggest Orthodox church in Western Europe. Built in 1868, some 50 years after Finland's annexation to Russia, the cathedral's red bricks were shipped in barges from the Bomarsund Fortress, which had been demolished in the Crimean War (1853–56).

On top, 13 gold cupolas create an opulent feel, which is continued in the Byzantine-inspired interior, making the church one of the most visible statements of Russia's effect on Helsinki's cityscape.

### 10. Minna Canth's salon

PROGRESSIVE THINKER

With the country full of famous residences turned into museums, it is a shame that Minna Canth (1844–97), the first woman in Finland who made a career out of writing and journalism, hasn't got a museum dedicated to her – especially as her home, Kanttila, is still standing opposite Kuopio's VB Museum and actively promoted and protected by a dedicated group of activists.

Still, you can visit Kuopion korttelimuseo, where Canth's progressive salon's setting has been recreated, partly using furniture that belonged to this groundbreaking writer and feminist. Luckily, at least Minna Canth's statue has a prominent spot in Jyväskylä's Kirkkopuisto (Church Park).

*For more on Kuopio, see page 144*

### 11. Hanko (Hango)

EASY BREEZES

Finland's history hasn't just been scuffles over borders, and great men (and women) dedicated to hard work. There have also been leisurely moments and celebrations.

One of the most famous spa spots in the early 20th century was Finland's southernmost city, Hanko (Hango), where the bourgeois flocked in hordes since the 1880s, and the military leader CG Mannerheim even owned a cafe there. Hanko (Hango) also had its casino and fabulous wooden villas, which adorn the city. Today, people still head here to enjoy the summer breeze on little beaches and the beautiful seaside setting.

*For more on Hanko (Hango), see page 100*

### 12. Senate Square

ASSASSINATION & ARCHITECTURE

Senate Square is Helsinki's empire-styled heart designed by the German-born architect Carl Ludwig Engel.

Engel didn't enjoy moving to Helsinki, but couldn't resist the task given by Tsar Alexander I of designing a new city.

Helsinki Cathedral is the obvious eye-catcher here, but many intriguing his-

SARIME/SHUTTERSTOCK ©

**Helsinki library**

toric events have taken place around the square, such as Finland's most notorious political assassination when the Russian General-Governor Nikolay Bobrikov was shot in 1904 in the yellow Government Palace, opposite the University of Helsinki's main building. By the square, there is the National Library of Finland, considered Engel's true masterpiece.

*For more on Senate Square, see page 48*

## 13. Vapriikki

TAMPERE'S BLOODY SPRING IN 1918

After gaining independence from Russia in 1917, Finland went through possibly the most traumatising period of its history, a civil war.

The bloodiest events were witnessed in Tampere between March and April. Here, the inexperienced 'reds' led by the amateur actor Hugo Salmela collided with the 'whites', led by the then-already-experienced CG Mannerheim, who later became the president of Finland.

Over 2000 reds lost their lives, half of them executed, the rest in battle or in prison camps. On the white side, casualties amounted to 700.

Tampere's Vapriikki museum, in the Finlayson area, has dedicated a permanent exhibition to the bloody events of spring 1918.

*For more on Vapriikki, see page 121*

## 14. Olympic Stadium

SPORTS, ARCHITECTURE & LONKERO

Helsinki's prime example of functionalist-style architecture is the Töölö Olympic Stadium. The 1952 Summer Olympics were a turning point in the city's urban lifestyle; war had destroyed the nation's leisure opportunities and infrastructure had to be upgraded to host the event.

This included, for example, a new airport, now Finland's main entry point; traffic lights; and the city centre Tennispalatsi ('tennis palace'), another functionalist-style masterpiece now hosting HAM (Helsinki Art Museum) and a cinema. But perhaps the most beloved innovation for the Olympics was Lonkero, a ready-made long-drink mix of gin and grape, which eased the lives of inexperienced bar staff who served thirsty sports enthusiasts.

*For more on the Töölö Olympic Stadium, see page 68*

## 15. Oodi Library

AN ODE TO LEARNING

Finland's first library was established in Vaasa in 1794, but the institution as it is now only arose in the early 20th century.

The library system, where everyone can borrow books, films and music – and nowadays games, tools and even rowing boats or sewing machines – evolved hand in hand with the country's inclusive and free-for-all education system. Both are now valued as key aspects of Finland's success in international surveys on education and reading-skill levels.

Although some smaller, remote libraries closed in recent decades, libraries are still valued here. One example is the Oodi Library in Helsinki city centre, awarded for its architecture.

*For more on Oodi Library, see page 53*

TOP LEFT: ALEKSANDRA SUZI/SHUTTERSTOCK ©; TOP RIGHT: LANA KRAY/SHUTTERSTOCK ©
BOTTOM LEFT: TELIA/SHUTTERSTOCK ©; BOTTOM RIGHT: BLUEORANGE STUDIO/SHUTTERSTOCK ©

# MEET THE FINNS

The relatively icy surface of the Finns might be hard to crack – but once you're in, you are in for a lifetime. PAULA HOTTI introduces her people.

**THE FINNS ARE** a trusting bunch, and this trust is extended not just to friendships but also towards the media and government. According to a 2021 report by OECD, 71% of the Finnish population trusts the government, compared to the OECD average of 41%. One reason behind this is considered to be the Finns' media literacy skills, scoring 75 points in the 2022 Media Literacy Index, followed closely behind by other Nordic nations. The skill is learned from an early age, as pupils learn to asses critically the information they are given. This affects everyone going through the school system here, as equal and free education has been one of Finland's core values for over a century.

In reality, a Finn may not come forth as a particularly trusting person: normally, there is a touch of reserve when meeting a Finn. It might take some time to break the somewhat cold surface and get an invitation to a local's home for a simple cup of coffee. But when you do achieve this, you have most likely got a loyal, kind and trustworthy friend for a lifetime.

This reserve is at least partly due to the fact Finns value their private space a lot, extending the same respect of privacy to others. Don't expect a Finn to sit next to you on the bus or share a spontaneous smile on the street.

Finnish humour is often described as dry, or even sarcastic, and jokes can be delivered with a straight face: it might take a short moment to realise you were actually told a joke. A good introduction to the Finnish way of life, humour and personal space are the comic strips *Finnish Nightmares* by Karoliina Korhonen.

Finns do enjoy rowdy parties and lively conversations too. The attitudes have been changing and the younger generations are typically more open, and even hug each other if they meet on the streets.

In general, Finns are also a very modest nation, with many proverbs to prove the dangers of bragging, from 'silence is gold' to 'if you reach for the spruce you will fall on to the juniper', pointing out that high aspirations end up in lousy results.

Then there is the oft-quoted line from one of Finland's most treasured poets, Eino Leino: 'Whoever is happy should hide it'. Which doesn't make sense for a country hailed as the happiest nation on Earth.

But maybe that's the Finnish way: a modest nation with a solid education system and a trusting attitude towards life, with no need to go shouting about it.

### WHO AND HOW MANY

Finland has a population of just over 5.5 million. The majority (86.5%) has Finnish as mother tongue, then Swedish (5.2%). Sámi is spoken by about 2000 individuals. There are some 469,000 foreign nationals living in the country.

**Clockwise from left: Winter sports, wooden bath in the forest, traditional Easter celebrations, Lahti market square**

## A VERY FINNISH CASE

I type this in my current home in Helsinki, but I was born in South Savo, where my 1990s childhood was a typical one: building tree huts in the forest, spending summer days on the city-centre beach, and cycling to school in -20°C.

This might sound a bit extreme, but it was a very typical Finnish childhood. But even then, I was dreaming of foreign lands and hoped that I'd have a little drop of some exotic blood.

Yet, as my sister recently did a DNA test, we turned out to be of 100% Finnish descent.

This also is very typical here, as for centuries the country has been quite a homogeneous one – a state of affairs that in recent decades has luckily been changing.

And, just when I had admitted my defeat of lacking diversity in my roots, my sister got contacted because of a connection to a clan in the Scottish Highlands – a drop of information that I happily cling to.

# THE SÁMI:
## TRADITIONS AND CULTURE

The only recognised indigenous people within the European Union area.
By John Noble

**THE SÁMI ARE** spread across Norway, Sweden, Finland and Russia's Kola Peninsula. Historically they have lived mostly in the northern parts of those countries. There are approximately 40,000 to 45,000 Sámi in Norway, 15,000 to 25,000 in Sweden, 11,000 in Finland and 2000 in Russia.

In Finland, Lapland's three northernmost municipalities (Inari, Utsjoki, Enontekiö), along with the Vuotso area further south, are considered the Sámi Homeland – 30,000 sq km of forests, fells and lakes with just over 10,000 inhabitants, about one-third of whom are Sámi. Today more than 60% of Sámi in Finland live outside this area.There are nine different Sámi languages, of which three are spoken in Finland. It's estimated that about one-third of Sámi people in Finland today speak a Sámi language. Since 1996, the Sámi in Finland have had constitutional self-government in the Sámi Homeland in the spheres of language and culture. This self-government is managed by the Sámi Parliament in Finland, situated in Inari village.

The Sámi are famously associated with reindeer herding, which is an important cornerstone of their culture. The animals are used for meat, clothes, crafts and transport. Although many Sámi no longer earn



Clockwise from left: Fresh fish, reindeer gloves, reindeer in Finland, on the Arctic Trail

their livelihood from reindeer herding – many pursue the same professions and occupations as the rest of society – reindeer herding retains a high cultural value, as do the other traditional Sámi livelihoods of fishing, gathering, handicrafts and hunting.

Today these activities are often modernised to make them more practical and cost-efficient. For example, Sámi reindeer herders use snowmobiles, ATVs, GPS collars, drones and helicopters in the tending and locating of their animals, just as Sámi artisans, while still working with natural materials, often employ modern tools in the making of Sámi handicrafts (duodji) – practical, handmade objects based on old traditions. Sámi who work in other professions often continue to make traditional handicrafts for their own use, or fish and forage to supplement their diets.

The Sámi today want the world to see them as the modern people they are, not as relics of bygone ages. One thing that is not part of their modern culture is the animistic religion that was replaced by Christianity several centuries ago. Touristic shamanism by non-Sámi distorts the cultural heritage with invented traditions.

The colourful traditional Sámi dress *does* remain an important part of Sámi culture. It not only identifies its wearer as Sámi, but its decorations, and the way it is worn, indicate which area the wearer comes from and can even reveal their family and marital status. Today it is worn mainly on special occasions. Sámi feel that they should be accorded due respect and privacy when wearing it, and especially that religious events like weddings, confirmations and funerals should be left in peace.

For more on this and related topics, see 'How to Travel Responsibly in Sámi Homeland', p211.

## VIEW FROM THE SÁMI PARLIAMENT

**Tuomas Aslak Juuso was elected in 2019 for a four-year term (2020 to 2023) as President of the Sámi Parliament in Finland, which is the official representative of the 11,000 Sámi who live in the country.**

There are three Sámi languages spoken in Finland: North Sámi, Inari Sámi and Skolt Sámi, of which the latter two are most endangered. Many Sámi lost their language in assimilation processes during the 20th century, but through language nest projects and active work, more people can regain the language of their families and continue to strengthen Sámi culture and arts. More than half of the Sámi live outside the traditional Sámi area, which has created challenges in ensuring the right to learn Sámi languages and receive services in Sámi languages everywhere in Finland, not just the Sámi Homeland.

Despite many advancements in the past decades, there are still serious issues with Sámi self-determination in Finland. The Sámi are recognised in the Finnish Constitution as Indigenous People, but both the UN Human Rights Committee and the Committee on the Elimination of Racial Discrimination have found Finland in violation of Sámi rights in recent years. Despite several attempts, Finland had at the time of writing failed to make the necessary amendments to the Act on the Sámi Parliament and the Sámi's right for FPIC – free, prior, informed consent on matters relating to Sámi culture was not fulfilled. The Sámi have often not been properly consulted when deciding on activities affecting the Sámi livelihoods and culture, like mining and other land use projects. The latest attempt to amend the Act was expected to be resolved during the year 2023. The Finnish government has also appointed a Truth and Reconciliation Commission to increase dialogue and trust between the Sámi and the state.

Traditional livelihoods remain crucial to the Sámi culture. In addition to reindeer herding, fishing, gathering, hunting and handicrafts, Sámi are also somewhat involved in other modern livelihoods, like Sámi tourism. Unfortunately, the ethical guidelines created by us for the tourism industry in 2018 – a step forward in ensuring a sustainable and respectful treatment of the Sámi and their culture – and our visitor guidance for travelling in Sámi Homeland (published in 2022) are not followed by all companies operating in Finland, and for example fake Sámi traditions and imagery are still widely used.

Above all, the climate crisis remains a major challenge to Indigenous Peoples around the world, and its implications are already frighteningly visible in the Arctic. Preserving our nature while also creating socially sustainable solutions to combat climate change is a priority for us all – and for that, the Sámi people need to be heard.

TOP LEFT: LITTLE ADVENTURES/SHUTTERSTOCK ©; TOP RIGHT: MARTINA LANOTTE/SHUTTERSTOCK ©

# CREATING ART:

## THE MANY SIDES OF FINNISHNESS

Bold lines, strong statements and striking melodies are omnipresent in the Finnish art world. By Paula Hotti

**FINNISH ART DIDN'T** only evolve in synchronicity with other aspects of society over time, but it was an essential building material in creating the notion of 'Finnishness' in the wake of the country's independence in 1917.

Naturally, where there are people, there is art.

In Finland, travellers can visit the sites of prehistoric cave paintings, such as the drawings in red on the Astuvansalmi cliffside near Mikkeli; medieval churches with beautiful decor (prime examples are located in Turku, Hollola and Hattula); and castles full of artsy artefacts in Turku, Hämeenlinna and Savonlinna.

Finland's medieval period lasted roughly from the 12th to the 16th century. Around this time the Finnish language got its alphabet when, in the 1540s, the reformist Mikael Agricola set down to work with his quill and translated the New Testament into Finnish and published the first book written in Finland, the *Abckirja* (ABC book). But the first novels in Finnish, alongside institutionalised art

 **Clockwise from left: Turku cathedral, Elias Lönnrot statue, Tuska Metal Festival, Moomins**

TOP LEFT: JAMO IMAGES/SHUTTERSTOCK ©; TOP RIGHT: MIKHAIL MARKOVSKIY/SHUTTERSTOCK ©

in other fields, only came into existence during the 19th century, when authors and artists set out to create the Finnish identity, looking through their romantic goggles at Finnish landscapes and folklore.

The project lasted from around the 1840s till the early 20th century and produced artists such as Akseli Gallen-Kallela, known for his scenes from *Kalevala* (1835), Finland's national epic written by Elias Lönnrot, who travelled around what is today Karelia (both in eastern Finland and on the Russian side), collected oral poetry and composed a consistent work from it.

Another influential painter from the time is Eero Järnefelt, renowned for scenes from the top of Koli peaks, which are now celebrated as a national park and a symbolic part of Finland's landscape.

In music, Jean Sibelius set the tone for Finland's emancipation project with his *Finlandia, Op 26,* which includes the often-performed 'Finlandia' hymn. The hymn, originally without words, was also part of a campaign against Russia's censorship and ever-tightening grip on Finland.

The Finnishness these artists created on their canvases, words and melodies had a clear focus: depicting an idealised image of the nation, with wild forests and high viewpoints.

Factories and cities were left outside the frames, although both modern phenomena were already found all over Finland towards the end of the 20th century.

Apart from these solemn works, there has been another influence in the Finnish art world.

When many were painting austere landscapes, Helene Schjerfbeck held a more delicate brush. Having spent her early career studying, painting and travelling in Paris and other parts of Europe, in later life she relocated mainly to small-town Hyvinkää and is now one of Finland's most esteemed modern painters, known for her still-life works and haunting self-portraits.

During the rest of the 20th century, the young nation's art scene kept diversifying.

In architecture, Eliel Saarinen and Alvar Aalto opened the doors of Finnish architecture and design to the world. Aalto was accompanied by his first wife, the designer and architect, Aino Aalto – with many stating the work of the two is often inseparable – and, after Aino's death, Elissa Aalto, also an architect.

Aalto became a forerunner of the mid-20th century modernism, with his buildings relying heavily on functional details and also with his invention of bent plywood furniture, influencing the aesthetics of international designers.

Saarinen's extraordinary railway station designed with Emil Wikström's stately statues will greet anyone arriving in Helsinki by train, whereas Aalto's work can be found in churches as well as in private and official architecture around Finland.

Today, you will find neighbourhoods with sombre and pastel-coloured 1950s blocks of flats anywhere in Finland as well as public buildings with bold straight lines combined with airy and wavy structures.

Finland has been in synch with the minimalist Scandi style, sometimes adding a playful twist, as Eero Aarnio has shown with his Ball and Bubble Chairs.

In literature, Tove Jansson's moody and philosophical *Moomin* comic strips morphed into books and animated TV series, capturing the imagination of old and young throughout the world.

Tom of Finland's gay erotica first found its audience in the underground queer world – first abroad (homosexuality was illegal in Finland till 1971), but later also in Finland, ending up adorning the official stamps in 2014.

Today, you can also buy duvets and pillow covers and other interior fabrics carrying his striking drawings.

Contemporary Finnish music is not just associated with grand symphonies, either.

Festivals, especially in the summertime, are a good opportunity to hear the diversity of music that this small Nordic nation produces, from world-renowned heavy metal to folksy instrumental and internationally touring rock and heavy metal bands.

Today, the Finnishness of the nation is as diverse as its artistic creators.

# TRIUMPHS & TRAGEDIES

How Finland is fighting to win the race against losing its most valuable asset – the nature. By Paula Hotti

**FINNS' CONCERN ABOUT** the state of Finland's nature had increased by 15% since 2020, according to a study in the summer of 2022 by the Ministry of Environment and the Finnish Environment Institute.

Almost half of the participants also acknowledged that they now know more about biodiversity than before.

The study also concluded that the COVID-19 pandemic deepened people's attachment to nature: now, 92% of the respondents think that nature is an integral part of Finnish identity.

This may not sound surprising, given that nature engulfs Finland, even its cities: Finland has 187,888 lakes over 500 sq metres in size, and over 75% of the land is covered by forests. Yet the country is not without its environmental challenges.

Every ninth species in Finland is endangered, due to the lack of biodiversity and the ever-narrowing living spaces.

Outdated mining laws make Finland seem like the Wild West, where land is up for grabs, regardless of the environmental costs.

Finland's marshes are also under threat, half of them on the verge of being lost, affecting up to 120 endangered species that call these landscapes their home.

**Swamp lakes in Finland**

Fortunately, Finland is historically a proactive country, at least on the NGO level, in tackling conservation and other environmental issues, even if it took a little while to put any tangible structures into play.

Finnish nature conservation has its roots in the 19th century, when the Finnish-Swedish Arctic explorer AE Nordenskjöld and the author and historian Zacharias Topelius spoke and wrote on the topic.

Yet it took until 1938, when Finland's first society to protect the environment was officially established as Suomen luonnonsuojeluliitto (the Finnish Association for Nature Conservation; FANC), before the country had a dedicated force to campaign for the environment.

**IN 2022 FINLAND GOT ITS 41ST NATIONAL PARK, SALLA IN LAPLAND, TO GIVE MORE SPECIES A FIGHTING CHANCE OF SURVIVAL**

In the 1930s, Finland also got its first national parks established on government-owned lands to protect the environment – exactly as Nordenskjöld had hoped some 50 years before.

Since the 1930s, FANC has had many triumphs: more national parks – such as Linnansaari, Oulanka and Lemmenjoki – and nature reserves were established in the 1950s. During the 20th century, the association also reacted to many international developments, such as informing on the dangers of the insecticide DDT in the 1960s and the limits of what was thought of as infinite growth in the following decade.

An important shift in nature conservation and awareness came about in the 1990s, as climate change and the limits of natural resources became evident.

More recently, in the autumn of 2022, the fells of Lapland witnessed the first successful nesting of the Arctic fox, for the first time in Finland since 1996. And the year before, over 170 fishers in the Saimaa Lakeland region received wire fish traps that are safe for the area's endangered seals, to prevent the frequency of young seal pups dying in the fishing nets used here.

Much of Finland's marshes have also been protected, due to vigorous campaigning by political parties, NGOs and actively participating private people; in Lapland, the Finnish state-owned enterprise Metsähallitus (Forest Administration) oversees 12 wilderness areas to protect their uniqueness.

In 2022 Finland got its 41st national park, Salla in Lapland, to give more species a fighting chance of survival. The year was also to witness a much-needed rewriting of Finland's 25-year-old law on environmental protection, but the final drafts were watered down, as the Central party lined up with the opposition, demanding changes to key aspects of protecting endangered species.

In 2022 FANC and the Finnish Greenpeace sued the Finnish Government – a first-time occurrence in Finland's history – as its actions are not in accordance with Finland's climate laws that aim at carbon neutrality by 2035.

With these developments in mind, and seeing the Central party's support numbers plummeting to single digits, it might be justified to say that all species living in this land of thousands of lakes may still have some hope.

**Linnansaari (p131)**

FAR LEFT: VLADIMIR MELNIKOV/SHUTTERSTOCK ©; LEFT: MMARTIN/SHUTTWERSTOCK ©

# INDEX

21982320934221

"Lapland (p187) is the land of the midnight sun, the polar night and the magical aurora borealis ('Northern Lights'). It occupies more than a quarter of Finland, mostly north of the Arctic Circle."

JOHN NOBLE

"In winter, Koli National Park (p152) witnesses the magic of crown snow-load, which transforms the foliage into an enchanting sight, heroically carrying the weight of snow."

PAULA HOTTI

All rights reserved. No part of this publication may be copied, stored in a retrieval system, or transmitted in any form by any means, electronic, mechanical, recording or otherwise, except brief extracts for the purpose of review, and no part of this publication may be sold or hired, without the written permission of the publisher. Lonely Planet and the Lonely Planet logo are trademarks of Lonely Planet and are registered in the US Patent and Trademark Office and in other countries. Lonely Planet does not allow its name or logo to be appropriated by commercial establishments, such as retailers, restaurants or hotels. Please let us know of any misuses: lonelyplanet.com/legal/intellectual-property.

LEFT: KADRIHARM, RIGHT: ERKKI MAKKONEN / SHUTTERSTOCK ©


## THIS BOOK

**Design Development** Marc Backwell

**Content Development** Mark Jones, Sandie Kestell, Anne Mason, Joana Taborda

**Cartography Development** Katerina Pavkova

**Production Development** Sandie Kestell, Fergal Condon

**Series Development Leadership** Darren O'Connell, Piers Pickard, Chris Zeiher

**Commissioning Editors** Lorna Parkes, Amy Lynch

**Production Editor** Sarah Farrell

**Book Designer** Norma Brewer

**Cartographer** Chris Lee-Ack

**Assisting Editors** Ronan Abayawickrema, Janet Austin, Andrew Bain, Melanie Dankel, Karyn Noble, Kathryn Rowan

**Cover Researcher** Gwen Cotter

**Thanks** Esteban Fernandez

Paper in this book is certified against the Forest Stewardship Council™ standards. FSC™ promotes environmentally responsible, socially beneficial and economically viable management of the world's forests.

Published by Lonely Planet Global Limited
CRN 554153
10th edition - Jul 2023
ISBN 978 178701 566 1
©Lonely Planet 2023 Photographs © as indicated 2023
10 9 8 7 6 5 4 3 2 1
Printed in China